3 4. 79

BUILDING AND MANAGING THE CORPORATE INTRANET

Building and Managing the Corporate Intranet

Ronald L. Wagner
and
Eric Engelmann

McGraw-Hill
New York · San Francisco · Washington, D.C.
Auckland · Bogotá · Caracas · Lisbon · London
Madrid · Mexico City · Milan · Montreal · New Delhi
San Juan · Singapore · Sydney · Tokyo · Toronto

Library of Congress Cataloging-in-Publication Data

Wagner, Ronald L.
    Building and managing the corporate intranet / by Ronald L. Wagner and Eric
Engelmann.
       p.   cm.
    Includes index.
    ISBN 0-07-066939-2
    1. Intranets (Computer networks)—Management.   2. Intranets
(Computer networks)—Design and construction.   I. Engelmann, Eric.
II. Title.
HD30.385.W34   1997   97-1071
658'.05436—dc21   CIP

McGraw-Hill

*A Division of The **McGraw·Hill** Companies*

1 2 3 4 5 6 7 8 9 0 DOC/DOC 9 0 2 1 0 9 8 7

ISBN 0-07-066939-2

*The sponsoring editor for this book was Scott Grillo, the editing supervisor was Ruth
Mannino, and the production supervisor was Tina Cameron. It was set in Vendome ICG
by Kim Sheran of McGraw-Hill's Hightstown, N.J., composition unit.*

Printed and bound by R. R. Donnelley & Sons Company.

McGraw-Hill books are available at special quantity discounts to use as premi-
ums and sales promotions, or for use in corporate training programs. For more
information, please write to the Director of Special Sales, McGraw-Hill, 11 West
19th Street, New York, NY 10011. Or contact your local bookstore.

 This book is printed on recycled, acid-free paper containing
a minimum of 50% recycled, de-inked fiber.

To Lisa.—Ron

To my parents. Thanks for the code and early programming.—Eric

Many of today's business limitations now exist only because people are accustomed to them. If we all could start over and learn our businesses from the ground up with the Internet and Intranets in place, most businesses would be structured and would function very differently from the way they are today.

CONTENTS

Contents

ACKNOWLEDGMENTS

We would like to express our appreciation to Bill Adler, Jr., and Lisa Swayne, Adler and Robin Books; Dick Connor, cmc; Brad Templeton, ClariNet Communications; Kody Kline, D.T.P. Extreme; Michael Sullivan, Haywood & Sullivan; Bea McKinney, askSam Systems; Frank Zerbel, AMT Learning Solutions; and Russ Rosenzweig, The Round Table Group; and The World Bank.

—RONALD L. WAGNER
—ERIC ENGELMANN

INTRODUCTION

The Internet has unquestionably and permanently altered the business landscape. It has changed forever how business interact with one another, how people communicate and how information of all types is distributed. It's used to sell products, provide access to research archives, deliver instantly updated statistics and reports and to send electronic mail messages across the globe in seconds. The Internet has arrived in full force and in our fast-paced world that opens an important question: What next?

Intranets

Intranets are internal versions of the globe-trotting Internet that form private networks that function almost exactly as their larger antecedent. Many Intranets rely on the Internet to connect remote offices within an organization, but an Intranet can be strictly internal and run completely upon a local area network (LAN).

LANs have been around for many years but, for all their widespread usage, they've been a pain in the neck for most businesses as well as for most users. One of the main problems with LANs has been the wide diversity of standards, software and hardware. Workers who master one LAN might move to another company and have to go straight to training classes to get up to speed on the new system. Worse, even without moving, management might decide to switch software vendors and trigger more training along with a huge loss of productivity.

Intranets have brought to organizations all over the world the ability to let workers use the LAN with familiar Internet software. It's a surprisingly simple process because most organizations have already developed Web sites for the Internet that provide access to the public to a lot of internal data. The next step is to extend that already ongoing process to include internal, private information, restrict access to the private data so that only users within the organization can see it and then use familiar Internet tools to let workers access it.

Thus, instead of having to create a complete parallel information system for internal use, all that's required is to point everyone's Netscape Web browser back into the organization and *violà*, the Intranet is born. Okay, there's a little more to it than that because of security reasons. But that's a task for your computer professionals—the average worker who's surfed the Web will need almost no extra training and no additional software.

As you'll see later, an Intranet can connect remote offices within any organization by using the Internet for long-distance information services. Previously, connecting remote offices with instant data interchange required costly, dedicated long-distance lines. Now the long-distance part is handled across the Internet easily and inexpensively. In fact, implementing an Intranet may result in no additional Internet costs!

So, if you're already spending the money on Internet service, why not also enjoy the unprecedented benefits available with an Intranet? This book first will show you the benefits to creating an Intranet.

After that, we include some important technical discussions that will help with planning, implementing and managing your Intranet. These chapters don't present a lot of in-depth technical detail—if we even tried to do that, you'd find this book outdated long before you bought it. To stay abreast of the rapidly-changing technical scene, you'll need to rely on magazines and Internet sites for information. So, we focus here on *principles* that will help you when you read those magazines and Internet resources.

Then—we assume you've agreed that your company simply *must* have its own Intranet—we'll present some crucial Hands-on lessons that will help employees get the most benefit possible from your Intranet. These lessons are important because the success of your Intranet cannot rest on the shoulders of your professional computer staff. Everyone is going to have to get involved in creating the Intranet. We'll show you how to get almost everyone to become self-sufficient Intranet content providers.

Okay, let's get started. We take you now to the World Bank in Washington, D.C. where you will see how a leader in the technology field has benefitted from implementing the Intranet.

BUILDING AND MANAGING THE CORPORATE INTRANET

Management
Guide

We begin this book with information that will help your organization make the decision to create its own Intranet. These chapters will point out the benefits and will show how an Intranet can bring a return on your organization's initial investment.

Chapter 1 presents some typical success stories that illustrate the benefits an Intranet can deliver. You'll get an inside look at one of the best Intranets, that of the World Bank. By using it as a model you'll also get plenty of ideas for your own Intranet.

This phase also will help management sell the entire organization on its decision to create an Intranet. We realize that organizational change can bring stress, but such stress is easier to manage when everyone can look ahead to the benefits that will accrue once the system is working smoothly.

We then offer guidance, in Chap. 2, on integrating the development of an Intranet into your organization. This includes outlining some necessary roles that will need to be filled, and a short discussion of what types of people you'll need in those roles.

The last three chapters of Phase 1 will help prepare you to understand more in-depth technical publications, such as computer magazines. After reading these chapters you'll have a better sense of what to look for when selecting Intranet hardware and software.

1

Intranet Success Stories

The Internet, the sprawling success story of the 1990s, fires the imagination of almost everyone with promises of communicating instantaneously from anywhere to anywhere, finding anything that is wanted, entertaining and educating, and doing it all cheaply. However, as wonderful as communicating with other companies, libraries, newspapers, and other parties can be, most corporate business information exchange is still internal to the organization.

For example, in the past the only places to find answers to customer questions, plus information about supplier contacts, advertising, accounting, in-house projects, and many other corporate matters was from file cabinets and dusty notebooks. Essentially that's still true, even though many businesses are now able to speed their communications and searching abilities with e-mail and PCs. Most technical advances of late are simply electronic versions of file cabinets and dusty notebooks.

But now, the Internet has brought about a revolution in the way information is stored and retrieved. Hypertext gives us the ability to link information that is related in ways that cannot be described by traditional computing technology. In turn, this linking ability has enabled us, through the Internet, to create the unprecedented information system called the World Wide Web.

The good news is that the hypertext of the Internet, if applied within an organization, offers a tremendous opportunity to greatly expand corporate productivity by putting the vast internal knowledge of the organization at every employee's fingertips, without heavy investment or retraining.

Intranet Defined

An *Intranet* is a network of computers, software, documents, and databases that generally works just like the Internet, except that it is only accessible to employees and selected guests. Because of this access restriction, an Intranet can be used to publish information that is proprietary, confidential, under development, or otherwise not ready for public viewing by customers and competitors. An Intranet will use local area networks (LANs), connections between LANs, and other means to connect the same Web, FTP, News, and other servers as seen on the Internet, but will restrict usage to internal users only.

The real strength of the Internet, and especially of the Web, is that it provides an easy and inexpensive way to locate and display information from any server anywhere in the world. The strength of an Intranet is that it can do the same thing with the many islands of information within an organization, at amazingly low cost.

No organization should have any technical problem with information storage. Today's computers give organizations plenty of storage power and solutions. The problem is with creating productive access to the stored information. An Intranet creates productive access to organizational information in two primary ways:

1. First, its user-friendly software enables users to quickly learn to locate and navigate through information resources, providing instant access to vast stores of current information.

2. Second, the structure of hypertext documents frees information authors from the limitations of linear information paths. Eventually, the structure of the information itself will change as people learn to create documents in a hypertext format that fully embraces hypertext's ability to link loosely related information.

Netscape's Intranet Services

To learn more about the basics of an Intranet, check out the Netscape home page at home.netscape.com (see Fig. 1-1). The Netscape website has many white papers on Intranet theory and on successful implementation strategies.

You can rely on the Netscape website as a valuable source of rapidly changing information on Intranets. From time to time you'll get updates on server hardware technology, server software developments, conversion tools, publication tools, TCP/IP developments, and ideas that will help strengthen your own Intranet implementation.

Opportunities for the Intranet

Most medium-sized or large-sized organizations have accumulated a variety of computer systems as computing technology has evolved. Mainframes, minicomputers, workstations, and PCs often are linked together via a potpourri of operating systems, applications programs, and user interfaces. Many corporate workers have become so sick of new systems and new applications that they are openly revolting and failing,

Figure 1-1

or sometimes even refusing, to use new software and systems. Comprehensive training for such diverse systems is nearly impossible because dozens of different courses might be needed to do a single job, and the systems change faster than users can schedule, attend, and assimilate new material from new courses.

The amount of available information also has expanded tremendously. It's not unusual for a large organization to have millions of documents and pieces of electronic information that required many more millions of dollars to produce. The corporate Intranet, more than any concept since the invention of the computer, makes it possible to easily and economically put this information in front of the people who need it without requiring impossible amounts of training.

Moreover, the information can be linked by hypertext, which gives it a different slant. Hypertext linking will create relationships between information that would have been impossible to take advantage of in the past. Your organization's productivity can soar to heights never-before imagined, because you'll be able to link information in innovative new ways that will create increased synergy for productivity improvements.

Restructuring the Information

Of course, the tremendous task of restructuring information to take maximum advantage of hypertext formatting still remains. But at least an Intranet will quickly bring far easier access to current information. Then, over time, an organization can modify its information so that the benefits from its Intranet access will steadily increase. A complete information overhaul, to maximize hypertext accessibility, might take a long time, but document-conversion software and automatic indexers will get your information online and cataloged. Meanwhile, most information will be available very quickly and inexpensively via basic keyword searches.

Converting all existing information into fully linked hypertext will be far too great a task for your organization's professional computer staff to handle alone. Fortunately, many excellent conversion applications are available on the market to help your organization quickly convert massive amounts of information into hypertext (see Fig. 1-2).

Unfortunately, even if your computer professionals had the time and resources, they probably would not be able to adequately decipher all the information and make it flow logically as hypertext. That's because straight conversion into hypertext isn't the real challenge; often, only the information's original authors will be able to convert it into well-executed, user-friendly, hypertext presentations.

Getting your organization's information fully converted and optimized might be a long-term project that will involve almost everyone in the organization. That's why most of this book is dedicated to

Figure 1-2

the hands-on aspect of creating hypertext documents. Beginning in Phase 2, you'll find a treasure trove of resources that will help almost anyone convert existing information and create new content in user-friendly, hypertext format.

The focus of the rest of Phase 1, however, is to help you understand the significance of an Intranet for your organization. We'll close this chapter with some real-world examples of what's being done via an Intranet today. Then, the next two chapters in Phase 1 will help you get everyone excited about having their own Intranet, and motivated to make it the incredible success that it can be.

Real-World Examples

Although Intranet technology is one of the hottest technologies now being pursued by corporations and other organizations, because an Intranet is usually meant only for internal access few people get to see examples that show a typical Intranet's many benefits. But Eric Engelmann, one of this book's authors, has been an insider at the World Bank as its Intranet has grown. By tapping into Eric's vast experience with the Internet and with Intranets, we'll show you many successful Intranet uses.

The World Bank (at **www.worldbank.org**; see Fig. 1-3) was a pioneer in using the Internet to realize its twin organizational goals of supporting developing countries and reducing poverty. Today, the World Bank has full TCP/IP connectivity for every worker and every PC in its headquarters, and for many of its offices located throughout the world.

TCP/IP connectivity at every desktop offers access not only to the Internet but, more important, to more than 10,000 computers within the World Bank. The Bank makes good use of this ability by offering a multitude of information services that were never economical before. While it would be impossible to show the 20,000 different information resources available on the Bank's many web servers, the following examples show some popular uses of Intranets.

Personnel Records

The Bank maintains a directory of all personnel, searchable by phone extension, location, unit, first or last name, e-mail address, and other

Figure 1-3

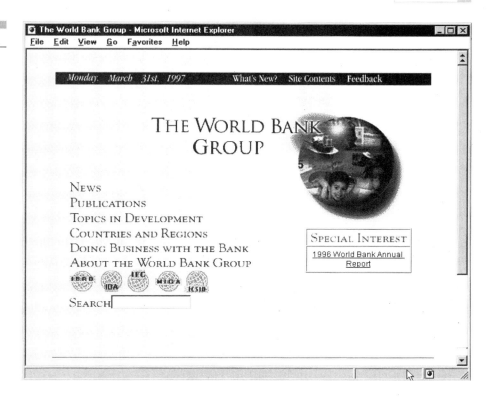

common variables. The directory includes up-to-date information on every staff member, including security ID photos (see Fig. 1-4). Can't remember the name of someone you met at a meeting? You can find him or her by scanning a list of attendees. Ever read a note with a phone extension and an illegible name? You can have the caller's name, organization, and photo in 15 seconds.

Organizational Services

An online *Yellow Pages* of services, such as key shop, housekeeping, printing, graphics, security, and hundreds of others is just seconds away via a web search (see Fig. 1-5). For example, if you need a videotape for a presentation you can find the organization that handles videos without making a series of frustrating phone calls, and probably just getting voice mail. Instead, you'll be able to type "video" into a search program on an Intranet, which will then locate a hypertext document that will show all

Figure 1-4

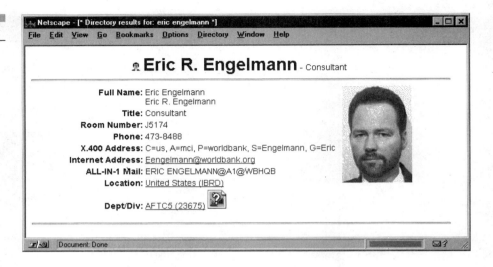

the related resources. Then you'll only have to click on a hypertext link to contact the people who can help you. You'll be able to display the location of their offices, perhaps complete with a color map, and you'll be able to request video services through an e-mail form built into the video services home page.

Project Status

Retrieving and understanding financial data used to require a computer guru, specialized software, and much patience. With an Intranet and Web browser, however, even the busiest managers now can get the data themselves in a minute or two. For example, the World Bank uses its Intranet to put loan status online for its many thousands of projects throughout the developing world (see Fig. 1-6).

Without an Intranet, a manager might spend more time tracking down the right person to ask than he or she now would need to locate the same information. And, before an Intranet, finding the right person to ask was often only the first step in a process that might require contacting several other people and waiting for several days, especially if the manager wanted to see the information during a holiday period or just before a weekend. Now, with an Intranet, anyone in the organization with sufficient access rights can check any inside information quickly, efficiently, and without help.

Figure 1-5

Figure 1-6

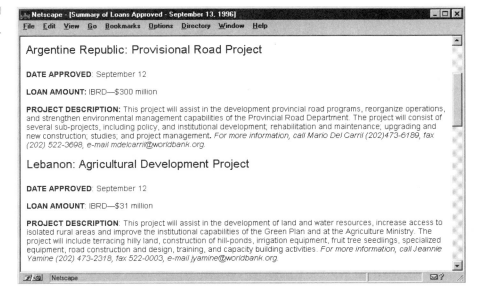

Newsletters

Newsletters often are used by management to keep an organization informed, directed, and motivated. Unfortunately, the costs of printing and distributing newsletters discourages their use. And even though desktop publishing has greatly reduced the lead time required to bring a new issue to publication, the lag time between completion of the camera-ready copy and the distribution of the printed newsletter can render much of the content out-of-date and no longer news.

A newsletter on an Intranet, however, allows full-color newsletters to be distributed to every desktop, instantly and with the very latest information (see Fig. 1-7). And, instead of merely summarizing important information, the online newsletter can jump readers to the original source with but a single mouse click. Moreover, errors, updates, and additions can be edited online to ensure that the newsletter contains the most current information possible.

Another major benefit of online Intranet newsletters is that they can be automatically archived for easy access at any later time. If your Intranet is equipped with the latest Web-searching technology, all content can be indexed into a search engine so that it can be located via a

Figure 1-7

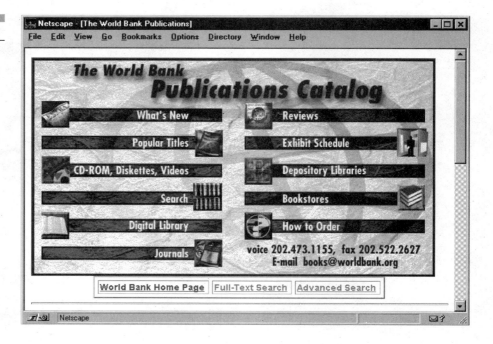

Figure 1-8

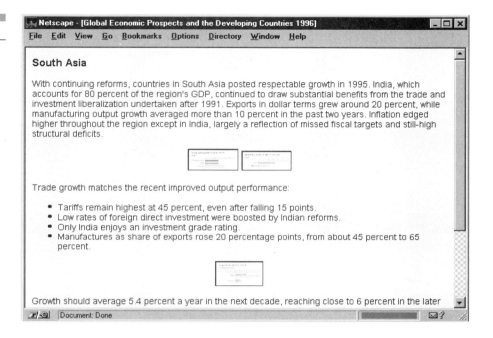

keyword search. As you can easily imagine, this is a vast improvement over trying to remember which past edition of the newsletter contained a key article you wanted to read again. If you can remember but a few words, you can quickly pull up the article on-screen. Then the information can be printed again, or copied and pasted into another article, a proposal, or a report. Or, it can be e-mailed anywhere in the world.

Meeting Minutes

Every organization suffers through necessary meetings, with minutes used to record conclusions and actions for attendees and for others who missed the meeting. An Intranet makes it easy for people who can't attend a meeting to find out what happened at any date (see Fig. 1-8).

Searchable, online archives of minutes are a big plus, too. As with online newsletters, online meeting minutes become instantly accessible, by keyword search, to every member of the organization who has access rights to the information.

Figure 1-9

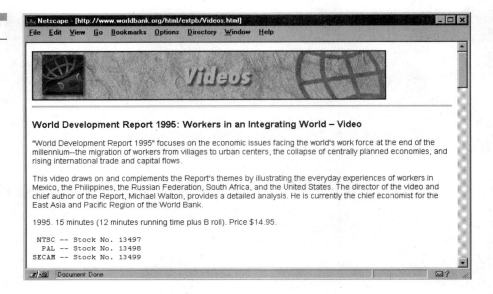

Training

Corporate training is fast evolving from having a linear structure and being rigidly formal to being just-in-time and individually tailored. An Intranet is a great way to distribute rapidly changing course schedules, class outlines, manuals, interactive online lessons, and even real-time videos (see Fig. 1-9).

The ability to create interactive, online lessons is perhaps one of the most exciting innovations available on an Intranet. Users will be able to study, fulfill training requirements, and take required exams, all online. For a multinational organization, this can be a tremendous boon that will eliminate the time zone problems associated with much monitored testing. As rapidly as the computer training industry is developing, you'll need to track current software and capabilities to stay abreast of this exciting technology.

Creating Online Lessons and Tests

Don't worry about the technical burden of creating online training programs and online testing. You won't need an army of HTML experts and computer wizards to create user-friendly lessons and tests, because there are some excellent programs that specialize in this type of Intranet content.

A top example is Interactive Brochure, created by AMT Learning Solutions. Interactive Brochure was designed originally to let you easily create interactive multimedia presentations that can work on your Intranet or over the Web. But now an expanded version also lets you create interactive training sessions. It includes a testing, scoring, and reporting system that can handle all functions online, sending crucial scoring information to corporate headquarters from any office in the world. It's a perfect way to handle ongoing training requirements at all your offices, and lets workers complete their requirements on their own time and in their own time zones.

For more information, contact AMT Learning Solutions at `www.amtcorp.com,` or e-mail a request to `amtsales@ amtcorp.com.`

Client/Customer Information

Keeping staff with an interest in a project up-to-date used to require a blizzard of memos or e-mail, with a lot of time spent filing and organizing the paperwork so that the information could be retrieved and used productively. An Intranet provides fast, one-stop shopping for the latest information. For example, the Bank's Africa region Web server stores information on each of the Bank's country partners, with status, contacts, and other information (see Fig. 1-10).

With an Intranet, instead of dozens—or perhaps hundreds—of workers tracking a client with individual files, your organization can give single-source access to everyone who needs to know. You'll be able to maintain a single location that holds all of the information, a traditional database system modified for Intranet access. Or, you can continue to let everyone on the project maintain individual records, but you can have them link their records across the Intranet, using hypertext, and create what is, in effect, a massive, complex, single record on the client or customer.

Such a massive record in the past would have been gross overkill and nearly useless, because its size would have restricted access. Now, however, an Intranet can index all the information so that every aspect of the client record can be accessed via a keyword search, even though parts of the record might be scattered across many computers in several countries.

Figure 1-10

Administrative Information

Every large organization maintains huge quantities of administrative manuals, benefits and compensation information, and travel or other information needed to support staff and the organization's mission. While the Bank still provides printed copies of these types of documents on request, many staff members have abandoned them in favor of electronic versions that don't clutter their offices or go out-of-date (see Fig. 1-11).

Creating a hard-copy manual of something as complex as today's health insurance benefits options can be an expensive and daunting task. The use of color graphics is imperative these days, to clearly explain to workers the many choices that are available. Then, for all the work and expense involved in producing a colorful manual, it can go out-of-date between completion and distribution of the printed version.

An Intranet version of an insurance manual, in contrast, can not only use graphics and color freely but can also link workers directly into the home pages of the providers themselves. What better way to handle workers' questions about complex insurance plans than to refer them directly to the source, via hypertext?

Accounting Expense Reporting

It's not unusual to hear workers in any large organization recount horror stories relating to accounting systems, manuals, and procedures. The Bank hasn't found a way to make budgeting painless, but it has saved staff time and has made information more accessible by putting procedures and contacts online on its Intranet (see Fig. 1-12).

Policies can be explained with clear, colorful graphics. Contact information for the accounting department can be published so that it requires only a mouse click to ask questions. Information can be collected on-screen from HTML forms that input the data directly into the accounting database. This obviously saves time by instantly placing the information into the organization's computer system, and by eliminating the time lag for hard-copy expense reports to be entered. But it also will reduce errors tremendously and speed reimbursement payments.

Outside News Services

The staff of every organization needs to stay informed on local, national and world news affecting their members' work. The Bank provides highly focused news clipping services with continuous updates of ClariNet

Figure 1-11

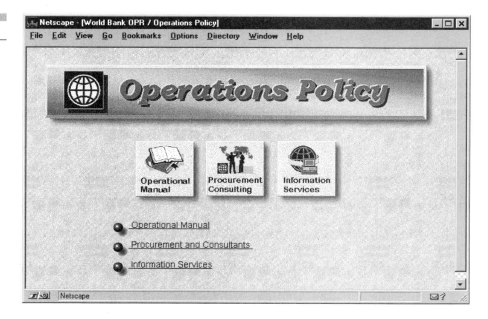

Figure 1-12

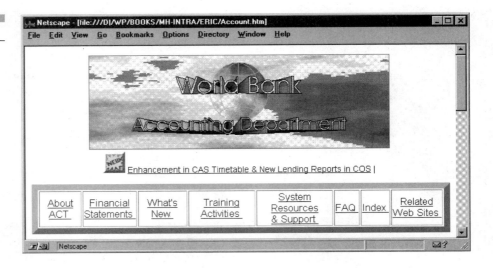

Figure 1-13

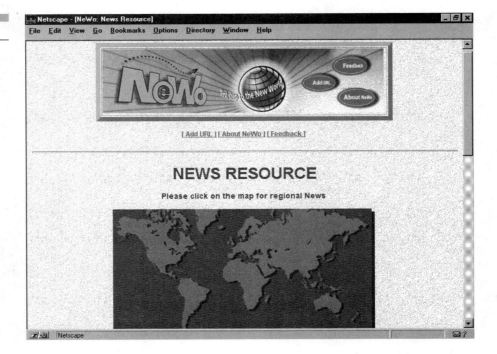

newsgroups. For example, the Bank's Africa region managers can follow the latest UPI and Reuters articles on West Africa with a few mouse clicks, without having to wait for the next day's newspapers (see Fig. 1-13).

These news services are available inexpensively and are affordable for almost any organization—you don't have to be as big as the World Bank to order tailored news delivery. Depending on the size of your organization, and its need for up-to-date news, you might want to simply make available direct access to the news service, or to the tailored reports. Larger organizations might have staff read and repackage the tailored reports, and might then publish on an Intranet only the rewritten material. Either way, you'll easily be able to give workers quick access to the latest information that might affect their jobs.

ClariNet

ClariNet e.News is an electronic newspaper that delivers professional news and information directly to your Intranet. It sends live news (including technology-related wire stories), timely computer industry news, syndicated columns and features, financial information, stock quotes, and more.

You can receive, on request, a free sample of selected articles that are posted to the Usenet newsgroup `biz.clarinet.sample`. If you want more information, contact ClariNet for a targeted sample of the news topics you want to track (see Fig. 1-14). If that isn't enough, they will give you a free, two-week trial of the e.News with no obligation.

With the e.News, you can put the Internet to work for you to receive the news that directly affects your life and your business. The e.News service combines the in-depth coverage of print media with the speed of broadcast media to give you the best of both worlds. Many U.S. media limit their international coverage for reasons of space and time, but e.News doesn't suffer from either of those limitations.

Your Organization

What about your organization? Perhaps you're thinking that you're not as large as the World Bank and you don't have comparable resources. Well, that's the beauty of an Intranet. You don't need a lot of resources.

Figure 1-14

Almost any organization of any size can use most of the examples cited here. Yours might be simpler versions, but the cost of implementation, whether large or small, can be low. And, you don't need massive computing power to handle these tasks, either.

Even more important, you don't need a staff of computer professionals. As you'll see in Phase 2, most of the technology that is employed on an Intranet also is in common use on the Internet. Thus, there are plenty of user-friendly tools that will help workers in your organization create Intranet content that everyone can access and use productively. And much of what they create will serve double duty as public Web content.

But before we move into the chapters on the "how" of creating Intranet content, we want to show you some of the "why" behind creating Intranet content. The next chapter will help you see the economic benefits that can come from implementing an Intranet in your organization.

Business Efficiency Tools

A well-implemented Intranet can boost employee morale and create a more harmonious and unified organization. And, an Intranet is a wise investment that can help the bottom line both by reducing costs and by increasing income. It can also deliver a wide range of benefits.

But the business efficiency that an Intranet can bring extends far beyond its simple bean-counting benefits. There is no way to measure accurately the cascading benefits that can come once an Intranet is implemented.

- Productivity increases, because employees don't have to waste time tracking down obscure information.

- Sales that might previously have gone to a competitor now can be closed, because sales representatives can answer nearly any question quickly.

- Errors will be prevented, because employees will have access to the latest information in all areas. Other errors will be prevented because much data reentry and transcription will be eliminated.

- Savings will come from quick access to tailored news delivery, and having the latest news might either derail problems before they become train wrecks or might open up new opportunities.

- Collaborative projects can be coordinated easily over an Intranet, so that everyone can work with the latest version, even workers who are traveling or live in distant countries.

- Quick feedback comes from employees once they discover a snag within a project, a program, or a document.

- Sharing information on competitors, including their stock performance and news that affects their industry and their pending business deals, can be very useful.

The list could go on and on. The important point here is that an Intranet will help the bottom line in countless ways that can never be measured. But, naturally, organizations need to base business decisions on something more solid than promises of countless unnamed, cascading benefits. So, we've prepared some direct, bottom-line factors that are easy to visualize and simple to translate into precisely how an Intranet can help your organization. First we'll explore ways in which it can reduce expenses, and then we'll show you ways in which an Intranet can improve revenues.

Expense Reductions

Most organizations spend lots of money on rent, telephones, utilities, travel, shipping, labor, computer hardware, and computer software. An Intranet will reduce expenses in each of these areas.

Unlike many business decisions your organization will make, the decision to implement an Intranet will be obvious. Few other decisions that your organization ever will make will generate a larger return on investment and will so quickly repay the start-up costs. Intranets can be implemented quickly and cheaply, and their benefits will improve the performance of every department in your organization. It's truly a no-brainer.

Rent and Utility Cost Reductions

To the extent that putting your company information online, using e-mail, and taking advantage of video conferencing can allow employees to work anywhere (including at their homes), you might be able to dramatically reduce your office space. Or, you might use less expensive space in areas closer to your customers, or with greater appeal to your employees. Telecommuting is one of the hottest new waves in organizations today, and it will continue to grow as technology improves. The Intranet will reduce costs, because fewer people in the office translates directly into lower rent and utility costs.

Another benefit of putting information online is that employees won't need to store so much information in their offices. This will reduce office clutter and thus cut floor space needs, which also saves on both rent and utilities. How much does your organization spend each year keeping its file folders comfortable and cozy?

And there's a bonus. Not only will your files consume less valuable office real estate, but they'll also be usable to everyone in the organization who has access to your Intranet—everyone in every office in every branch in every country!

Phone Bill Reductions

Your computer system might already be using dedicated data lines, yet employees can still run up enormous phone bills between offices. An

Intranet provides access and communication to any office in the world without additional, distance-based charges. Faxes between remote offices can be reduced, if not completely eliminated. Instead of printing a document and faxing it, employees can send the original document as an e-mail attachment. Not only does e-mail save on phone bills, but the recipient gets something even more useful than a fax. The original text can be edited, copied, and pasted or printed in a variety of fonts and on a wide selection of paper stock. People won't be limited to using paper that can be handled by their fax machines.

And, there's another exciting new development that one day will change the way we communicate: *Voice Over the Net* (VON). Today, it's only a crude technology and most office computers lack the required peripheral devices (see Fig. 2-1). But these days, crude technology becomes mainstream technology in a flash, so expect to be using VON over your Intranet very soon.

The promise of VON is that your staff soon will be able to bypass the telephone companies and convert workstations into digital phones, voice message recorders, and even video-conferencing terminals, all for far less than current telephone costs.

Figure 2-1

VON technology requires more bandwidth than the Internet can handle, and that's why you don't see it revolutionizing interorganizational communications. But Intranets are another story. Yours probably will have sufficient bandwidth to handle voice communications. If so, then you'll enjoy large savings in telephone bills. Or, more important perhaps, you might find that workers will no longer feel rushed to cut short their long distance calls, thus failing no longer to exchange important information that could affect a project or a sale.

Shipping Savings

Crucial spreadsheet numbers and files that might have been sent via Federal Express can be transferred across an Intranet instantly and at dramatically lower cost; e-mail can carry any type of file as an attachment, so you can send documents that contain graphics, clipart, charts, presentations, photos, and sound and/or video clips. Federal Express provides a wonderful service, but it's no match for instantly sending a document via an Intranet.

While there's a limit to the size of an attached e-mail file that you can send across the Internet—generally about two megabytes—your Intranet probably won't have restrictions on the size of e-mail file attachments (see Fig. 2-2). Thus, you could send very large computer files simply as e-mail attachments.

If your Intranet uses the Internet for access to remote offices, you might instead use the Internet's File Transfer Protocol (FTP) to send large documents (see Fig. 2-3). You can even set up an internal, anonymous FTP site that will allow any Intranet user to download important files at any time. In a similar fashion, the Web also can be used as a repository for documents that workers can download anytime. Your Intranet will ensure that these files remain confidential and can be accessed only by authorized Intranet users, and *not* by public Internet users.

If your Intranet relies on toll lines to provide connections between offices, transmission costs can be further reduced via compression programs. For example, consider two companies trying to work out a license agreement in a fast moving market. The Washington office could outline their terms and could send a document to Tokyo at close of business, via e-mail or FTP, where it would arrive at 8 AM for editing. The Tokyo partner could send electronic copies to the staff involved, and

Figure 2-2

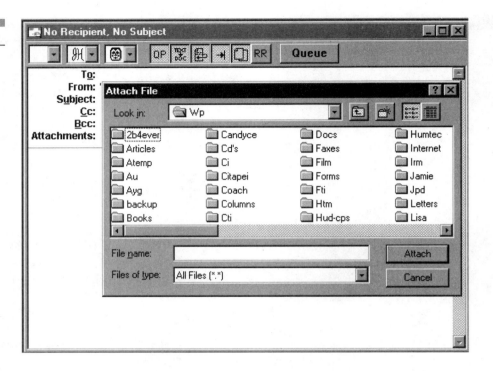

Figure 2-3

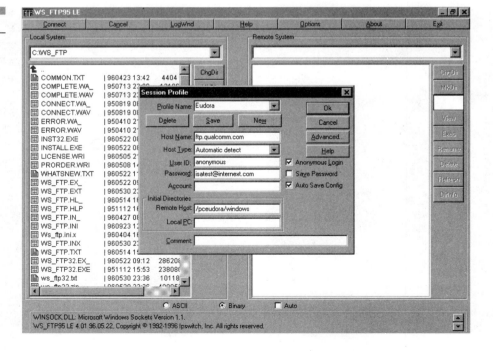

they could spend the day reading and annotating the electronic version of the document. They could then send it back to Washington at the end of their business day, making it available for a new round of editing at the beginning of the new day.

Compare this 24-hour cycle with the time needed for Federal Express (a minimum of four days). While a fax machine could substitute for some of this, the transcription delays and errors make it much less desirable. Faxes are no substitute for having the actual computer file that you can manipulate and reprint. Further, faxes suffer a continuous degradation with each transmission. After a faxed document passes through three or four editing cycles, it might become nearly unreadable. Of course, electronic transmission of the file ensures that it never degrades, no matter how many times it's sent, and the print quality is not dependent on the limited output quality of each person's fax machine.

Computer Software Savings

Computer software user licenses generally are based on one user at a time per registered copy of the software. Traditionally, this has meant paying a license fee for each employee who uses the software. An Intranet, however, can significantly reduce the number of copies of a software application for which your organization needs to pay, because an Intranet can give your organization the ability to legally share software among multiple users.

For example, first consider that the time difference between a branch office in Europe and another branch in California can be eight or nine hours. That means that one employee could use a software application all day in London, then at 5 PM, could logoff and go home. That copy normally would lie idle on a hard drive until the next morning. But now, that copy can be transferred via an Intranet to the California office and can be used all day in that office, then can be transferred back in time for the London worker to use it the next day in London. Software swapping saves money and still satisfies the licensing requirement to use each copy on only one PC at a time.

An Intranet also can bring some real savings benefits in the area of data backup. Many organizations have an elaborate system of tape backups that includes using a storage service to maintain archived copies of the tape off-site. But now, crucial data can be transferred via an Intranet to remote offices and can be stored on computers all over the world.

Using an Intranet as a data backup not only eliminates the need for an off-site tape storage service but is actually safer. If one office is destroyed in a widespread natural disaster, it's possible that the storage facility also could be affected. But having copies at several remote locations will ensure that data can't be lost to a single catastrophe, short of an invasion by alien UFOs.

And, there's a bonus to using an Intranet for data backup. If you ever need to restore information, you might encounter a lengthy delay in getting your tapes delivered and scheduling a computer guru to upload the data from the tapes. But over an Intranet, access time won't even be affected. You'll be able to access the data instantly over a remote server and continue working while the computer staff works out the technical problems.

Computer Hardware Savings

Here's a savings opportunity that will be most valuable within small-to-medium organizations: a reduced need for computer hardware. If your organization has several small offices scattered around, you might find it a serious financial burden to have to buy a complete set of computer hardware for every location.

For example, before an Intranet was available, each site might have needed an individual scanner and a color laser printer. But now, one scanner might be all that's needed for a dozen or more local branch offices. Images and documents can be delivered quickly via courier; you probably would have long ago scheduled regular runs for other documents. After delivery, the scanned image files can be sent out as attachments to Intranet e-mail.

Or, one color laser printer could suffice for several local branch offices. Here the process would be reversed. The files would be accessed via an Intranet, and then the finished documents would be delivered via normal courier runs. Of course, it's also possible that the color documents might need to be sent directly to a client or customer, in which case there's no need to return them to the office of origin. The office with the color laser printer could handle the mailing.

And there's a bonus here, too. Instead of having to train someone in every office in the specialized skills of image and document scanning, you can get by with only one person, plus an understudy, who can handle all the organization's scanning needs. Scanning is a difficult art to master, and producing truly professional results is not automatic. Entire Web sites are dedicated to scanning techniques (see Fig. 2-4). Thus,

Figure 2-4

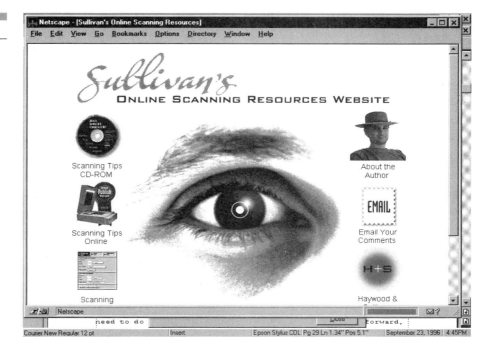

a central, single scanner would not only reduce hardware costs, labor costs, and training costs, but you would have all your scanning done by someone who could take the time to become an expert at that skill.

Labor Reductions

The single largest expense for most organizations is labor. If you implemented an Intranet, your staff members could locate in less time the information they need to do their jobs. And, because they could immediately forward, repackage, or otherwise use the information (because it would already be in a handy electronic format), they could be far more productive.

An Intranet will save labor on all sides of the personnel pool. The burden on workers will be reduced, because fewer people will be needed to handle, catalog, and transfer information. The burdens on management will be reduced because managers will be able to get information more quickly than ever before, without being dependent on an overworked staff.

Travel Expense Reductions

Airline travel can be a terrible waste of executive time, but even when travelers use a corporate jet, travel time includes downtime in which executives are not productive. Worse, jet lag can reduce the effectiveness of executives once they arrive, and its effects can linger for days upon their return to the home office. Furthermore, while they're gone, a vacuum can be created in their home offices. Typically, few people have ready access to traveling executives.

Fortunately, video conferencing, online audio, and electronic whiteboards can sometimes be used over an Intranet in place of increasingly expensive business travel. Even if the organization can afford the time and costs of travel, most executives could reach more of their organization, and be more effective, with technologies that let them be in multiple places at once.

Additionally, travel by employees who need to meet training requirements can be greatly reduced. Often, the only reason for employees to travel to a training site is so that a lot of people can have simultaneous access to one trainer. The Intranet can solve that problem in two ways. First, it can put the trainer and the students together through live video conferencing (see Fig. 2-5). Second (and this is more innovative), an Intranet can give workers interactive training lessons that can be accessed at any time, in any order, and can be learned at the pace of each individual student. That's a pretty nice benefit; not only are travel costs saved, but the training might actually be more effective.

Printing Cost Reductions

Company newsletters, procedure manuals, announcements, and other internal publications cost a lot to print. They also consume resources when they are delivered to desks for the recipients to look over, file, store, and then dispose of. All of these costs and personnel burdens accrue even though most of the material will never even be read. What a waste!

The Intranet makes the same documents available online faster, without the expenses associated with paper (see Fig. 2-6). Of course, some documents really do need to be printed and circulated, but these are only a small fraction of the mountains of paper cluttering most organizations.

And there's a bonus. While reducing printing costs, an Intranet actually can make the material more user-friendly. There's no way a printed

Figure 2-5

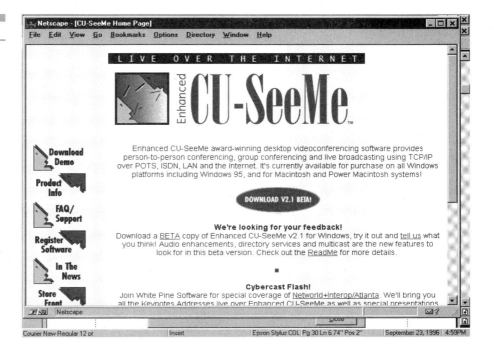

Figure 2-6

newsletter article can have a hypertext link that permits a reader to e-mail the author by merely clicking a mouse.

Security and Access Improvements

Most organizations have some information that needs to be kept secure, even from many of their own employees. This kind of sensitive information includes trade secrets, some types of customer information, some types of data on clients and customers, marketing plans, and some types of personnel information. While not everyone might need access to all this information, different segments of the organization might need access to specific pieces of it.

A properly designed Intranet can maintain an information access profile for each type of employee, allowing access to appropriate resources while blocking access to others. An Intranet authorization server can determine the authorization level of each user who makes a request, and then can notify information servers as to what data can be accessed.

There are, however, some serious data security risks associated with an Intranet. Just as a unified network with access to all corporate information from every desktop is simple and convenient for employees, everything is equally accessible to a hacker who can penetrate your security. Likewise, if large numbers of personnel feel comfortable with downloading and running new software on their PCs, a hacker can plant a program (called a Trojan or a Trojan horse, after the Trojan horse of legend) that can do anything the user's network privileges allow, including transferring files to the hacker's location at any time, day or night.

To control security threats, a layered security approach is used that is similar to the physical security present in office buildings. Just as company computers often need to be locked down to desktops, mission critical computers need to be behind restricted access doors, and secrets need to be kept in safes, an Intranet needs more than one guard at the door.

If your company is a security target, because of financial or political reasons, you should consider seriously the risk of Trojan-type programs. People with privileged access to sensitive computer systems and data should be cautious about storing passwords or clues on their systems. They also need to be cautious about leaving written copies of their passwords in obvious places around the office.

However, as serious as the hacker threat is, your organization is much more likely to be victimized from the inside, either accidentally or deliberately. Having all your customer and employee records online makes it easy for an insider to package the data and ship it out of the organization (or even out of the country) in seconds, something that couldn't be done when information was stored in physical filing cabinets. In an era of decreasing job security and angry ex-employees, a carefully planned backup policy is critical to long-term company survival. Since we will address the security issue more thoroughly in Chap. 6, let's move on now to ways that an Intranet can increase your income.

Income Increases

As important as reducing expenses can be for the bottom line, increasing income can have an even greater impact. Since a huge factor in increasing income is the effectiveness of your team, and because an Intranet can dramatically improve staff efficiency, your Intranet can help improve your organization's income.

An Intranet can make possible many projects that previously could not have been attempted. When an organization's talent is spread out all over the country, or all over the world, collaboration can be difficult. And, the cost of supporting a remote collaboration might have made many projects too expensive. Fortunately, many of those same projects now can be accomplished cost-effectively via an Intranet.

The Round Table Group

Remember, a typical Intranet can be connected to and can become a part of the greater Internet. This connection can bring you whole new levels of collaborative abilities.

For example, from its main offices overlooking Lake Michigan, Round Table Group (RTG) uses the Internet to coordinate worldwide connections between staff scholars and clients. RTG was conceived by Russ Rosenzweig while he was a student at Northwestern University. Russ realized that he had instant access to the ideas and opinions of the world's most respected scholars but that corporate leaders, policy makers, venture capitalists, and decision makers in general did not have the same access to information as the average college student.

Russ's solution was to bring together professors, decision makers, corporate leaders, and policy makers by creating a database of hundreds of professors spanning the breadth of the academic and professional disciplines, including economics, management, business, marketing, political science, international relations, government, sociology, criminal justice, and history. Individually, the Round Table Scholars are among the most respected and authoritative in their fields, publishing in prestigious journals, consulting for public and private firms, and teaching at more than 100 of the world's finest colleges and universities, including Northwestern, Harvard, University of Chicago, Yale, Brown, Emory, Oxford, Cambridge, Cornell, individual units in the University of California system, Georgetown, and Columbia.

Some RTG scholars are not university faculty but, nonetheless, are noted experts in their fields. Because of their association with government agencies, law firms, management consultants, news media, and other private corporations, RTG scholars are invaluable sources of current information and advice. Collectively, the RTG scholars make up one of the most learned think tanks ever assembled, except that they aren't "assembled" at all. Only a few years ago the RTG alliance would not have been possible, but in a few more years, similarly constructed virtual organizations will be common.

And now, you can *virtually* add the Round Table Group to your organization by linking a page on your Intranet to their Internet URL at `www.history.rochester.edu:80/rtg`. Your Intranet users then can search the RTG for collaboration partners in any field. These virtual workers will vastly widen the range of revenue-producing projects your organization can tackle.

So, an Intranet certainly will help you take on revenue-producing projects that previously weren't possible, but it also might enable you to take on new clients or customers that you previously could not afford to serve. And many factors of geography are eliminated by an Intranet, thus permitting your organization to look far beyond its local zip code for new business prospects.

Your Intranet also might enable your organization to increase revenue from existing projects for existing clients. If your offerings to existing clients involve providing them with information services, your organization might be able to grant direct access to your Intranet to certain trusted clients and customers (an Extranet). Since these clients would be receiving premium information access, you could charge them a premium rate for services you previously provided in hard copy format.

Increasing Revenue

Here's a website to which you might want to link your Intranet: **www.marketing-coach.com** It's maintained by author Ron Wagner in conjunction with Dick Connor, CMC, who has written several books on how to increase your organization's revenue. His best-selling books are *Getting New Clients, Increasing Revenue,* and *Marketing Your Consulting and Professional Services,* each of which is featured in his Marketing Coach website.

The Marketing Coach site is a rich source of Internet links to valuable Internet marketing resources. Of course, Dick himself is available as a marketing consultant. He specializes in helping organizations increase revenue and get new clients by showing them how to increase the value they deliver to their clients and customers.

Turnaround Time Improvements

Information, numbers, facts, and news can be exchanged in real time to ensure that only the very latest material goes into proposals and reports. An Intranet can give full corporate access to remotely located workers, regardless of the distance or of the time zone in which they work. One popular way to take advantage of a global Intranet is to use time zones to extend the workday. Suppose you have a job that takes 16 hours and can be split among many workers. If the first worker in New York works eight hours and sends the partially completed job to the Paris office at 5 PM, the Paris worker could start at 7 AM Paris time and have the job completed by 3 PM Paris time, or 9 AM New York time.

In global companies, U.S. staff members have jokingly proposed that all senior management be relocated to Europe so that approval cycles could be reduced. This tongue-in-cheek theory is based on having workers complete their tasks, then having management review and approve the work during the night so that workers could return in the morning to have instant access to approved projects. Normally, the approval cycle could run well into the next day so that the original worker might not get the approved project back until the next morning.

The Intranet also can help management track the progress of remote workers. ISDN and other new, high-bandwidth communications options offer sufficient bandwidth for work-from-home for maternity leave, inclement weather, and temporary building shutdowns (moves, repairs, renovations, natural disasters, and civil disorder).

Even holiday shutdowns can be worked around with an international Intranet. For example, the Fourth of July in the United States can easily create a four-day holiday period in which little work is accomplished. But workers in other countries can keep advancing an Intranet-based collaborative project. So the U.S. workers return to work to find the project has continued to move forward. Remember, as you think of ways to implement your own Intranet, you'll need to forget a lot of common practices that you've accepted in the past. Many business limitations now exist only because people are accustomed to them. If we could all start over and learn our businesses from the ground up with an Intranet in place, most businesses would be structured and would function very differently from the way they are today. This means that many projects can be turned around now in far less time than we've expected in the past.

Customer and Sales Support Improvements

An Intranet makes it possible for the very latest information to be online and available to tech support and sales personnel 24 hours a day. In this age of ever-shortening product cycles and ever-widening product lines, up-to-date information simply can't be provided any other way.

You might be thinking that this sounds more like an Internet function than an Intranet function. Yes, that's largely true because a lot of your customer support now can be provided across the Internet. Internally, however, your sales representatives and technical support staff will have better access to inside information and will be able to handle customer questions more quickly and more accurately. Keeping customers satisfied with your products and services is a surefire method of increasing revenue through repeat business, and perhaps through positive word-of-mouth.

Feedback-to-Management Improvements

Discussion groups cut through bureaucracy and offer better access than any "open door" policy ever has offered. With information about every department's plans and progress online on an Intranet, managers can drill down to the information they need without waiting for requests to move through channels and wondering what details might have been "filtered out."

With more timely input and with deeper access to inside information, managers also can ensure that the organization delivers maximum value to its clients and customers. And delivering value will increase revenue, because money follows value.

Training Improvements

Technology training seems endless. Few people can afford the time to get a week of detailed training on a single computer application program, such as annually overhauled new word processors, spreadsheets, and graphics programs, much less the endless new systems and upgrades devised by armies of computer professionals dedicated to improving their companies' competitiveness. But training is an important factor in your organization's bottom line. Without proper training, employees will lag in the skills required to constantly help the organization increase its revenue by focusing on the value it can deliver to its clients and customers.

What your employees need to deliver value is training specific to a particular need, immediate and tailored to the skills they need to service your clients and customers. The Intranet enables your organization to push into the new frontier of *computer-based-training* (CBT) that gives your organization just-in-time training on everything but athletics. When an employee uncovers a customer need that he or she cannot fill, then Intranet training can get that person up to speed quickly and perhaps even enable him or her to land additional business.

An Online Training Example

Want to see an example of an online training course? The Internet has plenty, but a good place to start is at the Newbie Cyber Course (see Fig. 2-7). It's a permanent, ongoing training site on the Web, designed especially for new Internet users (*newbies*). It's an extremely well-done treasure trove of information, and it's free. Of course, it also can help you with ideas for your own Intranet-based training system.

Figure 2-7

Today's reengineering of business processes is requiring all employees to constantly improve their skill sets and adapt themselves to new ways of doing business. When so many recommendations, common problems, frequently asked questions, procedures, and latest software versions are already online, users can often find help even when their technology support people are working on other problems.

New policies and procedures can easily be placed online and updated as frequently as desired, without the considerable expense of printing, distributing, and storing bulky paper manuals and memoranda. When procedures and examples are online in hypertext format, users can follow a hypertext link to see examples of a completed form, read why a process is necessary, send feedback on the form for evaluation by business process engineers, and complete and submit information without ever printing and mailing anything. Most important, the user learns by actively doing, which is critical for retention.

For other types of training, CBT on an Intranet lets people quickly locate online training materials. Training producers can maintain just one copy of the training materials on a server, saving the time and labor to update hundreds or thousands of hard copy manuals that have outlived their shelf lives.

The distinction between help desks and training is blurring, and Intranets will continue that trend. Increasingly fewer employees will need formal training, because they will essentially have interactive access to instructional help available around the clock. Is this training, or is it help? It doesn't really matter what you call it; the bottom line is that an Intranet will enable your organization's employees to say "Yes" to clients and customers more often than ever before.

The next step is to begin looking at the process of actually implementing an Intranet in your organization. The next chapter gives you a look at issues that managements need to handle to ensure that an implementation goes smoothly and produces a valuable, productivity-enhancing business tool.

CHAPTER 3

Implementing an Intranet

It's important to recognize that many of the benefits you've read about so far will not materialize immediately. The benefits will have to wait for staff to be trained, information to be made available, and for traditional corporate culture and old habits to change to the Intranet way.

The manager who looks only to next quarter's results might abandon an Intranet before it got started. While investments in hardware, software, and training to implement your Intranet will be low, your corresponding investments in time and patience will be much larger.

Intranet implementation also will be a full-circle process. The more widely an Intranet is implemented, the more people can access it and the more information will be on it. The more it is used and filled with data, the more valuable it will become to everyone using it. Thus it will be used more, which will lead to even more valuable content, which will lead again to increased use.

While many successful Intranets have started quietly, if not spontaneously, planning and management will help ensure success with the fewest false steps and the least expense. One day your Intranet will be an indispensable business tool. Keep that in mind as you suffer through the inevitable start-up problems and delays. And, try to stay focused on the benefits we've described in the first two chapters.

Management

The key to starting or expanding an Intranet is management commitment. That will keep the process going, which is one of the most important aspects of Intranet development. Create a comprehensive plan at the very beginning, share the overall vision with everyone in the organization, let everyone in the organization know that you're completely committed, then don't look back.

Here are some specific actions that the organization can take to enhance the implementation process.

Assign Clear Responsibility

Demand that managers of data stores be responsible for making data accessible to Web browsers. Large corporations are often riddled with "data silos" run by data managers who have little interest in getting the information to users efficiently. Their job so far has been to protect the data that are in their charge. Expect resistance to forcing information managers to throw open their silos.

Insist on Universal Access

State as policy that all information of use to others in the organization should be placed online. We guarantee that such a policy will raise fears in many areas within your organization; empires are threatened by open access to information. Remember, open information toppled the Berlin wall and shredded the iron curtain. Your organization most likely has a few of its own little Berlin walls, and the guardians of those "virtual walls" will be afraid that an Intranet will put them out of business.

Ease the Fears

Revise incentive and reward structures to encourage publishing and participation in online discussions. It's not unusual for employees not to want useful information controlled by them to be placed online, but not all resistance is designed to protect empires. You might discover fears that users will find the information so useful to the organization's bottom line that they will burden the author with requests for more.

And there's another angle: Many people fear criticism or blame once their data become public. An Intranet just might expose a certain amount of "dirty laundry" within your organization. So far it's been hidden away and everyone has stayed out of trouble. Now, along comes this Intranet thing and everyone is supposed to decorate it with pretty graphics and show their treasures to everyone else.

With the right positive incentives, however, people usually will *want* to help others, thus making the entire organization more effective. Just have patience when you sense early resistance. And, give people time to clean up their acts without having to let everyone else see them perform before they're ready.

Emphasize Content over Form

Some staff members might look at your Intranet as an opportunity to become the artists they wanted to be before they had to earn a living, and thus might spend huge amounts of time tweaking graphics and page appearances. Technical staff often encourage this thinking by pushing the technology envelope with animations, tricky page layouts, 3-D graphics, and the latest Web fads. So many exciting things are happening on the Web that people who publish plain, basic information sometimes feel that their information doesn't look professional enough if it doesn't also dance and sing.

Resources only should be spent on page design when the page will be widely and frequently used. And even then, everyone needs to remember that the value of an Intranet is *wide* distribution and easy access. Certainly many of the pretty graphics and colors enhance accessibility. But watch the development closely to make sure that form isn't winning out over function and content.

Also, fears about workload will be eased if it's made clear that the organization's aim is not to create a stunning web structure. It's far too easy for staff members to say they don't have time to put information online if they believe they are expected to spend hours enhancing it with colorful graphics.

Get Everyone Involved

State as a principle that content publishing should be done by the content producers, with technical staff working as coaches and technical problem solvers, not HTML coders. If the content producers can't write or organize their information, deal with *that* problem.

The bulk of this book (indeed, the entire Phase 2 section) is devoted to hands-on lessons that will help everyone put content online. You will find chapters that describe the full spectrum, from simple conversion of existing word processing documents to color, graphics, sound, video, and animation. You cannot expect the computer professionals to carry the entire burden; an Intranet is far too widespread for such a restrictive mind-set.

And there's another angle: Don't let your technical people get between the information and the people who need it. Make it clear that the job of the computer professionals is to help educate the organization's content providers. You'll find that the content providers know best what needs to be published and how best to present it, while the computer professionals might tend to focus more on style and technology.

Develop an Appearance Template

Technology is changing fast, but there's no reason for every menu in an organization to look different than all the rest. Users should spend their time accessing and using the content, not figuring out how to navigate a hodgepodge of Intranet pages.

One good way to set an appearance standard is to have your Intranet's home page and several key screens created by an HTML professional who is experienced in Intranet implementations. These can serve as templates for everyone else. In fact, you could make public the location of various templates that content providers can follow. Templates not only create a standard look but speed HTML authoring chores.

Getting a Jump on Standardization

Today's advanced Windows word processors, such as WordPerfect and Word, have template functions built in. Remember, we've already said that an Intranet will involve a lengthy process of unfolding. For users who might not be placing content on an Intranet for a while, you can create word processor templates that they can use right away to create content that is destined later for an Intranet. Content created from those templates will be easy to convert to HTML documents later.

Advanced users will find that dedicated HTML editors also include Web page templates. HotDog Pro, profiled in Phase 2, begins each new HTML document with a template dialog box (see Fig. 3-1). If your organization's templates are loaded into the HotDog template directory, standardization will be a snap.

Standardize Your Web Browser

Now here's a touchy subject. We're not going to say that you must force everyone to use the same Web browser; you wouldn't be able to accomplish that even if you banned all but one. But different Web browsers render different appearances to Web pages, and you absolutely cannot tolerate having your organization's content providers saddled with the

Figure 3-1

burden of creating double sets of HTML pages to cater to both Netscape and Internet Explorer users.

The solution is to designate a design Web browser; this most often is Netscape. You then would use Netscape as the standard for testing Intranet web page design and appearance. But if a page works well in either of the two mainstream Web browsers, it's basically going to look fine in the other; the differences these days are quite subtle. The setting of a standard will squelch the dual-track system before it ever gets started, and before it eats up vast amounts of time with the testing and reworking of Web pages.

And, while we're on the subject of browsers we recommend that you don't get tunnel vision over using Netscape Navigator. It's not a lock. Look seriously at Microsoft Internet Explorer. As this book is written it still lacks a couple of important features that are currently built into Netscape, but has additional features that Netscape lacks. And, as always, Microsoft is working furiously to pass the competition. There's a very good chance that the momentum soon will swing over and make the Internet Explorer the most widely used Web browser.

Budgeting

Most of the cost of an Intranet will be in labor, but you'll also need to buy some hardware and software. Your technical professionals probably will be able to identify the hardware and software best suited to their backgrounds and to your organization's needs. Departmental Web servers generally will be well served by a recent model PC and Windows NT.

Computer professionals generally prefer UNIX systems for Web servers that will handle frequent information requests from throughout the organization. But a UNIX Web server will seriously undermine the point of Phase 2 of this book, which is to get nearly everyone involved in publishing Intranet content. At best, UNIX will require intervention by professionals to publish completed content pages to the Web server. Opting for Windows NT will ensure that most users can quickly learn to handle minor Web server publishing and maintenance tasks, and that will translate directly into labor savings.

Assuming you already have an organization-wide local area network, you might have to modify the software on each workstation to support the industry standard TCP/IP protocols needed for a standard Intranet. You might also need some additional network infrastructure to support TCP/IP and increased network data traffic. Here are some approximate guidelines.

- Web server hardware: $3000 to $50,000
- Server software: free to $4000
- Browsers: free to $20 per desktop
- Remote access: $15 per employee, plus modems and phone charges
- Network hardware (routers, DNS, modems, firewalls): free to $50,000
- Database software: either an inexpensive option included as standard on a normal upgrade or a very costly addition

Labor

Just as document publishing in an organization often involves a wide range of skills of a variety of staff, publishing on an Intranet will generally involve a variety of people in an organization. All of the roles listed below might be assumed by just one person for a small organization, or by separate people (or even by teams of people) for a very large and well-funded system.

Funding and Mandate

A sponsor, usually a senior manager, provides budget and political support for an Intranet venture. Yet, even with the media hype over the wonders of the Web there will be no shortage of people protecting existing IS structures and budgets, and these people might see an Intranet venture as a threat to the status quo. A sponsor will know how to get the resources the team needs, how to protect them from bureaucrats who might otherwise interfere, and how to ensure cooperation by reluctant content producers and controllers.

Infrastructure Deployment and Maintenance

It's best to have a technical professional design and establish the Web server on which documents will be placed. If your organization doesn't already have a local area network with TCP/IP support, your network specialists will need to establish one. Depending on your plans, it might be necessary to upgrade the network with routers, dial-in modem access, and security devices. The "webmaster" will often be expected to be the hardware and software expert (the "web architect") as well as the system director, coach, teacher, and taskmaster, so solid communication skills are critical. If your web architect lacks the high-quality people skills that are commonly missing in good systems people, you'll need to have someone who *does* have these skills work closely with the architect to ensure that necessary information gets out to the content producers. Engineers enjoy tinkering a lot more than writing directions to help people actually use the tools they've created, and they seem to always have a lot of urgent jobs that prevent them from completing the documentation.

Content Selection

This is the process of identifying and prioritizing the documents, spreadsheets, databases, photos, videos, sound tracks, and other items that should be made available. This includes deciding when the content needs to go online and to whom it needs to be accessible. Will it be available organization-wide or only within certain regions or departments? Will it be available on the Internet as well? If so, will Internet access be unrestricted or will it be password-protected and limited to clients and customers, members, or some other selected groups?

Everyone in the organization should make proposals for Intranet content, including access rights. Management will then approve or disapprove the content proposals. Don't do this from the top down, because lots of information might be hiding in those hidden data silos we mentioned earlier, about which management might be unaware. There might be some pleasant surprises if the proposals for Intranet content come in from the grass roots level within the organization.

Content Production

The continuing need for content production is the greatest challenge an Intranet faces in the startup phase. If you don't have content to begin with, you won't have readers, but people will often *stop* generating content, too. This can quickly turn into a vicious circle that leaves your web server a *ghost* server. To get content, it helps to make production easy for the content producers, and even to have the tech staff do some of the content production work, at least during the startup phase. The following are content production tasks your people will need to do.

Generation

This can often be a draft text or other raw data for publication. Anyone who generates documents would be involved here. In an organization in which staff members are empowered and hierarchies are flattened, most documents will be created directly, by whoever needs to be involved. In more traditional structures, the manager's administrative assistant might prepare raw documents for management review and approval.

Design

This is the process of defining how the document should be presented. Design personnel must consider how to make the document fit with others published, and what results are expected from readers. Should the documents inform them? Persuade them? Make them act? For documents with small circulation, these are not big issues and are generally handled by the content producer. For documents with wide distribution, publishing professionals should assist just as they probably now do for printed publications.

Editing

This step eliminates spelling, grammar, and other language problems. This is handled by the same people who edit paper documents. Ideally, content producers' existing writing skills will be strong enough for internal documents. If they are not, an Intranet deployment might furnish an opportunity to sneak in a writing skills course that will have great benefits to the organization.

Expect to encounter some resistance, however, from some of your traditional paper-document editors. Many of them are in their profession because of a lifelong love for books and printed material. But now they're going to be forced into a computer world; in fact, they might be pushed far beyond that and clear out into cyberspace. There's a good chance that much of their editing work will now have to be done directly on HTML documents.

Keep in mind that none of them entered this profession because they wanted to edit Web documents. These folks are going to need the chapters in Phase 2, and they're going to need some understanding and support as they move into this new realm of editing.

Style

This is the control of the appearance of the information. People with a good sense of color, balance, and flow can help the idea of the document be effectively communicated with the right fonts, colors, use of photos, emphasis points, and other tools. For most documents, a few minutes' coaching by the webmaster and a short list of general design principles should be sufficient.

For documents that will be read often by many people in the organization, a design professional should be consulted. This is a good idea anyway, as we mentioned earlier, because you can have the professional come in early in the process to create templates that will serve as models for the rest of the content.

Either way, the person in this role needs to have a solid knowledge of HTML coding techniques, as well as communication skills and a good sense of esthetics. So, either find one or create one by developing someone already in your organization.

Technical

Computer specialists assist in providing technical support and training in producing web documents. Note that this is just a small part of publishing. The important elements are in the roles we just mentioned above.

Where databases and interactive web pages are needed, the technical staff assumes a much larger role. For most database applications, a programming background is a big plus. Just as the introduction of the PC in the 1980s resulted in a lot of amateur database applications that were poorly designed, the web offers new opportunities for writers and artists to easily create database applications that everyone in an organization can become dependent on. It's important to get your organization's systems people involved early, before you discover you've grown a mission-critical application that is nearing collapse because of poor initial planning.

Content Organization

This issue involves both technical staff and management. Files must be stored somewhere, and must be organized for ease of access and archiving. Web documents on a single server can easily number in the tens of thousands. A good directory structure will assist staff and provide easy access to material. Some tips on directory structures are given in Chap. 4.

Planning

To get the most from an Intranet, extensive planning is essential. While there are many success stories of spontaneous and "underground" corporate Websites graduating into successful Intranets, planning will reduce false starts and save your organization lots of labor and money.

However, Intranet software and hardware is changing very rapidly, and long-range technology planning is simply meaningless. In other words, we're all learning. Every Intranet being created today is, in some sense, an amateur affair that one day might graduate and become a truly professional system. None of us really yet know what we're doing.

The type of planning that pays off is the type that defines nontechnology issues. Focus on planning who will do what, how content will be updated and verified, how to handle menu conventions, and how to manage change. If you can count on one thing about your Intranet, that thing will be *change*. The technology behind an Intranet is really a nonissue. Technology can easily be handled by any competent, well-informed network professional.

Your challenge is to rethink your organization's communication environment and personnel structure from the ground up, with your own Intranet in mind. How would your organization look today if Intranets had been around as long as telephones? Wouldn't it be a totally different place? So, try to think out into the future to the day when an Intranet is a mature tool. See that vision, and you'll be on your way to creating it.

4

Server Layout
and
Maintenance

Many people think that extremely fast hardware is needed for even modest Web servers. For basic text page serving functions, however, inexpensive hardware will usually suffice. However, when Web servers are responsible for hit counters, database queries, and other types of programs in addition to delivering Web pages, hardware requirements can grow dramatically, thus rendering your hardware obsolete rather quickly. Keep this fact in mind when sizing your server; by oversizing your server you could be wasting money. Buy what you need to do the job and plan on upgrading every two years, just as you update your server software and tools. What do you need? We can't provide the ultimate answer to such a fast-moving, fast-changing question, but here are some real-world examples from the World Bank, a year after its Intranet was widely deployed.

The World Bank's Africa Region Web server serves about 1200 people and is available to the rest of the 10,000 people with access to the World Bank's Intranet. It makes some use of graphical counters and image maps, does light database access (using Allaire's Cold Fusion and a variety of Microsoft Access databases), Perl forms to e-mail, and stores more than half of its 2000 files on Banyan LAN servers. This server runs Windows NT 3.51 on a Dell 120-MHz Pentium PC with 64 Mbytes of RAM and a 2-Gbyte hard drive with PCI SCSI controller and 16-Mbyte Token Ring connection. The server gets about 9000 hits per weekday from about 750 people, totaling about 50 Mbytes of file transfers. During peak hours of the day (2 to 4 PM) the server rarely shows more than 10 percent CPU utilization for sustained periods, and little, if any, delay to visitors.

The World Bank's largest Intranet Web server supports about 10,000 potential visitors, all of whom have Web browsers on their PCs. It receives approximately 70,000 hits and transfers about 250 Mbytes of data each weekday. The Web server hardware is an older model DEC Alpha 3000/500, with 256 Mbytes of RAM, and it averages about 10 percent CPU utilization.

Obviously, your results might vary. The point of these two examples is that, despite claims from people who sell computer systems, until your organization gets used to using the Web frequently for its information needs, the power of the hardware you use doesn't matter much. Put your initial resources into posting content that will attract visitors, and upgrade as the content causes traffic to increase.

That said, it's likely that use of your Web servers will eventually achieve critical mass and require a serious outlay. Servers that begin as experiments can rapidly become mission-critical, as documents and databases migrate to your Web from previous data stores. And, as your Web servers become critical parts of your business processes, a single hour's downtime might have a serious impact on productivity. Adding a backup server that mirrors or replicates the primary server, preferably in another building or room, can help ensure that downtime never exceeds a few minutes.

As critical servers proliferate in large organizations, there is a trend to move these back inside the "glass house" (traditional corporate mainframe group), in "server condos" with the same attended-support that core systems enjoy. Given the historical conflict between these groups, and the freewheeling nature of the PC desktop crowd, traditional computer solutions won't work for everyone and almost certainly won't make sense during the early life of your Intranet.

Server Software Selection

There are so many server choices, and their technology changes so quickly, that it is pointless to recommend a particular Web server program. Instead, we'll focus on discussing principles for server selection for your organization's Intranet.

Standardize Server Software Where Possible

Early Webmasters were pioneers and might react fiercely to any suggestion that their organization should have a standard Web server. But even if you can't get them to agree to use common server software, you will still benefit from standardizing software on any new servers. Many options are available, and new ones are being introduced too quickly for us to name a favorite, but we list below some of the incompatibilities between Web servers, which are the main reasons to standardize.

CERN versus NCSA Image Map   For example, Purveyor uses CERN-style image maps and most others use NCSA style. When users want to move pages from one server to another, they have to rewrite their map files. As the HTML 3.2 specification gets widely implemented in the browsers on your desktops, use of client-side image maps will eliminate this problem. Netscape 2.0+, Microsoft Internet Explorer 3.0+, and future versions of the Notes Web browser all have (or will have) HTML 3.2 client-side image map support.

CGI Program Uniformity   Different tools are used on different servers. Each server might use different methods for forms, databases, access counters, and other CGI applications. The result is that moving pages from one server to another often involves rewriting any portion of a page that uses these server-specific features.

SSI   Server-side includes (SSI) might be implemented on some servers and not on others. Or, some might implement only a subset of the commands available on other servers.

Security   One server might offer security to the file level, another only to directory level. One might offer IP address access while another might use passwords. Others might interface well with authorization servers planned by your security experts, but several standards for encrypting transfer of information from the browser to the server also exist. For most organizations, internal encryption hasn't been an issue to date. If your organization is very large, and if trade secrets travel across your Intranet, encryption is an issue to consider. Internal security issues can be quite complex, but having a server/browser standard makes encryption implementation a lot easier.

Log Files   If you want to analyze access log files consistently, you'll want logs in the same format. Most servers offer the option to use the "Common Log Format," so format won't be an issue in most organizations.

Administrative Tools   Most Web servers come with a variety of administration and maintenance tools. Using the same server throughout the organization helps Webmasters support each other.

Match Your Technical Staff's Expertise

UNIX   The authors' biases might be showing, but in actual practice, running a UNIX server seems to require *two* UNIX experts. That's because there's a tendency for many UNIX experts to endlessly optimize and customize their servers to the extent that only *they* can handle maintenance, and a new Webmaster would rather start all over from scratch. The most popular of all Web servers on the public Internet are Apache and NCSA, both running on the UNIX operating systems. They are much less popular on Intranets within corporate firewalls.

Windows NT   Windows NT has become a popular platform for Web servers, and dramatic advances in performance, scalability, and reliability of Windows NT systems planned by traditional mini/mainframe vendors such as DEC make its future quite bright. In many ways, Windows NT is also very similar to the Windows workstation with which your technical and not-so-technical staff are already familiar.

The bad news on Windows NT is that many of the tools available free with UNIX systems (courtesy of armies of university computer science students' work over the last decade) have to be purchased. While fierce competition is quickly adding more tools to NT Web servers, UNIX systems are still more flexible. The good news is that you'll find better documentation and support for the commercial products, including those for NT, than you will for most free software.

The authors, based on personal experience, recommend WebSite (see Fig. 4-1) and Purveyor for departmental servers. Microsoft's Internet Information Server shows great promise, especially for organizations that have only Windows/Intel workstations and that wish to develop advanced applications. Netscape's broad cross-platform support and commitment to standard protocols is a huge plus for organizations with more diverse hardware and operating systems, and its SuiteSpot product appears to be designed to save lots of time in administration of your Web server, usually the most expensive factor in operating a server.

Macintosh   In general, Macintosh software is designed to be very easy to install and use. Unfortunately, the focus on ease-of-use sometimes

Figure 4-1

makes a negative impact on flexibility, third-party support, and scalability. Nonetheless, if your Webmaster is an experienced Mac user and your organization doesn't plan to do a lot of programming, Macintosh can be an excellent choice for a departmental Web server platform.

NetWare If your organization uses NetWare, you should seriously consider using IntranetWare from Novell. Novell also claims higher performance than equivalent Windows NT-based servers, but there's a toll to pay for ease-of-use.

Oracle Oracle is making a big push to be *the* corporate database publishing server. If your organization has Oracle programmers and databases, chances are that Oracle servers will be a big part of your Intranet.

Virtual Drive Capability (Banyan, Novell Drive Access)

Whatever your existing network might be, it's a big plus for users to be able to save Web pages to network drives the way they always have done, without having to learn about FTP at the same time. By letting users store their content on network drives you can decentralize a large portion of server administration. Servers that support virtual drives will make a user's network drive directory appear to be a local subdirectory on the Web server.

For example, `N:\html\test.htm` might become `http://hostname.domain.com/dept1/test.htm`, because `dept1` substitutes for the `N:\html` network directory. This dramatically simplifies your efforts to get technophobic authors to publish their documents, because the authors need only do a SAVE AS to the `N:\HTML` directory for search engines and menu maintainers to find and index them. They'll never know they're interfacing with a Web server.

APIs

If you plan to do serious software development for your server, and if efficiency is important, a built-in Application Programming Interface (API) will generally offer better performance than adding third-party development products. Most commercial Web servers now offer APIs.

Even if you don't plan to do any programming, you might want to install programs written by others that require a particular API. Using a server API instead of add-on CGI programs will often make server applications run two to three times faster. Using an API means that your server won't have to load program code from disk every time a user needs it.

If you use a proprietary API, however, it will be considerably harder to move an application to another server that doesn't use the same API. Although moving to another server might seem a remote possibility today, the rapid evolution of the Web and Intranets makes moving a stronger possibility than you might anticipate. In general, try not to do anything that will block future moves to take advantage of technological improvements.

Multimedia Servers

Multimedia poses a number of problems for Intranets, mostly relating to bandwidth. You can read a good discussion on the differences between real-time data transmission and normal data transfers at **www.starlight.com/starlight/html/wp.html** (see Fig. 4-2). If you decide to place sound and, especially, video clips, on a Web server, it's probably a good idea to have them on a separate server so they won't interfere with the speed of text and database delivery on your conventional Web server.

Figure 4-2

Directory Structure

Because of the many hyperlinks set by users between Web documents and bookmarks, changing directory structures on an actively used Web server is quite disruptive. This is especially true for those who have the least ability to manage bookmarks and keep up with change. If you must move something, leave a short file behind that points to the new location and includes precise steps for updating bookmarks within your organization's standard Web browser. Careful planning of directory structures will save you and your visitors a lot of grief as the number of Web files and authors grows.

Images, Maps, HTML

Some Webmasters like to keep image files and other non-HTML files in a directory separated from their HTML files. The advantage is that it's easier to share and update common images, saving disk space and minimizing the labor needed to update logos and other common images. While this is great for the technically savvy authors, it is a major hurdle to new authors, who already have enough to learn without having to struggle with multiple directories. Disk space is cheap; your authors' labor definitely is not. It's also easier to move documents when all the local link files they refer to are in the same directory with them. Based on our experience, departmental server Webmasters should do everything possible to make publishing easy, to encourage production of more of the content that encourages visitors.

For a large organization's central servers, where much of the content is widely used and more technical support can be allocated for document preparation, keeping separate directories for graphics makes more sense. Just be careful that the technical order desired by computer specialists doesn't trample on the needs of the less vocal, content-producing community. These people are most critical to an Intranet's success, not the techies. Force the techies to find solutions that make publishing easy for the producers.

In a large organization, some benefits also come from using a consistent directory naming structure from server to server. For example, if CGI scripts are kept in the same directory on each server, authors will be able to move documents from server to server more easily. Keeping log files in a standard log directory, with server information in another, makes it easy for visiting Webmasters to see how your server is organized, and to "borrow" ideas for their own server. For example, an HTML file with descriptions of the tools used to build and run the server is kept in the `\tools\tools.htm` file on some of the production servers on the World Bank's Intranet. While there is often no mention of this on a menu, the Bank's many Webmasters know how to retrieve it.

Newsletter Directory Structures

Documents that are produced frequently and are archived are the most frequently reorganized. Webmasters and users often put each new issue in the same directory at first, then realize that there is a problem when they get to the thirtieth or one-hundredth issue. Directory clutter can become especially severe when authors add lots of graphics and support files to each issue. We've found that creating a separate subdirectory for each issue, with a parent directory with indexes for each year's issues, keeps things simple. A useful naming scheme is the issue date with format YYMMDD, or something similar so that files sort well by issue. Better still, use YYYYMMDD, since the year 2000 approaches.

Emphasize Relative Links

Even with the best planning, you'll probably have to reorganize files during company reorganizations, and if file numbers grow dramatically. Using relative links whenever possible will minimize labor needed to relocate files. New authors generally find relative, absolute, and external links quite confusing. The beginners generally aren't a problem, because they tend to use tools that handle link creation for them. But the authors who open their pages with a text editor are likely to use unnecessary absolute and external links. Make sure links of the form `../../menu.htm` are taught in postelementary Web-publishing classes.

Virtual Drives

Virtual drives can allow access to removable network and CD-ROM resources and can make publishing much simpler for nontechnical authors. A virtual drive lets a server **N:** drive appear to be a directory on the Web server drive. For example, a Windows NT Web server can access a NetWare file service for a finance division in another building, and has assigned a drive letter `N:` to this file service. If HTML files are stored in the HTML directory of this service, and if a virtual path `~finance` were asigned to the actual path `N:\HTML`, Web browsers could find a file `menu.htm` with the URL `http://hostname/~finance/menu.htm`.

The real power of virtual drives lies in letting users save their files onto their regular network drive and having them instantly published. With many new applications offering viewers for native application formats, and with others letting users SAVE AS in HTML format, publishing to the Web can't get much easier. And, users can't claim they don't have time to learn how to publish documents for the rest of the organization to share if all they have to do is save a copy to a particular directory of their network drive. For important documents that will be heavily accessed, this isn't the best solution because the data will have to be transported across the network twice before it reaches the requester (once from the network drive to the Web server, and then again to the Web browser user).

Multihoming

It's often easy for staff to remember a single word that goes to a logical group of information. For example, if your Intranet has a host called **directory.domain.com**, users would only need to type **directory** or **http://directory** to go to the server that contains the organization's directory Web server. Similarly, if the finance department has its own server, a user might type **finance** to load the home page for that server. Setting aliases on your Domain Name Server allows a single machine to have multiple, user-friendly names. If your server supports multihoming, you can assign multiple IP addresses and host names to the same machine and the server software will automatically load the Web pages associated with the host name.

Multihoming also can be useful for moving blocks of Web pages from an overburdened server onto a new machine, without having to change any hypertext links or bookmarks. Unfortunately, there are practical limits on how many host names can be placed on a server. If you want to exploit this, plan carefully with your Web server software provider.

NOTE: *Techie staff members often prefer nicknames for Web servers that have nothing to do with their function. Because of their close association with these machines they have no trouble remembering their names, and might not understand the benefits of naming servers by function. For example, the staff responsible for the World Bank's central Web servers liked the names* zoom, amaretto, and silk *for directory, staging, and discussion group servers, rather than the* directory, staging, and discussion *names that users would prefer.*

PURL Links

A rapidly growing Website will often need restructuring, and international growth may lead to needs for mirrors of Websites. For users who create bookmarks and search engines, and for others who record your URL locations, any movement of documents produces the "404" FILE NOT FOUND server error. Persistent URLs (PURL) use a PURL server as the reference for the actual location of a Web document. If a resource is physically located at `http://www.wdn.com/ems/index.html`, it can be advertised as located at `http://purl.com/ems/index.html`. The PURL server at `purl.com` locates `ems/index.HTML` in its database and sends a redirect to the actual location on `www.wdn.com`. If the page ever gets moved, only the server at `purl.com` needs to be updated, not all the bookmark lists and search engines.

FTP Server

Authors need to get their files to the server. If putting them on their regular LAN drives isn't practical, you'll need to find a way for them to copy files to the server drive. FTP software is available for every type of workstation and most Web server platforms. If your Web server is a Windows NT machine, you can use a shared drive to let Windows for Workgroups, Windows 95, and Windows NT workstations use simple file copies on the shared drive. For UNIX servers, NFS offers similar functionality but requires NFS software, which might or might not be installed on workstations. Netscape 2.0 and later allow FTP uploads from within the browser.

The main problem with using an FTP server is the growing password crisis. As organization staffers become more mobile and more dependent on many different data stores with separate security systems, users' ability to manage their password portfolio is failing. As the number of Web authors grows, managing their directory write permissions and passwords can become a significant, and unwelcome, part of an administrator's workday. Authentication servers might someday handle the password problem, but the access permissions labor demands will remain. Again, if FTP is a hassle for users, they won't create and update content and your Intranet will not be as good as it could be. Make access as simple as possible for them.

News Servers

You can configure your own news server to feed your Intranet. There are a lot of factors to consider before offering newsgroups, and you'll need to be constantly ready to change the mix of newsgroups very quickly. Many newsgroups are controversial, at best, with many of them being totally unacceptable on a corporate Intranet.

Don't forget to advise users that newsgroups are for business use, especially if you don't impose any censorship. Even if you don't intend to enforce a "business only" policy, a warning helps avoid blame for content and abuse. At the minimum, publish a disclaimer that the organization is not responsible for the content of articles in newsgroups.

Options

Your two options are to let your users use the news server of your access provider, or to maintain a local news server. A local news server gives faster response and lets you filter newsgroups that are objectionable to most organizations, such as the **alt.sex.** hierarchy.

Getting a Feed   You'll generally get your Usenet news feed from your ISP, but can also buy one from another provider. Typical cost is $50 per month, in addition to the base cost of your connection, and this will bring you a raw, live news feed.

As an alternative, you could offer popular and noncontroversial newsgroups on site (for best performance), and contract with an ISP for access to a complete set of newsgroups. This distances the organization from censorship issues and relieves the system from needing storage for large numbers of newsgroups your staff rarely (if ever) read. For example, `alt.net` offers 18,000 newsgroups for $5 per month per account.

Excluding Problem Newsgroups   When deciding which newsgroups to include and exclude, make sure your decision is based on business principles. A full news feed and high-speed access often are seen as nice benefits. Management often imagines (sometimes correctly) that staff will spend too much time on hobby newsgroups and neglect their work. If your workplace reward system doesn't motivate staff to focus on their work, you can either fix the workplace or make users request that specific newsgroups be added to the feed when they discover what they need for their jobs.

If you have a large organization, responding to requests to add newsgroups ends up being a bit of a burden for the administrator and is frustrating to staff who are then delayed in accessing a newsgroup. Furthermore, without being able to browse through lists of available topics, few workers will ever know of a newsgroup to request in the first place.

With more than 26,000 newsgroups in existence, and many more coming, it can be quite time-consuming to consider which newsgroups to include and which to exclude. Your staff is unlikely to use more than a small percentage of them. Besides the disk space and bandwidth used to collect and store them, large collections create delays for users browsing lists of newsgroups.

If you decide to include all newsgroups, be aware that many users might object strongly to the `alt.sex.` newsgroups. Many others will object to fringe political and "hate" newsgroups. Still others will be unhappy about any of the growing number of politically correct and anti-PC subjects that inevitably are discussed in various newsgroups. The point is that, if you decide to provide a full feed, be prepared in advance with a sound business rationale. Here are some options for policies.

- *Use an uncensored feed.*   This saves labor and removes the possibility of criticism for including any particular group after excluding another. Be prepared with a censorship statement proclaiming that you don't censor, stating why you don't. If you do decide to provide a full feed, consider a satellite service, which uses a small, roof-mounted dish to get all news feeds for as little as $30 per month.

- *Remove all sex newsgroups.*   Typically, here is where substantial wasting of time and network resources will occur. Binaries take up lots of space and might be seen as contributing to sexual harassment in your workplace.

- *Remove newsgroups to which any staff member objects.* This gets management and administrators out of the censorship/selection role, but might cause problems for the person suggesting the newsgroup removal.

Proxy Servers

Instead of giving everyone direct access to the Internet, you can configure a proxy server. Proxy servers fulfill a number of roles, from aiding your security efforts and controlling unauthorized Web usage to speeding up Web access at users' workstations.

For Limiting Access

If your organization can't focus users' work time on doing their jobs, instead of spending company time on recreational Websites, you can use a proxy server to block access to problem Websites. Unfortunately, there are so many prurient Websites that blocking all of them will waste a lot of your administrator's time. Some organizations block access to all sites and allow access only to specific sites on request. This can be a real administrative nightmare if your organization is large, and can make things very inconvenient for users. An alternative is to let your staff know that traffic logs are routinely analyzed for abuse.

Reducing Web Traffic and Costs

If you have a field office connected with a slow- or medium-speed connection (often shared with voice communications), you might benefit by installing a proxy server with a large disk cache on site. Users at the remote site would use this proxy server as an intermediary to fetch Web documents from the source or from their large disk cache. With a field office of 100 people who visit a remote Web server every day, many megabytes of traffic a day might be saved.

Staging Servers

Staging servers let users put their files on a server identical to the production server, for testing. After they have finished testing the files, they advise the Webmaster to copy the files to the production server. This is especially useful for new services that will be placed on external servers, because it provides more opportunity for management feedback and broader testing.

Access Control

Many Web server programs offer access restriction to directories or individual files, based on IP address and/or passwords. But users have to remember passwords and the Web administrator has to assign them, which can take a lot of time.

The problem with IP address checks is that they can be spoofed by knowledgeable users, and yet they can block legitimate users who try to access the page from a different workstation. IP address blocking works well for parents of small children in a home environment, but it's not a serious tool for blocking savvy Web users.

One solution is to invest in a secure-token type of system. In this system, users are issued a credit card—sized password generator into which they enter a PIN number when logging into the network. The password produced is sent to an authentication server that either confirms or denies the user. All data systems in the organization can then use the authentication server entry to decide whether to allow or disallow access.

Today this sort of system is mostly used to allow dial-in or access to an Intranet from over the Internet, but there is a great deal of demand to extend it to cover all data systems. There are many different technical approaches to providing security for information, and the subject is technically too complex to cover in a single chapter.

In any implementation of security, it's important to keep a few general security concepts in mind. First, there is no completely secure system. If any person can get information out of it, it can be compromised, at least by the person authorized to read the data. If no one can get data from it, there's no reason to bother with storing the data in the first place.

The principle to keep in mind is that there is a tradeoff between the expense and inconvenience of security measures and the various losses a data thief might cause you. It's unlikely that a thief would be motivated to employ a large network of workstations to crack a system that contained information only on bicycle inventory at a local store. However, it's reasonable to expect that the National Security Agency would deploy vast computing resources to get the names and missions of foreign spies or nuclear terrorists.

As the CIA's Aldritch Ames clearly showed, if your data are an interesting target, unauthorized access from the Internet is only one of many possible security breaches. Carefully weigh the benefits and costs against the risks of each exposure. Many organizations opt for segmented security on their networks, with looser and more flexible security for low-risk data sources and much tighter security for bigger targets, such as financial systems or marketing and research data.

Search Engines

Putting tens of thousands of documents online doesn't mean users will be able to find them. The problem of finding information gets even more complex when files are scattered across many Web servers. Chances are good that much of the information put online was on network file servers even before an Intranet was established. The Intranet just made it easier to find and display the information, but that's the whole point. Your Intranet's main function is to provide user-friendly access.

If your users can't find information easily and quickly, your Intranet is crippled. Next to getting users to actually publish their data, providing good search tools will be the most critical factor in your success.

There are two basic methods for helping users find information on Web servers, by menu and by free-text or keyword search. A well-implemented search plan includes both. If possible, offer free-text search across all pages in a given subject area, or on a particular server. For example, a user might want to find the issue of a newsletter that discussed a new field office in Paris.

Regardless of how you design your Intranet, it is critical to provide a means for content producers to register their own Web pages. If you don't, a huge amount of your time still won't be sufficient to fully index the content that even a modest-sized organization can produce.

For menu-oriented searches, the Yahoo! model of letting users pick the menu their link should be added to, and completing a form for Webmaster review, is most efficient. Users generally have a pretty good idea where their entry should appear and usually can do a better job of describing it than the Webmaster, who might be totally unfamiliar with the material or its subject. The Webmaster receives the request and either adds it to the menu (automatically, via a database, or manually via copy-and-paste) or replies to the author with recommendations for changes.

For indexed, free-text search engines operating on a single server, such as WAIS, Verity, and Excite, indexing can be as easy as running a batch file once a week to build indexes. If your organization has multiple Web servers you need to provide a single, consolidated index to avoid forcing users to switch servers and repeat the same query.

`Ht://DIG` offers an Intranet-wide search index. It builds an index with a Web crawler indexing program to produce a result like Lycos, but its usage is restricted to Websites within an Intranet.

Netscape's Catalog Server offers additional capabilities. For the latest information, visit `home.netscape.com/comprod/server_central/product/catalog/index.html`.

Of course, free-text searches don't work well when the your document collection becomes very large. Creating intelligent searches is a major research area for computer scientists. As this is written, it appears that metatags will play a prominent role in many emerging search systems. While no standard exists yet, Excite's lead in metatagging will likely produce a subset of future standards.

Maintenance Tools

Given the popularity of Web servers, it's no surprise that a wide variety of tools exist to help you manage them. Because Intranets are so new it will be a while before these products mature. Server producers are working hard to add time-saving maintenance features to their products, but third-party products generally have more to offer. Three common problems for Webmasters are broken links, failed servers, and orphaned files. We'll give examples of tools that help with these problems.

WebAnalyzer builds a picture of an entire Website. Its most useful feature is its ability to identify broken links and documents that are missing titles. The downside of encouraging content producers to self-publish is that your site will become riddled with broken links and defective HTML files. There is no real substitute for having content producers hand check their files and link destinations occasionally, because the content of a page you link to might change.

Another frequent occurrence is that the actual location of a page might have changed but the server responds to the request for it with a redirect to the new location. This is normally transparent to the browser user, because most browsers will recognize the redirection information returned for the initial request and will load the page from its new location. However, in addition to the extra delay this causes (slower response from the user's point of view), the redirection information will eventually disappear, turning this into a broken link. CyberSpyder Link Test will warn of these so that the original link can be changed to point to the new location. Other link test tools include SiteCheck, SiteSweeper, WebArranger, WebMaster, WebMapper, and Webxref.

 NOTE: *You might wish to invest in software that periodically checks a Web page and e-mails or pages the Webmaster when it doesn't load. This is mostly used for large Internet Web servers, but might be worthwhile for large corporate Intranet Web servers as well. For example, see* **www.tvisions.com/webpager.**

WebSite and WebMaster offer the ability to locate files in a Windows/Windows NT directory structure that don't appear to have links from any other Web pages. Users tend to create test Web pages and forget to erase them when the production page is working. A list of orphaned files generated by maintenance programs of this type can be sent to content producers with a request for cleanup.

MIME Types

By using a standard set of MIME types, users throughout your organization will be able to load sound, video, word processing, spreadsheet, presentation, and many other types of files without struggling with configuring their browsers.

The MIME (Multipurpose Internet Mail Extensions) types were originally used for e-mail but now play an important role in delivery and display of files on the Web. Both the server and the browser have to be properly configured for painless transfer and presentation of a file. A set of common MIME types is generally loaded when your Web browser and server are installed, but important data types for your organization are probably not included.

For example, if your organization uses Excel worksheets you might want to ensure that your Web browser and servers are both configured with a type *application/x-excel* for extensions of *xls.* The *x* indicates that this is not a formally recognized MIME standard type. You could dispense with this at the risk of offending standards purists and define the type *application/excel.* A third option would be to define both, so your users would be able to automatically load and display Excel worksheets on Intranet and external servers.

Unfortunately, MIME type registrations are in total chaos. For example, it's easy to find Web servers that list Video for Windows file types as *video/x-msvideo, video/avi, video/msvideo,* and lots of other configurations, because "standard" types don't include Video for Windows and, in fact, include only a few of the many types of files in existence. Basically, you are on your own until an industry standard emerges. However, at least within your own Intranet you can configure all Web servers to use the same MIME-type definitions for which you've configured your Web browsers.

CHAPTER 5

Intranet
Discussion Groups

Online discussion groups are often touted as offering some of the greatest opportunities made available by groupware and an Intranet. Proponents generally cite key benefits, such as problem and knowledge/solution sharing, open discussion and feedback, announcements, and communication across unit boundaries. While Intranet discussion groups offer great opportunity, successful discussion groups require some help to be the tremendous asset they have the potential to be to an organization.

There is a tendency among technology people to see successful discussion groups as a technology problem, and to be frustrated when their work isn't fully used. We'll cover software technology briefly, but dealing with technology is not the real challenge with regard to Intranet discussion groups. The real challenge involved in making discussion groups work is people-oriented, and that's the focus of this chapter.

Software

Several types of software support discussion groups. Each of these has features appropriate to different business objectives. You should carefully consider your needs before establishing a discussion group using one of these technologies, because picking the wrong one will either limit its effectiveness or force a later conversion to another type of software, disrupting users.

Usenet News

Your organization already might have an internal news server. Most large organizations will have at least one that offers local access to Usenet newsgroups. Once you've got a news server it's a simple matter to add local newsgroups, whose messages will be available only within your Intranet. One major advantage to using local newsgroups for discussions is that your users might already know how to read and post to newsgroups. If they don't, teaching them will help prepare them to take advantage of more than 26,000 public newsgroups.

Public Usenet Discussion Groups

Using public discussion groups presents a number of opportunities and problems. For a discussion of issues and solutions regarding which of the 26,000+ newsgroups your organization should provide in house, see Chap. 4. Note that public newsgroups are second only to IRC in chaos. Few companies are brave (or is it foolish?) enough to formally communicate with clients and each other in these forums. Trolls (people who try to start flame wars or disrupt others), lunatics (yes, there are disturbed people on the Net, just as there are everywhere else), spammers, and incredibly rude people require great patience and skill to handle while the whole world is watching.

If your people are up to it, there is a great opportunity to listen to the uncensored views of your existing and potential customers. For example, O'Reilley, the author of the popular WebSite Web server software, makes good use of Web server newsgroups. He answers questions and criticisms in a way that positively reflects on his company and builds a sense of community. But for most organizations, private newsgroups will offer the most productive discussion forums.

Listservs

Listservs are e-mail forums for discussion, in which each poster's message is sent to all people on the list's distribution database. This type of forum is nowhere near as desirable, except that it can be used to include key clients and customers who would otherwise be unable to participate in your internal newsgroups, because they would normally be outside your organization's firewall.

Anyone who can send and receive Internet e-mail can read from and contribute to the list. Listservs can also be used to store and retrieve old versions of newsletters, meeting minutes, or any other type of file.

Web-Based Discussion Groups

These are among the most rapidly developing Web applications. A CGI script on a Web server maintains a database of messages and organizes and delivers them on demand. Some generate the HTML versions of the messages as they are written; others generate them from stored text on-the-fly.

Some advantages of Web-based discussion groups include the ability to customize their appearance, the ability to control access to limited IP addresses or to users who know a password, and the opportunity for users to embed HTML code for hypertext links to other resources.

Depending on the software used, advantages over newsgroups might include powerful searching and sorting capabilities, a bidirectional e-mail interface, more control over the layout and functionality of every forum, control over the privileges of users and moderators, and tracking of registration information, postings, and the viewing history of every user.

Groupware

Groupware products such as Lotus Notes and some new, elaborate, Web-based products also offer discussion groups, often with many additional features that might be worth their high prices. These additional features might include calendars, archiving of discussions, security, and replication onto notebook PCs for travelers.

Making Your Discussion Group Work

Interactive communications forums, such as listservs, newsgroups, Web discussion groups, and groupware conferencing hold great promise for your staff's potential to exchange news and opinions, offer feedback, and engage in dialog supporting your organization's mission. The idea is so compelling that the first reaction of many "newbies" to this type of communications medium is to want to form one for their own group as soon as possible. They mistakenly believe that the benefits of the new forum will immediately begin to flow by virtue of the forum's mere existence.

Unfortunately, constructive dialog rarely happens just because an electronic forum exists, any more than building a conference facility in a city will automatically cause people to meet there and hold meaningful discussions. The history of the Usenet, for example, is littered with newsgroups that became virtual ghost town communities. At any given time approximately one-third of all newsgroups are empty. Not only does no discussion occur in such forums, but their very existence inhibits creation of an active forum on the topic in question once the most likely visitors learn that no discussion occurs there.

This chapter lists the authors' ideas for creating and maintaining active online communications, based on their experiences in the BBS and online communities since 1982. Following these recommendations will by no means guarantee that a forum you establish will be successful and long-lived, but they will almost certainly help.

What Gets Posted?

- *Meeting announcements.* A newsgroup offers a good way to reach people who don't know about a meeting, but not a good way to notify or invite a known list. You will reach your targets in a more timely way via e-mail. The best strategy is to use e-mail for your regulars and recruit new members in the newsgroup.

- *Announcements of new information resources with links to full documents.* Newsgroups can be especially useful for announcing new Web pages and major updates. Note that placing complete texts in discussion groups is usually poor practice.

- *Feedback requests and discussion.* Management often wants to solicit staff feedback on projects and organizational procedures, which can be one of the most valuable uses of discussion groups. An online, asynchronous meeting with automatic minutes can occur between people who come from wide-ranging time zones and have impossibly busy schedules.

- *Suggestion boxes.* These can't do much harm when there is a physical box and folded paper, but a public box could, in some situations, cause a problem. An organization of any size is likely to have a few people with highly unusual ways of presenting their (sometimes absurd) ideas. The keeper of the physical box can take ideas in any form and adapt them as necessary. In an online forum, these ideas are immediately seen by everyone, without being edited or modified in any way. This might mean that the writing style used to express an idea could prevent the idea from being fully considered. It could also mean that crank messages from unhappy staff could get posted in ways that damage morale.

- *Polls.* Polls in an online forum won't be scientifically valid, but at least they're voluntary. Keep them short and simple if you want maximum responses.

- *Review requests.* Posting a note or an idea for peer feedback can be useful for both the poster and the reviewer. The reviewer gets an early look and a chance to help shape the idea, while the poster gets feedback and, possibly, some consensus building.

Who Posts?

- *Technologically competent staff members.* These people understand how to post messages and how the posting process works, and they generally feel comfortable with the technology. They will probably benefit a lot more from an etiquette oriented toward generalized customer relations and business communications than from technology training.

- *Technologically challenged staff members.* These people are new to the idea of posting messages and might be afraid of doing something wrong or embarrassing themselves. (Make sure these people get sufficient hands-on training in posting messages; fortunately, we've provided a whole chapter on newsgroups in Phase 2.) To help them learn, your organization can establish a test or training discussion group wherein users can practice posting. Technology-oriented people seldom appreciate that there are a large number of technophobes who have been hiding from technology change, much as adults who can't read will hide their limitation from others. Use discussion group training as an opportunity to review basics, such as how to copy and paste text, how to do a spell check, and how to create and save text to a directory.

- *Thread starters.* These people look for opportunities to start message threads, either because they really like to post, like to see their names online, or are simply eager to help the discussion group succeed. These people are extremely useful to a discussion group and should be strongly encouraged.

- *Lurkers.* Lurkers are people who read messages but never post anything of their own. They might fail to post because they don't have anything to say, but more often because they see no personal advantage to posting and imagine a variety of risks.

- *Technical writers.* These people have good writing skills and are confident that their grammar and spelling won't embarrass them.

- *Poor technical writers.* These are people whose writing skills in the language the forum uses are weak, or who are uncertain of their writing. Training for them should focus on the importance of their ideas and content, and practical use of spelling and grammar checkers. They often won't want to admit they are nervous about their writing, and some sensitivity will be needed to address this issue with them.

Starting the Conversation

Imagine going to a meeting with a group of people you have never met, whom you can't see, with additioinal rooms filled with people listening to you remotely. Imagine also that you can't read or hear a word from any of them until the next day. Would you be comfortable speaking? Would your coworkers? For many people, posting to an online discussion is something like this imaginary meeting. You don't know who's reading what you write and you won't get any immediate feedback.

Given the very unusual nature of the dialog in an online forum, getting a conversation started and keeping relevant parties engaged is a major challenge. Fortunately, many tactics can be used to keep the discussion going long enough for lurkers to become posters, and for the timid to develop enough confidence to post. Some methods are more aggressive than others, and might even seem distasteful to some people.

Post a Charter The discussion group's charter should be posted prominently within the discussion group and should include the kinds of things that may be posted, who may post, the moderator's job and authority, the group's distribution and archiving, and, if appropriate, a Frequently Asked Questions (FAQs) section that spares group regulars from repeatedly having to answer common questions.

Management Involvement People follow their leaders. If managers post questions and answers, especially if their replies to posters indicate an appreciation of the posters' efforts even when management makes it clear they disagree, they (the managers) will have strongly encouraged posting.

Online Experts

Some authorities on discussion groups emphasize the importance of having an expert active in the group, who can answer questions and direct people to relevant resources. While having such people can be valuable, the world has become so complex and fast-changing in most fields that there no longer can be a single expert. A great advantage of a discussion group over a phone call to the expert is that a poster can reach many experts in many related fields at once.

Still, if your organization has recognized experts in discussion group subject areas, encourage them to visit frequently and answer questions. Advise your designated experts, however, that their presence actually could inhibit open discussion, and might even reduce the value of the group, because some posters will be reluctant to expose themselves to correction. The expert will have to straddle the fence between straightening out misconceptions that could hurt the organization and offering help to people who genuinely desire it.

War Chest of Discussion Subjects   Posting a new message subject every two or three days will encourage people to visit the forum frequently to see the new topic, and to reply to existing responses. If you can't identify a dozen topics for discussion in advance you probably shouldn't be creating a newsgroup. Note that if you post all the subjects you've thought of all at once, people won't be encouraged to visit regularly. Pace yourself and start a new thread periodically for a few weeks, until forum activity becomes self-sustaining.

Shills   The idea might seem distasteful to some, but shills can be used during newsgroup startup to demonstrate the ideal communication you want. A manager could post a question on the pros and cons of an option he or she is considering, and the shill would post a reply. The manager provides positive feedback to the poster, thus encouraging others to post. The perfect shill would be someone without great technical skills (e.g., a noncomputer professional or a computer novice), with marginal writing skills (leave an obvious grammar or spelling mistake in place), and from a relatively lower rank in the organization, though shills from all ranks are even better. A typical thread might run something like this:

DIRECTOR: "We're thinking of meeting with XYZ Company to have them handle our shipping. Any comments?"

SECRETARY IN ANOTHER DEPARTMENT: "We have to keep using the Post Office anyhow, because the manuals are sent the last Saturday of each month by Express mail and are delivered on Sunday, so they can use them first thing Monday."

DIRECTOR: "Good point! Thanks! I'll ask publications and printing if the printing/shipping schedule can be altered."

Preannounce the Newsgroup   Make sure people know that the newsgroup is coming, and what its role in the organization will be. Reannounce after you've prepopulated the discussion group.

Prepopulate the Newsgroup   Announce the starting date and remind people by e-mail an hour after you've populated the group with the first posts and a couple of replies. This way no one's first impression of the group will be that "no one's posting anything." Critical mass is essential. If people, especially the coveted "early adopters," visit and see no activity, they might never come back and you will have lost the people most likely to take a chance on posting a message.

Don't Divide a Newsgroup Too Soon   Don't create a newsgroup for each vice-presidency level until the organization-wide newsgroup is overflowing with messages. Don't create departmental newsgroups until the VP newsgroups are overflowing. Ten newsgroups with one message each per week will die fast. Yet the same messages in one newsgroup might make that single group viable. Later on, as things heat up it's a lot easier to divide successful newsgroups than to resurrect dead ones by trying to put them back together.

Keeping the Discussion Going

Once your discussion group is recognized as a good place to post, the moderator's job shifts somewhat to that of a facilitator. Usenet has a long history of dealing with the complex human relations of online dialog. A moderator's job requires a little technical knowledge and a whole lot of people skills. The moderator must be clearly identified and should have clearly stated authority to mediate.

Catch Problems Early   While Intranet discussions will generally lack the kinds of people problems found on the Internet's public newsgroups, the Intranet is not immune to them. You'll need to decide in advance how you will deal with various problems, so that no long delay in acting occurs after a problem post appears.

The moderator needs to keep conversations focused on the group's area of interest. For example, a discussion group about organizational change can easily produce a comment about ensuring that diversity gains are retained, which might evoke a comment about achievement and merit as the proper sole determining factors, given past efforts at diversity, which can quickly spill into a forum discussion that management would not see as constructive.

Remember, some people will write things to an online forum that they wouldn't dream of saying in person. Users tend to overreact to controversial statements, especially when there are no visual cues to show lack of hostility. It's the moderator's job to coach proper online behavior through private e-mail and occasional public reminders to the group as a whole, on proper "netiquette."

Seven Keys to Becoming a Good Newsgroup Moderator

Make sure the newsgroup receives sufficient new posts to keep discussion interesting. If traffic diminishes it's the moderator's job to start a new thread, or to restart dead ones.

For threads that facilitate business decision making, state a summary of the arguments and the conclusion or decision they led to. These completed decision threads will normally be moved off-line to a Web page, with a pointer from the discussion group.

Here are seven tips for newsgroup moderators:

1. Move incorrectly posted messages to the proper discussion group(s).
2. Remove errant posts (e.g., blank messages and huge binaries).
3. Market the discussion group. Recruit new posters.
4. Split large groups into subgroups and terminate groups that no longer fill a business purpose.
5. Keep conversations focused on the group's designated topic.
6. Moderate poster behavior.
7. Retire and archive older posts.

An existing netiquette guide often is more readily accepted than one written by the moderator. If the group has a lot of newbies, frequently post extracts of, or pointers to, etiquette guides. If violations are isolated, send private e-mail to the violator(s) with pointers to specific sections of resources such as:

- `archive.phish.net/ftpspace/phish/text_files/ netiquette`
- `www.albion.com/nqhome.html`

Make Everyone Feel Welcome   A subtle and polite reminder to a violator is usually all that's necessary on an Intranet. There is generally no need to use the extremely direct methods that sometimes are necessary on public, Internet newsgroups. Moderators with lots of BBS or Internet experience should remember that the people they chastise on an Intranet are on their own team. You *want* these people to post! You just want them to post in constructive ways.

Don't beat them, entreat them.

Start almost any message to posters with a "Thanks for contributing!" Look for ways to make posters feel they are members of a special group of those with the vision, willingness to take risks, and willingness to spend time to improve the bottom line of the organization. A short recognition note to the manager of a frequent poster with a copy to the poster can support the poster and remind managers of the discussion group's importance.

In some groups the moderator might be the only one with the ability to post messages. Posters would then send messages to the moderator for possible inclusion in the discussion group. This method introduces a time delay and might precipitate thoughts of censorship, but might also be useful in some discussion situations, including those in which staff might raise concerns about management decisions and performance. The moderator can also make postings anonymous, and can direct appropriate messages to management anonymously rather than to the group.

NOTE: *The moderator also might need to retire old messages, possibly archiving them for organization historians. Remember that, if a business decision and the basis for it are discussed and concluded online, there might be no paper record for future reference by legal, managerial, and historical researchers.*

Summary of Posting Guidelines

We'll close with some important factors for consideration by anyone in your organization in a position to offer advice and exercise authority over the posters to an Intranet discussion group. Explain to these people very well—and well in advance—that the purpose of the discussion group is to get ideas out in the open.

1. Write offenders via e-mail to discuss problems. Do not post such notes publicly, as this will likely embarrass the poster. And, public posting might elicit a public flame or, worse, scare away some of your most precious resources, coworkers who post regularly. If you attack anyone, others might fear that they could receive a similar public lashing if they err.

2. Strongly encourage frequent use of facts and logic in addition to common courtesy. Unless you know the person well, even off-line corrections of grammar and spelling won't be appreciated. If the writing is so poor that its meaning can't be discerned, carefully craft a request for clarification. Discussion groups are about ideas. Don't get distracted by writing styles and details. If you're overly picky about grammar, a million-dollar idea might never get posted because the author might not have the time to write up the idea to your exacting standards.

3. Respond to flamers or other problem postings via e-mail and *never* in the discussion group. If you do, then you could be blamed for starting and/or participating in a flame war.

6

An Active Intranet

Limitations in traditional communications media (i.e., before hypertext became common) have restricted and conditioned us to linear, unidirectional information distribution. But the human mind is not restricted to accepting information in only one unidirectional manner.

Clearly, our abilities to grasp information have exceeded the abilities of our information distribution media. Television is a good example of a unidirectional, passive medium. You get one channel at a time and your only option for interaction is to change the channel or turn off the television.

By contrast, the first generation of Websites allowed visitors to select the information they wanted by clicking on links to other pages. While this kind of interactivity is a big improvement over the limitations of television, early Websites still lacked the sophistication in interactivity that people are able to process.

Newer generation Websites can record a visitor's interests, and present individually tailored pages. Thus, the latest generation Websites permit consumers to become producers and directors of information content, even though they did not create or store the information.

New Web enabled application software (such as Microsoft's Office 97) transform applications into Web browsers and Web publishers. Dealing with two-way publishing poses a large number of interesting questions for technology and management staff.

- Who decides who can publish what?
- How will quality and approvals be maintained or indicated?
- What methods will you use to put content online, then review, edit, catalog, index, archive, and retire it?

Publishing Decisions

In the past, "published" information was generally information of relative importance to large numbers of people. The increasing flood of knowledge, coupled with increasing hyperspecialization, means that there are now many pieces of information that are important to only a few people, but which can still make an important contribution to the organization's bottom line.

Data storage costs are now so low that there are few economic reasons to limit the amount of information you store. Unfortunately, many Webmasters still cling to the idea that they should personally edit and enhance every document on their Web server.

Many traditional managers might feel uncomfortable with their staff publishing casual documents that the manager has never read or approved. While it's certainly possible to have management read and approve every document prior to publication, and to hire an army of HTML editors to put the documents online, such tight control is rapidly becoming impractical and might seriously limit productivity, competitiveness, and creativity.

More to the point, it's often not worth the bother. If a spreadsheet or document will only be viewed by three people, why spend 30 minutes enhancing it? The organization is better served when the manager produces and enforces guidelines, and authors just save files as word processing documents, spreadsheets, or HTML files into the directory designated for publication.

Even menu updates and document descriptions are probably best left to the author. For example, consider the mechanism used by Yahoo! to organize their menus. The submitting author recommends menu placement and the Webmaster reviews and either agrees to the placement or puts it elsewhere. This provides more accurate menus because authors generally know best the categories in which readers are likely to look. And, it saves Webmasters' time for technical problems rather than wasting it on reading and classifying unfamiliar information.

Substance over Form

There's a strong temptation by technocentric Webmasters and managers to imagine that adding animated graphics, movies, sound, and a lot of special effects will attract and entertain visitors and make their Website a success. There's some truth in this feeling, but before we discuss how to use all the cool new technology, let's do a quick reality check.

Most TV commercials cost hundreds of thousands of dollars to produce and use full-color, full-motion video, high-quality sound, and professional direction. Yet many TV viewers reach immediately for the remote control if they aren't especially interested in the subject matter of the commercial. Compare that behavior with investors who will go out of their way to peer through small-font, heavily abbreviated stock market quotes printed on cheap pulp paper in the local newspaper. The point is that, if you provide the information people want and need, they will consume it if they can locate and access it.

Provide a flashy site for the sake of flash or technology alone and you're likely to end up pleasing only yourself. The most important function of an Intranet is to distribute timely, easily accessed content that is relevant to users' needs and interests.

That said, judicious use of graphics and special effects can make documents easier to read, and the latest technology novelty will often attract some classes of users to your site, at least for a moment, giving you a better chance to present your message. In an Intranet, you can often provide popular content to draw visitors in and expose them to less glamorous items they might otherwise not see. For example, an organization acronym database might be used as a draw to the corporate facilities services page in much the same way that popular television programs expose viewers to consumer products.

Data versus Information

There is a nearly infinite ocean of data around any business. But remember, except for statisticians, people need information and not data. Data are merely one input used to produce information. It's okay to put data stores online for the occasional researcher, but it's far more useful to provide the kind of summary data that facilitate decision making. A content author who knows how information will be used can provide additional value by formatting the information within the likeliest decision framework to help users make choices that meet their needs.

For example, you might produce a Web page with pricing for new PCs, which managers would use to select options for their units. Added value might include a graphic showing price/performance trends over the last two years, plus locally valid benchmarks for each price category of PC. A Java applet could accept inputs from users and could help them discover the best buy for their needs.

To convey information, keep in mind that most people learn and retain information far better if there is some sort of action along with it. Get your users involved and have them learn by doing. With that in mind, let's discuss some of the issues you'll encounter when you do apply action-oriented enhancements to your Intranet content.

Multimedia

Yes, we are going to discuss multimedia, even though we've said that most of your Intranet content doesn't justify any more than merely posting and indexing it for quick, widespread access. This discussion will deal with the information that's best presented via enhancements. Let's begin with some technology basics.

The good news about putting a Web server on an Intranet is that an Intranet Web server (on any LAN) can deliver data far faster than a typical home-user modem or even an ISDN line. Internet Service Providers (ISPs) typically connect to other ISPs with T1 lines that have a maximum capacity to transmit 1.54 Mbits/s (millions of bits per second). Most Web servers easily can saturate this connection with a single, large file transfer running at 200 kbits/s, or 1.6 Mbytes/s. This is why Web server performance often isn't as important to the Web server field as many newcomers expect it to be. The bottleneck for simple Web servers is the data pipe size (even then, the upstream ISP usually won't be able to accept the full bandwidth of the data pipe they sold the client).

An Intranet will generally communicate over a 10-Mbytes/s Ethernet, a 16-Mbytes/s Token Ring, or a 100-Mbytes/s fast Ethernet network. Compare this to 28.8-kbytes/s (.0288-Mbytes/s) modems or even ISDN lines (.128 Mbytes/s). This means you have more freedom to use graphics, audio, video, and large files in general.

However, don't get too excited until you've done a reality check on your network. Typical connections between offices, over a WAN, might be limited to 1.54 Mbytes/s, 128 kbytes/s, or even 56 kbytes/s. Low-end servers might deliver only 200 kbytes/s, barely enough for full-speed Video for Windows for one user. Specialized servers can deliver more data, often 75,000 to 100,000 hits of average-sized files per hour, but an unswitched Ethernet link, with collisions, is "full" when average traffic reaches about 30 percent of capacity, or 3 Mbytes. That's only about 300 kbytes/s. The good news is that switched hubs (which avoid Ethernet collisions), MPEG (and other highly compressed) video, and Fast Ethernet (100 Mbytes/s) are being deployed rapidly, and the ability to deliver many video channels at once might be ready by the time you have created your content and your users are ready to access it.

As you shop for real-time video and audio products, keep in mind the differences between the types of continuous data streams and "bursty" data, such as Web pages, images, word processing files, spread-sheets, FTP files, and newsgroup articles. If video and audio data streams don't arrive at the speed they are played, the user will experience dropouts or jerkiness, often making the data stream unusable, and at best annoying.

Good audiovideo servers ensure that enough bandwidth is reserved so that acceptable traffic rates are guaranteed. They also guarantee that audiovideo streams don't interfere excessively with the bandwidth needed to transmit normal data, such as Web pages. To make this work well you might need to install special software on both the server and the workstations; you might also use protocols for bandwidth reservation (RSVP) and multicasting (GARP). A great deal of work is now being done by standards organizations on quality of service (QoS) and Policy Management Architecture (PMA) for Internet communication.

Interactive Websites

Interactivity, which generally involves tools with which you can exchange information with visitors, provides lots of opportunities to careful Webmasters. The most important of these might be to use the Web to let visitors exchange information with each other, using the discussion groups concepts presented in Chap. 5. In addition to dispensing information to visitors, you can use your Intranet to collect information, both passively and actively.

Passive collection can be done from access logs, which might produce information about the host name and IP address of visitors, the files they viewed, when they viewed them, the browser they used, and what they were looking at immediately before they visited your site. In addition to providing feedback to Web authors, logs can be used to determine what percentage of your users are actually using different versions of their Web browsers, information which could help you plan training and product introductions.

Here's a word of warning on logging information. Users are often quite surprised to discover that managers can review what they have viewed, and even get the address of the last Web page they visited before they came to an Intranet site. One user was quite upset to discover that a temporary worker, who happened to be a practicing Satanist, had used her PC to surf the Web and had inadvertently produced records of visits by the absent worker's host ID.

While visit records are useful, collecting actual input from visitors is much more valuable. There are several ways to let visitors provide information. In order of increasing complexity for the Web author and Webmaster, these are `mailto:` URLs, forms whose input is formatted and mailed, and forms whose input is stored in a database for later analysis.

"Mailto" URLs

A Web author can add a mailto fill-in form to a Web page by just placing a `mailto:userid@mailhost` in the HTML code, where `userid` is the mail ID of the person who should receive the mail and `mailhost` is the host and domain of the mail server your Intranet uses, usually named `mail`.

The disadvantage of using `mailto` links is that there's no way to control what the user types. Users might omit or mistype information you need to identify them or fill their requests. One tip that might work for your browsers is to append a `(source)` to the end of the `mailto` address, so you know what Web page the message came from. For feedback from the `Travel Plans` menu, for example, the link might be `<a href=mailto:yourname@domain.com (travel menu)>`. Make sure you send confirmation of receipt back to the sender, who might be uncertain the message was delivered. New users are often certain they'll do something wrong, so a little reassurance can go a long way toward making them feel like Internet experts.

Develop a set of responses that you can quickly edit for specific questions, with at least enough responsive text so the recipient will think an actual person read his or her note. Users really hate electronic form letter responses to questions (even more than voice mail), but don't mind thank you notes for routine data submissions.

Forms and Mail

Most Web servers also will be configured to support mailing the output of forms to an e-mail address. Although forms require more skill from the Web author and might involve installing and configuring forms processing software on the server, there are a number of advantages to using them instead of `endmailto` URLs.

Perhaps the biggest advantage is the control over user-data entry. Depending on server software, or on the browser script-processing capabilities, you might be able to validate individual data entry fields and force the user to give you all the information you need before mailing will be permitted. Remember to ask for only the information you really need. Users have lots to do besides filling out lengthy electronic forms. Do what you can to convince them that their input is significant and truly appreciated.

Forms and Databases

The most useful (yet most complex) method for acquiring information from users is to have the data from input forms placed into a database on the server. Software that does this also will allow queries on the database that are sent to the user as a formatted Web page. The Web browser thus becomes the client in a client-server transaction system. Virtually every major database vendor is making it possible to easily link Web browsers to their databases, transforming formerly impenetrable corporate data stores into easily clickable information providers.

File Transfer

A fairly recent addition to Web pages is the ability to transfer files to a server directly from a Web page. This ability can be used to let people easily upload documents, databases, spreadsheets, or other files, including Web pages they've produced.

Real-Time Conferencing Products

Discussion group and conferencing products were discussed in Chap. 5. Discussion groups are all delayed "posting" types of interactions. The Intranet also offers more immediate, real-time discussion abilities. Tools to do this include text-based products for Internet Relay Chat, voice, and even video-conferencing software. Before installing any of these, check with your network security experts to see what impact this will have, and whether firewalls will allow that type of traffic to a particular port. Many organizations don't allow the type of traffic that many of these new technologies require.

Internet Relay Chat (IRC)

This type of software lets as many users as you wish communicate with each other by typing in real time, with all members seeing each other's typed words. A variety of products offers the ability to exchange ideas in real time, with optional recording of everyone's input. Some include whiteboard and other interactive features.

When using IRC, don't be discouraged by the heavy public use of IRC channels by adolescents. There's no rule that says that IRC must be used only for worthless chats among bored college students; there is real business value in chat software when it is used correctly.

IRC is excellent at maintaining anonymity during brainstorming sessions in the early stages of product design or development, marketing strategies, and any other business phase in which creativity and spontaneous ideas need to be encouraged from people who might otherwise think their new ideas are either silly or likely to upset vested interests. IRC also can be used for audio and video conferencing. You'll also find that chat sessions are far cheaper than conference calls, and they work a lot better than phones when you have more than three participants. Send e-mail to `csamsi@clark.net` to get a global site license for the most popular IRC software, WSIRC.

Voice Over Network (VON)

Live audio includes Voice Over Network (VON) and streaming audio. VON software provides a way to bypass expensive long-distance telephone charges and is now seen as a threat by certain telephone companies, some of which actually asked for the software producers to be regulated as telephone companies in the United States. Despite the hype, current Internet VON products simply don't work as well as traditional telephone connections, and probably won't carry many business calls for some time. When you compare the value of the time invested by the people engaged in the conversation against their long-distance bills, sacrificing the sound quality and ease-of-use of a conventional phone to save 20 cents per minute on long-distance usually doesn't make sense. Of course, if the VON software provides features the phone company doesn't offer, or if the hardware-software combinations improve to equal the features of conventional telephones, or if your telephone connection is two dollars per minute, the equation changes.

A representative VON product is Vocaltec's (**www.vocaltec.com**) Internet Phone 4.0. This product includes voice messaging, simultaneous voice and data connections, document conferencing, text chat mode, Web integration, file transfer, and other capabilities.

Video Conferencing

Video conferencing on your Intranet can range from limited and inexpensive to TV-quality video . . . and serious money. To watch video you need only a PC with a good video card, processor, and software. To hear the audio that accompanies the video, you need a sound card and headphones or speakers. To transmit video from your desktop to another, you need a camera and a video capture card.

The most popular software for entry level video conferencing is CU-SeeMe, sold commercially by White Pine Software (**www.wpine.com**). At the time this was written, a single workstation license was $69. Hardware costs include a $100 to $500 video camera and, usually, a video capture card worth $200 to $300. You can get a complete, prepackaged system with color camera, Enhanced CU-SeeMe, and video capture card lists for $400 from VideoLabs, Inc. (1-800-467-7157).

Another low-cost video-conferencing product is VDOnet Corporation's VDOPhone. Thought it was initially available only for Windows 95, support for other operating systems and computers is planned. VDOPhone will run on connections from 14.4 modems to T1 connections, where it can deliver 15-frame per-second, full-color video, and full-duplex sound.

At the other end of the price/performance spectrum is PictureTel (**www.picturetel.com**) which specializes in high-end, high-performance desktop video conferencing at prices from $1495 to $5000 per workstation, plus ISDN charges. A top-of-the line ATM-based system will cost about $12,000 per workstation for a turnkey system that produces video that's comparable to live TV. Their low-end product for Windows 95 and an 128K ISDN connection (Live200p) includes software, a plug-and-play card, and a headset for $1495.

The industry is moving toward standards-based software such as T.120 and H.323 for video conferencing, which will allow users of competing products to connect to each other. White Pine already is committed to supporting standards in upcoming releases of Enhanced CU-SeeMe, and also will provide interoperability to Microsoft's recently announced NetMeeting communications and collaboration software. The big impediments to more widespread video conferencing appear to be high costs and access to affordable, reliable bandwidth. The Intranet offers great bandwidth, but its bursty nature often produces disturbances in video stream delivery that distract participants from the content of the conversation. According to video-conferencing specialists, users often demand high resolution, color, and at least 15 frames per second (fps), but generally can forget about picture quality, frame rates as low as 10 fps, and simple color, after the first couple of minutes of a meeting. What does irritate them are disturbing artifacts in the video stream. Until guaranteed bandwidth over LAN connections is available, you'll want an ISDN or ATM connection for widespread, business-oriented video conferencing.

Training/Learning Applications

Interactive training/learning applications are naturals for your Intranet. They promise a self-paced, seven-days-a-week, 24-hours-a-day, globally accessible, inexpensive method to deliver training on almost any subject, but especially those of interest to large organizations. Training might be *the* killer application for an Intranet, at least until desktop video conferencing becomes commonly available and affordable.

The strong trends in corporate training are to just-in-time training, "learning" (as opposed to training), and providing multiple teaching methods to meet different individual learning styles. As the amount of knowledge a modern worker needs continues to grow, the distinction between formal training and "help" applications is narrowing.

Three classes of training can be delivered on your Intranet.

1. *Formal education.* This is the realm of principles, fundamental skills, and background knowledge. Formal education topics include subjects such as reading, writing, arithmetic, and comprehension courses, such as how to use an operating system or the basics of telecommunication, accounting, or contracts. While the Web can be used to teach these subjects, it is much better at the other two types of training.

2. *Application training.* Typical application-training material might include *Introduction to Netscape,* using Solomon Accounting Software or a custom-made corporate application, such as a leave accounting system.

3. *Specific need.* This is the type of training that blurs into what traditionally has been found in application help files. Example subjects would include how to create a company-standard, formatted document index in WordPerfect or Word, how to complete an equipment pass, and how to use the organization's FTP site. This type of training lets you document business processes that no one else could document for you. It has traditionally been very expensive to deliver, because authors had to work too hard to produce a user interface, get the application to each user's desktop, and train the users on how to use the training application. A Web browser at each desktop radically changes production and delivery costs, allowing a real revolution in this class of training.

To make these types of training successful, it's important that authors, a category that will include a lot of people who have had no formal background in education or learning theory, understand how adults learn. As content producers generate content, they need to understand that they aren't just documenting a process, they are *teaching* a process.

Learning Summary

Don't waste time on creating lectures as text. Adults need a "learning space" through which they can navigate to locate specific items that interest them. Motivation is critical to adult learners; they simply won't bother with material that does not have obvious relevance and immediate positive benefits.

To get adults to learn, you must use real-world examples in all online training, and you must use pointers to Web resources. Customize Web resources to exact user needs. When soliciting feedback or input from adults, make sure the form is printable and that it includes a mail address. This is especially important if you want answers requiring contemplation, and when the clock is ticking with online charges for the student.

Get adult learners to partner with others. Create a commitment between partners to help each other learn, so that each student will remain on schedule in the face of potential discouragement or the interposition of other priorities.

Adults learn by comparing new knowledge with past experiences, unlike children who learn exactly the task at hand without filtering it through a lifetime of related experiences. So, you can reach adults by using analogies and examples from existing knowledge whenever possible; this is a very important point.

Adults also need immediate feedback on progress. Adults further benefit from real tests of understanding rather than multiple-choice questions. Arrange real-world, practical progress measurements.

Many adults are driven by fear of failure, which is claimed to be the strongest factor in adult decision making. Keep this in mind when you design training material, and make sure that users cannot fail their first experience in a training program.

When building process-training pages, be sure to describe reasons for the process, unless security reasons limit your ability to openly publish such information. If you can't document the rationale for a process it probably is a good candidate for reengineering.

Also, keep in mind that adults learn in many different ways. Some have a strong need to read about a subject before beginning learning. Some need to watch others. Others learn by doing, diving into the material without abandon. Fortunately, the hypertext environment of an Intranet provides an opportunity to accommodate all styles simultaneously. Use it to the fullest and you'll enjoy an Intranet environment that will catapult your organization to unprecedented heights of productivity and competitiveness.

Next up is Phase 2, in which we give you hands-on lessons that can be used throughout the organization to help everyone learn the basics of how to use an Intranet aggressively, and how to become Intranet content providers.

Employee
Hands-On
Guide

Your organization's computer professionals serve as a bridge between the demands of a productivity-driven management and the needs of employees who want to do their best on the job. Computer personnel can't handle the entire task alone. They will need to rely on nearly everyone's pitching in to put information content on an Intranet, and to set up their own home pages. If other users merely wait for the computer staff to do everything, your organization's Intranet will lag far behind your competition. That's where these chapters will help.

This phase includes hands-on exercises and valuable resources that will help individuals create and maintain Intranet contents. It will help all employees to use an Intranet to boost productivity. The lessons, tips, and resources in these chapters will guide employees toward Intranet self-sufficiency.

Even if your computer professionals are able to handle the entire workload, other employees will learn from these chapters what can and what cannot be done on an Intranet. They then will be better able to outline desired projects for the computer staff. But that's not the focus. The focus is on making nearly everyone self-sufficient so they can publish content on an Intranet without delays or misunderstandings.

CHAPTER 7

Windows
for
Intranets

To use an Intranet and the Internet productively, employees need to be quick and efficient in Windows. They will encounter a lot of information that they'll need to cut and paste, save, transfer, and organize. The lessons in this chapter can transform even the most timid user into an aggressive power user. These hands-on lessons are based on Windows 95, the new standard in PC GUI interfaces.

Your Intranet will deliver a bewildering assortment of windows all over everyone's screens. To work efficiently, users must know how to quickly and easily transfer information between any two windows. These hands-on lessons will create a cadre of productive Windows power users who will enjoy and use your Intranet even more.

Without knowing the principles developed in these lessons, many users will be scribbling notes on the side and doing a lot of retyping. But with the expertise these lessons will deliver, no one will ever need to retype anything that can be seen on the screen.

Simplifying the Work Load

Windows brings the same philosophy to software controls that people experience with renting cars. When people rent a car they look for common controls. The heater controls in a rental car are not exactly the same as their own car, but they expect to find controls that adjust the temperature, defrost the windows or vent warm air to the interior, and set a fan speed.

Windows has a term for this design philosophy. It's called *Common User Access* (CUA).

CUA is the principle under which all Windows programs provide common user access by using common user controls. In other words, when using Windows software, users who focus on the commonality—and not on the differences—will learn faster, will learn more, and will be more productive. If you get all users to approach new applications the way most people approach a rental car, your Intranet will enjoy instant acceptance.

In the rest of this chapter, we will cover what we call "advanced basics." The tips presented here have been proven to be important productivity-enhancing tools. Some people have used Windows for years without knowing these advanced basics. They have paid—usually many times over—for the time it would have taken to learn the features when they first learned Windows.

Window Types

Let us begin by identifying the two basic types of windows found in the Windows operating system. You and your computer communicate constantly. You communicate what you want and the computer tells you what it's doing. When you use Windows, all communications with your computer pass through a window. There are three basic types: Application Windows, Document Windows, and Dialog Boxes. For this lesson, start Windows on your computer. We'll begin with the Program Manager.

Application Window

Every application runs inside its own window (Netscape is an example of an *application*). The easiest way to identify an application window is by the icon in the upper-left corner. Application windows use the same icon as the icon that you used to start the application (see Fig. 7-1).

Most application windows can cover your entire screen. There are exceptions, but remember, we are focusing on common principles.

Shortly, we'll show you how to access all your open applications windows and give you a variety of ways to switch between them, enabling

Figure 7-1

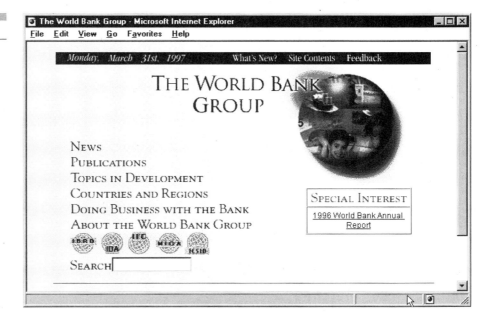

you to easily run multiple applications. Running multiple applications is called multitasking. Windows 95 has some powerful new multitasking features, yet retains some of the best ones from Windows 3.1.

All application windows can be closed by pressing ALT+F4, or by double-clicking on the application icon in the upper-left corner.

Document Window

Many applications have windows within them that are called *document windows,* though they are not always for documents. Spreadsheet applications, for example, use document windows for individual spreadsheets. An internet e-mail application such as Eudora use document windows for its IN, OUT, and TRASH boxes.

The icon in the upper-left corner of a document window is different than the main application-window icon. Document windows cannot cover the entire screen because they are limited to filling the maximum amount of screen space being used by their parent application window. You cannot place a document window on your Windows 95 desktop because you cannot drag a document window out of the borders of its parent application window.

A document window can be closed by pressing CTRL+F4, or by double-clicking on its icon (see Fig. 7-2).

If an application uses document windows, it lists them on the menu bar under the Window menu item. You can use this list to switch to any document window within the current application window. Using this list makes it impossible to ever again "lose" a window because, even if you cannot see the window, its title will be listed under the Window menu item.

Start Button

Just in case you've missed all the Microsoft commercials, we'll define a term that will be used throughout this chapter: the START BUTTON. It might be visible now on your screen in the lower-left corner. If so, click on it when you see the command ACTIVATE THE START BUTTON. If it's not visible, moving your mouse pointer to the bottom of the screen should display it by activating the Taskbar. The Start Button is on the Taskbar. The Start Button can be moved and reconfigured. Let's look at some options.

Figure 7-2

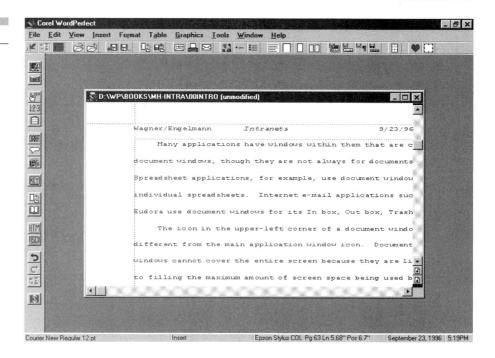

Place your mouse over a blank area on the Taskbar, then drag-and-drop the entire Taskbar to any edge of the screen. It will remain there for subsequent Windows 95 sessions, until you move it.

Right-click the Taskbar and click PROPERTIES, then make sure that both ALWAYS ON TOP and AUTO HIDE are checked. This will hide the Taskbar until you touch the edge of the screen with your mouse.

Grab the edge of the Taskbar and stretch it wider to accommodate more full-sized buttons.

Objective: Activate a window.

❑ Activate the START BUTTON.

❑ Click RUN.

❑ Type `c:\windows\progman.exe` and press ENTER.

This will be a reunion with an old friend, the Program Manager. If your Program Manager is in another directory or on another drive, you can use the browse button to navigate your files.

❑ Click WINDOW on your Program Manager.

❑ Click any window on the list that you cannot see open.

The menu windows can display only nine document windows at once. If your application has more than nine document windows the last item on this list will be **More Windows...**

Dialog Boxes

Dialog boxes look much like application windows and document windows but they behave quite differently. Dialog boxes are activated within an application window to let you input instructions to your computer. You cannot switch between dialog boxes as you can between application or document windows. They are used one-at-a-time only, but there are exceptions, of course.

Few dialog boxes have all of the standard windows controls. Still, it is usually easy to understand how to handle them once you know the advanced basics and focus on commonality, not on the differences.

We'll give you four simple techniques that are easy to learn and can increase productivity, yet are overlooked by legions of experienced Windows users. The first lesson is for dialog boxes that have text entry boxes (see Fig. 7-3).

Objective: Improve speed when typing within text entry boxes.

❑ Click on any application icon on the Program Manager.
    Remember the title shown under this icon.

❑ Press ALT+ENTER.

The highlighted text on the top line means that your cursor is on that line. Also, you're in a special, momentary state that can lead to different results, depending on your next keystroke. Don't waste your time

Figure 7-3

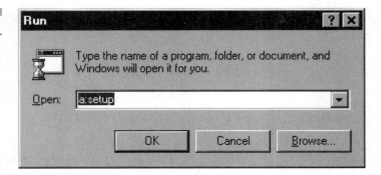

using the mouse to position your cursor when you see this state; it is already in the text entry box.

❑ Press END.

The highlight will disappear and you now can edit the existing text. (Actually, any cursor movement key will "set" the text in this box.)

❑ Press ENTER.
❑ Press ALT+ENTER.

Again, don't waste time using the mouse because the first non-cursor-movement keystroke clears the text box. Type the original title.

❑ Press ENTER.

The next two lessons will enable you to make dialog box selections more quickly, using the keyboard instead of the mouse.

Objective: Improve speed when using any dialog box.

❑ Press ALT+ENTER.
❑ Press ALT+I.

The letter I on the Change Icon button is underlined. When you see an underlined letter on a button label, you can press ALT plus the letter instead of interrupting your workflow by picking up the mouse.

❑ Press ENTER twice to return to the Program Manager.

If the dialog box does not have any text boxes, you don't need to hold down ALT to activate a button. Let's demonstrate that principle.

❑ Open the Accessories group and double-click on NOTEPAD.
❑ Press F5 to enter the date and time.
❑ Press ALT+F4 to close Notepad.

You will be asked if you want to save the changes. Again, don't bother picking up the mouse.

❑ Press N to say No.

You will exit Notepad immediately without saving.

❑ Minimize the Accessories group.

Using these keystroke techniques can save you a lot of time over the years. They also will reduce physical stress by eliminating unnecessary

Figure 7-4

mouse use. Here are more exercises that demonstrate simple, time-saving keystroke techniques.

Objective: Quickly jump to a specific, known listing.

❑ Open the Main group by pressing ALT+W, then press the number on the line that says MAIN.

❑ Use your arrow keys to highlight CONTROL PANEL.

❑ Press ENTER.

❑ Use the arrow keys to highlight REGIONAL SETTINGS (see Fig. 7-4).

❑ Press ENTER.

Most likely, ENGLISH (UNITED STATES) is highlighted.

❑ Press s.

Notice that the list jumps to Spanish.

❑ Press s repeatedly and check the list each time.

You will scroll through all the language options that begin with "s". Eventually, pressing the letter will cycle you back to the first option that begins with that letter. Most users make changes on lists such as this one by using the mouse to click on the drop arrow at the end of the list, and then using the scroll arrows to meander to the desired entry. Then they click on it, then they move their mouse pointer over and click on OK.

❑ Press ESCAPE to dismiss the dialog box.

Pressing ESCAPE for most dialog boxes is much faster than clicking on CANCEL.

❑ Press ENTER to bring back REGIONAL SETTINGS.

❑ Press UP ARROW. The list will scroll through the options.

❑ Press DOWN ARROW repeatedly until you return to ENGLISH (UNITED STATES).

❑ Press ENTER to close the dialog box. This works for most dialog boxes and is much faster than clicking on OK.

❑ Press ALT+F4 to close the Control Panel.

You now will be back to the Program Manager . . . and you did all that without the mouse!

Using keystrokes is not always faster than using the mouse. When you already have the mouse in hand you might save time by continuing to use it. Still, you can increase speed overall by using keystrokes and your mouse together, depending on which is faster for the task at hand. Later, you'll see more keystroke examples, including some that will give you access to some crucial Windows commands even when they're not available on a visible menu.

Window Controls

When you learned basic Windows techniques, you learned how to use the icons in the upper-right corner of a window to maximize the window and to restore it to its previous size. When you get deeply into Internet software, you might have windows all over your screen and you will not always be able to see the maximize and restore buttons on all of them. Instead of dragging a window around to bring these icons into view, you can double-click anywhere on the window's title bar to maximize it. Or, if a window already is maximized, double-clicking on its title bar will restore it to its previous size.

Objective: Learn a shortcut to maximizing a window.

❑ Double-click MAIN again to open it.

❑ Double-click anywhere along its title bar to maximize it.

While we're here, let's go over a few important points.

Notice that the Main window covers all of the other windows in this application. Such maximization often occurs accidentally when users inadvertently double-click on a title bar. At this point, they fear that their other windows are lost. But that won't happen to you once you've completed this next lesson.

Objective: Learn how to switch document windows.

❑ Click on WINDOW.

❑ Click on any window other than MAIN.

❑ Click on WINDOW.

❑ Click on MAIN.

None of the other document windows were gone, they just were hidden by one maximized document window. Even in this state, you still have full access to every window. Of course, these sample windows don't contain documents, but the document windows in your word processor will behave exactly the same, so you can use this technique to manage multiple documents or spreadsheets.

While we're in this state, let's make one more important observation. Notice that the title bar no longer says PROGRAM MANAGER. It now says PROGRAM MANAGER - [MAIN]. That's because a document window can never fill the screen. A maximized document window cannot extend outside its parent application window, so it must share the title bar with its parent.

Look for this state when you're experimenting with new applications or when it seems that you've lost something. If you see two titles on the title bar, here's the interpretation:

1. The first title is the application window title.

2. The second title—in square brackets—is a maximized document window.

If any document windows seem to be missing, they simply are being covered by this one maximized document window, and you can switch to them via the WINDOW menu. Now let's look at a couple of quick ways to make all of your document windows visible again.

Objective: Learn to use Cascade and Tile to find "lost" windows.

❑ Click WINDOW, TILE to Tile the document windows.

❑ Click WINDOW, CASCADE to Cascade the document windows.

❑ Press ALT+W, then press T to Tile the document windows.

❑ Press ALT+W, then press C to Cascade the document windows.

❑ Press SHIFT+F4 to Tile the document windows.

❑ Press SHIFT+F5 to Cascade the document windows.

Every open document window now has been neatly cascaded down from the top of the application window and all minimized document windows have been arranged at the bottom of the application window. These principles often are essential to successfully using Internet applications, especially a mail program that might use dozens of document windows for its mail boxes.

Whenever anything seems to be missing, click WINDOW, CASCADE (or press SHIFT+F5) and you'll get your bearings again.

Miscellaneous Keystrokes

Next we'll present some keystroke tidbits that can help speed your work in Windows 95. One even might bail you out sometime if it appears that you need to reboot your computer.

ENTER key

On most dialog boxes, pressing ENTER is the same as clicking on the highlighted button. We've seen countless users pop up a dialog box that needs a single line of text entry, then pick up the mouse to click in the box (when the cursor is already in place), then put down the mouse, then type the text, then stop, pick up the mouse again, move the mouse pointer over to a button that already is highlighted, and then click. Spare yourself the agony; usually, you merely need to type the line and hit ENTER!

Of course, you have to make sure that the highlighted button represents the action you want to take, but it almost always does.

There are exceptions, of course. Some text boxes allow multiple-line entries. In many of these, pressing ENTER will start a new line of text. The basic principles still apply though, because, if you'll notice carefully, you'll see that there are *no* highlighted buttons on this type of dialog box. Thus, pressing ENTER can't activate a highlighted button because there isn't one.

Some multiline text boxes use another key to make new lines, such as CTRL+ENTER. Your clue will be to check whether any dialog box button is highlighted. If one is, then pressing ENTER *will* be the same as clicking on that highlighted button, and you'll have to find out what other key is used to create new lines in the text entry box within the dialog.

TAB key

Closely related to the current subject, the TAB key can save you a lot of time. TAB moves the focus within a dialog box from item to item. It's much faster than using the mouse. We'll show you a quick example, although you'll probably see it will be of more benefit within large dialog boxes that have more entries than are used in this exercise.

Objective: Learn to speed your work using TAB.

❑ Open any group on the Program Manager.

❑ Press ALT+F.

❑ Press ENTER twice.

This dialog box now will let you add a new application to the Program Manager. You'll add one, then delete it. First, notice that the cursor is in the top text box.

❑ Type `Solitaire.`

❑ Press TAB.

❑ Type `sol.exe.`

❑ Press ENTER.

❑ Press ENTER again to start solitaire.

❑ Press ALT+F4 to exit solitaire.

That was quick, wasn't it? Your hands never left the keyboard. Yet millions of users would have clicked in the first window, then typed `Solitaire`, then stopped typing and picked up the mouse, moved it over the second text box and clicked, then put down the mouse and typed `sol.exe`, then stopped typing, picked up the mouse, moved it over, and clicked on OK. You will fill in lots of forms on the Internet and you can blaze through them if you'll type the necessary information, press TAB, type again, press TAB, type again, press TAB, then press ENTER when you're done. Avoid the mouse when completing forms.

Note, also, that using SHIFT+TAB will cycle you backward through the available items in a dialog box, which is useful when you need to return to a previous entry.

A final quick lesson while you're here.

Objective: Learn how to delete an application icon.

❑ Make sure the Solitaire icon still is highlighted.

❑ Press DELETE to delete the icon.

❑ Press ENTER to confirm the deletion.

Don't confuse this with eliminating a program, because this action deletes only the icon. The application itself still occupies space on your hard disk. To completely eliminate most programs you'll need an uninstall program. Windows 95 can uninstall any programs you've added through the Add/Remove Programs feature.

ALT key

You've already seen how to activate menu items by holding down ALT and pressing the underlined letter. But ALT has a broader effect than that. Pressing ALT always activates the menu system, whether you press a letter while holding it down or not. You can tap and release either ALT key, then you can press any underlined menu letter.

This is a critical property of Windows. Most likely, you sometimes will tap an ALT key by mistake. Many Windows 3.x users who did not know this principle have rebooted their systems after inadvertently pressing an ALT key. Once the menu system has been activated with ALT, Windows is waiting for you to hit one of the underlined letters. Under Windows 3.x, this gave users the impression that their system had frozen. Fortunately, under Windows 95 only the first keystroke counts, and if it's not a valid menu letter the menu system is deactivated until you press ALT again. Try it yourself, using the Program Manager.

Objective: Learn to activate the Windows menu system.

❏ Continue to use the Program Manager.

❏ Press and release either ALT key.

The menu item FILE will be highlighted.

❏ Type **X**.

Your computer will beep, but FILE no longer will be highlighted. In Windows 3.x, this condition persisted until you pressed ALT again, or hit a valid letter.

PRINTSCREEN key

You can copy an image of the entire screen, or of any active window, onto your clipboard. This sometimes is a great help when you find something on the Web that you want to transfer to your word processor. PRINTSCREEN captures the entire screen and ALT+PRINTSCREEN captures the active window. Let's do a quick demonstration of both, again using the Program Manager.

Objective: Learn to capture screen images.

❏ Continue to use the Program Manager.

❏ Press PRINTSCREEN.

❏ Open your ACCESSORIES group.

❏ Double-click on WORDPAD.

❏ Press CTRL+V to paste the screen image into WordPad.

You might want to use the image's handles to resize this image for a better look, but you'll see that you've captured the entire screen.

❏ Press CTRL+N to start a new document.

You'll see a dialog box asking you to specify the new document type. You'll capture just this dialog box to the clipboard and paste it into the new document.

❏ Press ALT+PRINTSCREEN to capture the New dialog box.

❏ Press ENTER, then press N to close WordPad without saving.

❏ Press CTRL+V to paste the image of the dialog box.

You might find countless uses for this as you the surf the Net. It can be a wonderful tool. Or course if you don't have a dialog box active, then even ALT+PRINTSCREEN will capture the entire screen.

❏ Press ALT+F4 again to exit.

❏ Press N to confirm you don't want to save.

Switching Windows

This lesson will make sure you know how to use the full power of Windows. Remember, the word "windows" is plural. You can have a lot of them open at once, but since you can only work with one at a time, you need to know how to switch between them to activate the one you want. The techniques are different for switching between document windows and application windows.

Switching Document Windows

You already have seen this principle, so here is just a reminder. Remember, document windows can exist only under the control of an application window. If your application window can support multiple windows, it will have WINDOW on the menu bar. Here's a summary of some of the methods you can use to switch document windows:

▧ Click on any visible document window.

▧ Click WINDOW, then the name of the window you want.

▧ Click WINDOW, CASCADE.

▧ Click WINDOW, TILE.

▧ Press SHIFT+F5 to Cascade.

▧ Press SHIFT+F4 to Tile.

▧ Press ALT+HYPHEN, then press T to cycle to the next available document window.

▧ Press CTRL+F6 to cycle through all available document windows.

Switching Application Windows

Here are the key principles to observe to become a Windows expert. Without them you don't have a chance of keeping up on the Internet. You cannot afford to run one application at a time and exit each one before starting another. First, let's start several applications so you can practice using these methods.

Objective: Learn to switch between open Windows applications.

❑ Use the Accessories group that is still open from the last lesson.

❑ Double-click on WORDPAD.

❑ Click on any blank space on the Program Manager.

❑ Double-click on CALCULATOR.

❑ Click on any blank space on the Program Manager.

❑ Double-click on PAINT.

❑ Minimize Paint.

❑ Click on any blank space on the Program Manager.

❑ Double-click on CLOCK.

You now have five applications open; now let us learn to switch back and forth between them. Move your mouse pointer to the bottom of the screen. This activates the Taskbar that shows every active application.

❑ Click on WORDPAD on the Taskbar.

❑ Move your mouse pointer to the bottom of the screen.

❑ Click on CLOCK.

You get the idea. Now we'll learn another technique that doesn't require use of the mouse.

❑ Hold down either ALT key.

❑ Keep holding down ALT while pressing TAB.

Use this ALT+TAB method until an application you want is highlighted, then release ALT. Pressing ALT+TAB once returns you to your last application; thus you can use ALT+TAB to jump back and forth between your Web browser and your word processor, a big time saver if you frequently switch between them.

Now we'll summarize the methods you can use to switch application windows. Most were covered in the exercises, but you might want to test others. Choose the method you prefer. Here's the summary:

■ Click on any visible application window to make it active.

■ Activate the Taskbar and click on the desired application.

■ Use ALT+TAB to cycle through all open applications, and release ALT when the desired application appears. Use SHIFT+ALT+TAB to cycle backward through all open applications, and release ALT when the desired application appears.

■ Press ALT+ESC to cycle between all open applications. This is not as direct as ALT+TAB and you might have to cycle through a lot of windows to get to the one you want. It always cycles through in order, by contrast to ALT+TAB, which starts with your most recently used application.

Hiding the Taskbar

If you are hooked on using the mouse but are tired of giving up screen space to the Taskbar, you might want to do the next hands-on exercise. We'll show you how to reconfigure the Taskbar so it will be hidden until you need it.

Objective: Learn to hide the Taskbar.

❏ Position your mouse over a blank area on the Taskbar. The next step won't work correctly if your mouse is over any of the buttons on the Taskbar.

❏ Click the right mouse button on a blank area on the Taskbar.

❏ Click PROPERTIES.

❏ Make sure ALWAYS ON TOP is checked.

❏ Make sure AUTO HIDE is checked.

❏ Check SHOW CLOCK (optional, but why not?).

❏ Click OK.

The Taskbar now has been reduced to a thin line at the bottom of the screen. You probably can't see it because it's gray and the status bar on your current application is gray. With some applications, though, you'll notice the line.

❏ Move your mouse pointer to the very bottom of the screen.

This activates the Taskbar so you now can use it normally.

❏ Click on PROGRAM MANAGER.

Modifying the Taskbar

Once you've hidden the Taskbar there's no need to limit it to its normal narrow width. And, you might prefer it somewhere other than at the bottom of your screen.

You can widen the Taskbar simply by dragging its border as you would with any window. Figure 7-5 shows the Taskbar at the bottom of the screen, but widened to three rows. If you open a lot of applications at once, their Taskbar buttons get too small to read. Widening the Taskbar can keep all of your buttons full-size, but you definitely will need to activate the AUTO HIDE feature outlined in the previous exercise.

The Taskbar can be positioned to any edge of the screen. To move the Taskbar, activate it, grab it someplace other than on a button and drag it to the desired side. It will remain there for future Windows sessions until you move it again. Figure 7-6 shows the Taskbar moved to the left edge of the screen and stretched out wide enough to display the full name of all the buttons. This configuration actually makes more sense than the default because after you click START, SHUT DOWN is at the bottom of the list where you're unlikely to choose it accidentally.

Figure 7-5

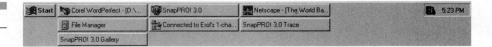

Figure 7-6

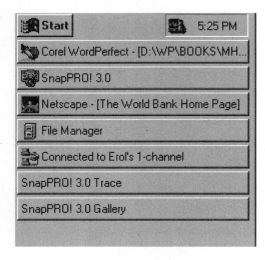

Window-Switching Exceptions

As you might expect, there are exceptions to the methods we've shown here for switching between windows. A popular example is Netscape's bookmark window. Netscape also has the WINDOW menu item on its menu bar. So, you would expect that each of the features under WINDOW would appear in document windows.

But here's the exception. Each feature under the Netscape application window actually is a separate application and runs in its own application window. Yet, you can use WINDOW to switch between these different Netscape applications.

That's something you would expect to be able only to do using application-switching tools or techniques, such as the Taskbar or ALT+TAB. Of course, those *do* work; the point is, you can also use them in addition to the WINDOW menu item.

And, even though they appear under the WINDOW menu, these windows are closed with ALT+F4 instead of with CTRL+F4 as you would expect. Thus, you can see that without understanding the difference between document windows and application windows, you might get confused. Let's see Netscape's exception in action.

Objective: To see an application window that you might expect to be a document window.

❑ Start Netscape.

❑ Click BOOKMARKS, then GO TO BOOKMARKS....

This window is an application window, even though you might have expected it to be a document window. Let's see more.

❑ Press ALT+TAB.

You now see an extra icon on this list, next to the Netscape icon.

❑ Press TAB until you've cycled back to Netscape, then release ALT.

❑ Click the icon on the Netscape Bookmarks window.

Note that the keystroke to close it is ALT+F4 and not CTRL+F4.

❑ Click on CLOSE to close the Bookmarks window.

If you can't do this exercise now, keep these techniques in mind because you will encounter windows that do not behave normally. Knowing these principles will help you deal with their oddities.

Boosting Your Productivity

We've shown you how to quickly switch between document windows, but quick-switching methods are no match for not having to switch at all. So now we'll help you set up your Windows for maximum productivity. You can greatly increase your productivity by grouping your most frequently used icons into a single, primary folder on the Windows 95 desktop. Once you've created this new folder, you'll keep all other folders closed because you rarely will need them. Here's a good example of a primary folder (see Fig. 7-7).

Creating a Primary Folder

Follow these steps to create your primary folder on the Windows 95 desktop. Most users find this folder to be a tremendous productivity enhancement.

Objective: Add a primary folder.

❑ Move the mouse to the Taskbar and click the right mouse button.

❑ Click MINIMIZE ALL WINDOWS. ·

❑ Right-click the desktop.

❑ Click NEW, FOLDER.

❑ Type **Primary** and press ENTER.

You now have created a new folder.

Adding Your Productivity Icons

Now that your primary folder has been created, it's time to add your most frequently used icons. Using the Internet aggressively will have you running lots of applications, so you'll want them available for speedy access. Adding icons to your primary folder won't be any harder than playing Solitaire, so let's do it.

Objective: Add your best productivity-enhancing icons.

❑ Open the folder that contains your word processor.

You need only one icon in this group, so copy that one to PRIMARY.

❑ Use the right mouse button to drag and drop your word processor's icon into PRIMARY.

❑ Click COPY HERE to copy the icon into PRIMARY.

❑ Close your word processor folder.

❑ Open the group that contains your Internet icons.

Here, you might need several of these icons or you might need several different folders. Use the right-button drag-and-drop method to copy all your frequently used icons into PRIMARY. As a minimum you will want your main Internet connection icon (Netscape, for example) and your e-mail icon (Eudora, for example).

Adding Icons to Your Primary Folder

Look at the example pictured in Fig. 7-7 for ideas about which icons to include in your Primary folder. Here are a few suggestions:

▪ File Manager, Print Manager.

▪ Calculator, Notepad, WordPad.

▪ Others might include your word processor, Netscape, Eudora, your Usenet reader, your network e-mail, a calendar/scheduler, Contact Manager, a spreadsheet, a graphics drawing package, a database application, a file viewer, backups, and a scanning application.

When all your Primary applications are in one folder you won't waste time hunting for the right folder or browsing through multilevel

Figure 7-7

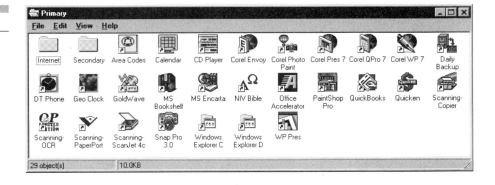

menus on the Windows 95 Start button. As long as you never close your primary folder (always use the MINIMIZE icon instead), the Taskbar will have **Primary** on it. And you'll be able to use ALT+TAB to return to **Primary** quickly to start any of your favorite applications.

Of course, the Windows 95 desktop lets you to create a folder for any application and put it on the desktop. But, a single primary folder reduces desktop clutter and lets you find your most important applications with the mouse or with ALT+TAB.

You might have a second tier of applications that you need regularly, but not daily. If so, create a folder entitled **Secondary** and copy the icons you want into that folder. You probably will keep SECONDARY minimized instead of closing it, so that it, too, will be visible on your Taskbar.

Fitting in More Icons

You can get more icons inside each group if you'll change the icon spacing within Windows. The examples listed in the next exercise work well with a screen resolution of 800 × 600. While this is a common setting, yours might be different and you might need to experiment with different settings. Consider these icon-spacing numbers as starting points.

Objective: Get more icons in a group by changing icon spacing.

❑ Right-click the desktop.

❑ Click PROPERTIES, APPEARANCE.

❑ Click the ITEM drop list, then click ICON SPACING (HORIZONTAL).

❑ Change the number to **36** (or whatever you want to try).

(See the Window Screen Resolution section below for more information about the effect of screen resolution on the numbers you enter here.)

❑ Click the ITEM drop list, then click ICON SPACING (VERTICAL).

❑ Change the number to **42** (or whatever you want to try).

❑ Click OK.

❑ Open your new **Primary folder**.

You will *not* notice any immediate changes; it's a little quirk of Windows 95. To put the new spacing into effect,

❏ Right-click the folder.
❏ Click ARRANGE ICONS, BY NAME.

Windows Screen Resolution

The example of a Primary group shown in Fig. 7-7 uses a screen resolution of 800 × 600 pixels. Pixels are dots on the screen. As the number of pixels in your resolution increases, the image quality improves and you get more information on your screen. There are, however, two trade-offs.

First, if the resolution gets too high, the text and icons will be too small to use. The ideal solution to that problem is to get a 21-in. monitor. Since a 21-in. monitor alone costs more than an entire PC with a 15-in. monitor, few people have them. You probably won't want to go above 640 × 480 on a 14-in. monitor. Most people are happy with 800 × 600 on a 15-in. or 17-in. monitor. With a 17-in. monitor you might even go up to 1024 × 768. The highest resolution in common use today, 1280 × 1024 makes the text too small for most users on any monitor smaller than 19 in.

The second trade-off is a penalty in computer memory. The high resolutions require lots of memory and can render some systems inoperable. The 800 × 600 setting is a good balance between resolution, readability, and computer memory requirements.

Menu Fonts

While we're on the subject of screen appearance, we'll give you a little-used tip that your eyes might appreciate very much. You can change the font face, font size and font attributes on your Windows 95 menus. One of the options, applying bold to the menu words, is especially nice. Here's a short hands-on exercise that will walk you through making your menu words bold and, while you're there, will let you make other changes as well.

Objective: Change fonts for Windows 95 menus.
❏ Right-click the desktop.

❏ Click PROPERTIES, then APPEARANCE.

❏ Click the ITEM drop list and select MENU.

❏ Click the BOLD button on the FONT line.

You now can make any other changes you might desire. You can change the font face, font size, and font color.

❏ Click OK to accept the changes.

As an alternative, if you're undecided you can click APPLY to see the changes take effect immediately and then make other changes if desired. The CANCEL button, however, will not undo any changes you make if you have pressed APPLY.

Displaying All Open Applications

Windows 95 lets you see all of your open applications at a glance (Fig. 7-7). You can Cascade or Tile every open application to get an overview of everything that's running. Windows 3.x also had the same feature, but Windows 95 has a bonus: after seeing the applications, you can Undo the Cascade or Tile action and restore all windows to their previous state. In Windows 3.x, you had to restore each one individually, which was a lot of work.

Objective: Learn how to see all open applications at a glance.

❏ Right-click the Taskbar.

❏ Click CASCADE.

❏ Right-click the Taskbar.

❏ Click UNDO CASCADE to restore all windows.

❏ Right-click the Taskbar.

❏ Click TILE HORIZONTALLY.

❏ Right-click the Taskbar.

❏ Click UNDO TILE to restore all windows.

NOTE: *Here's a caution about exiting Windows. Never turn off your computer or reboot it when Windows is running unless it has frozen and there is no other way to recover. Windows does a lot of clean-up work when it closes down. When you turn off your computer while Windows is running you can end up wasting a lot of hard disk space with stray files. Even worse, it's possible for Windows to become corrupted and require reinstallation. Always use the Taskbar to click START,*

click SHUT DOWN, *then click* YES *or press* Y *to confirm. Even then you should wait for the message that tells you it's safe to turn off your computer.*

Special Switching Techniques

As you might imagine, there are many other ways to start and switch applications. The switching techniques we've shown you so far are generic and will work with all copies of Windows. Since starting and switching applications is so important when you work on the Internet, we'll now show you some specialized alternatives.

Windows Resources

When you begin freely using ALT+TAB you will begin to run Windows with a lot of simultaneously open applications. If you're using Windows 3.x, you might begin to encounter system problems, such as hang-ups that you never before have experienced.

One way to keep Windows running reliably is to keep an eye on the system resources. Here's how you can check system resources at any time:

Objective: Learn how to check the system resources.

❑ Activate the Taskbar and click START.

❑ Click SETTINGS, then CONTROL PANEL.

❑ Double-click SYSTEM.

❑ Click PERFORMANCE.

❑ Click OK, or press ENTER to dismiss the dialog box.

❑ Close CONTROL PANEL.

Unlike Windows 3.x, Windows 95 does not suffer from serious resource limitations. You can expect to run five major applications simultaneously without any problems.

However, just for the fun of it, check your system resources sometime immediately after you have turned on your computer and started Windows. They should be above 80 percent. If they are not you probably have a lot of fonts loaded or some out-of-date drivers. Check with the manufacturers of some of your computer's components, especially your video display card, and make sure you have the latest driver. We've seen some quirky, unreliable systems become stable simply because the display driver was updated.

For example, one computer had serious problems with hanging up when using WordPerfect for Windows. The owner blamed it on a recent WordPerfect upgrade. But the problem was with the video display driver that was designed long before the manufacturer knew about Windows 95. Installing an updated video display driver restored the system's reliability.

Microsoft Windows Key

New keyboards today are sporting a couple of new keys designed specifically for Windows 95. Perhaps you got a new computer with your Windows 95, and it has the new keys. If not, you'll find that a new keyboard is inexpensive and even can help decrease physical stress. Microsoft makes one of the best ones, the Microsoft Natural Keyboard. Plenty of others are available, however, including models with a built-in Glide-Point mouse pad and mouse buttons. Choose the one that feels best to you; just make sure it has the new Windows logo keys.

Pressing either Windows key activates the Start button. In Windows 3.x, this key performs the same function as the CTRL+ESC keystroke. Once the Start button menu is activated you can press ESC or either ALT key to cancel it.

Most Windows keyboards also have another new key. It has a menu icon on it because it is designed to activate context-sensitive menus within applications. Within true Windows 95 applications it performs the same function as right-clicking the mouse. In Windows 3.x applications the results are unpredictable.

CUA Keystroke Summary

Here's a summary of some of the keystrokes that will help you the most when you're working on the Internet. Having every one of these techniques in your repertoire will make you a maestro of the Internet, and you'll be able to work with it to new heights of productivity.

SHIFT Key with the Mouse

You also can use the SHIFT key with your mouse to quickly select multiple items on a list. From earlier hands-on exercises in this book, you should still have the Program Manager open. We'll use that again for examples.

Objective: Learn to select a series of items on a list.

❑ Click WINDOW, MAIN to open the MAIN group.

❑ Double-click FILE MANAGER.

❑ Select any directory with a long list of filenames.

❑ Click on a file near the top of the list.

❑ Hold down SHIFT while you click an item near the bottom.

All files between and including the two on which you clicked will be selected.

❑ Click on one file near the top of the list.

❑ Hold down SHIFT while you press the DOWN ARROW key.

This, too, will highlight files in sequence.

CTRL Key with the Mouse

You can select a random assortment of files on any list using the CTRL key with your mouse.

Objective: Learn to randomly select multiple items on a list.

Use the same list you used in the previous lesson.

❑ Click on any file.

❑ Hold down the CTRL key while you click on another item.

Every click adds another item to the selection. Almost any file function you perform will be performed on this entire group of selected files (see Fig. 7-8).

❑ Continue holding down CTRL while you click on more items.

If you want to deselect a selected item, click on it again while holding down the CTRL key.

❑ Click on any item without holding down CTRL.

SHIFT Key with Cursor Movement Keys

Here's one of the best Windows tricks of all. It's hard to imagine using the Internet without this feature. Any cursor movement key selects text if SHIFT is depressed.

Figure 7-8

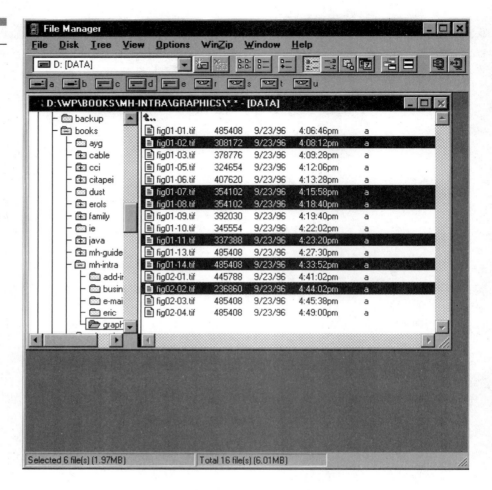

Here are some examples that will greatly boost your speed. To see this technique in action, it will be best if you open a file with some text. The exercise begins with your opening a document you can use to practice these keystrokes. We'll have you continue to use the Program Manager icons.

Objective: Learn to quickly select text using keystrokes.

❑ Click WINDOW, ACCESSORIES to open the group.

❑ Double-click WORDPAD.

❑ Click FILE, OPEN or click the OPEN icon.

❑ Navigate to the Windows directory.

Typically, this is `c:\windows`, but might be different on your system.

❑ Double-click the file **Exchange.txt**.

❑ Move to the bottom of the document with CTRL+END.

❑ Hold down SHIFT and press CTRL+HOME to move to the top of the document.

This selects all the text in any document with but two keystrokes, CTRL+END, or SHIFT+CTRL+HOME. This is a time-saving, valuable trick on the Internet and an excellent way to capture entire documents. You'll use it often. Press any cursor movement key to deselect the text. Try a couple of more examples to reinforce the concept.

❑ Press CTRL+HOME to jump to the top of the document.

❑ Press DOWN ARROW to go to the first line of hyphens.

❑ Hold down SHIFT then press DOWN ARROW four times.

This will select the entire title heading at the top of the document. You now could perform any number of operations on this text, just as if you had selected it with your mouse.

❑ Press DOWN ARROW to deselect it and move to the copyright line.

❑ Hold down SHIFT then press END.

This selects the entire line. You can do this in either direction. Let's try it now.

❑ Press END to deselect the line.

❑ Hold down SHIFT and press HOME.

❑ Press DOWN ARROW to deselect the line.

❑ Hold down SHIFT and press CTRL+END to select from the current cursor position to the end of the document.

❑ Press CTRL+HOME.

This deselects the text and positions you back at the top of the document for the next exercise.

Using the SHIFT key to select text is especially important when copying URLs and addresses. Try this with your cursor in a single-line text-entry window. We'll have you copy a line of text into the clipboard and then Paste it into this document.

Objective: Learn to copy the contents of a text entry box.

❑ Continue to use WordPad.

❑ Click FILE, then SAVE AS....

The text in the Filename box already is selected, so you could copy it now, but don't. Now you can see how to do it if the text is not selected.

❑ Press END to move to the beginning of the line.

❑ Press SHIFT+HOME to select all the text on that line.

This is an improvement over the frustrating method of trying to drag your mouse across the entire line without missing the first or last character. Even if you use the mouse to click in the text-entry box, finishing with the keystrokes might be quicker.

❑ Click at the far right of the text entry box.

❑ Press CTRL+C to copy it to your clipboard.

❑ Press ESC to cancel the SAVE AS dialog box.

❑ Press CTRL+V to paste the filename into the current document.

(You'll use this technique countless times on the Internet as you copy URLs and paste them to other applications or locations.)

❑ Press ENTER to start a new line for the next exercise.

Bold, Italics, and Underline

Nearly every windows application uses the same keystrokes to emphasize text with bold, italics, and underline. Let's practice, using the same document you used in the previous lesson.

Objective: Learn the keystrokes for bold, italics, and underline.

Use the same document as above. Don't worry about the mess we're making of this document. When you're through you simply will exit without saving.

❑ Press CTRL+B to turn on Bold, and type some text.

❑ Press CTRL+B to turn off Bold.

❑ Press CTRL+I to turn on Italics, and type some text.

❑ Press CTRL+I to turn off Italics.

❑ Press CTRL+U to turn on Underline, and type some text.

❑ Press CTRL+U to turn off Underline.

❑ Select the title header again, using SHIFT+DOWN ARROW.

❏ Press CTRL+B to bold the existing text.

❏ Press CTRL+I to italicize the existing text.

❏ Press CTRL+U to underline the existing text.

All three of these font attribute keystrokes are "toggles." That means that if the associated attribute is off, the keystroke will activate it; if it's on, the keystroke will deactivate it. Using these keystrokes will be much faster than interrupting your typing to grab the mouse, find a button, click, put down the mouse, and then return to the keyboard.

❏ Press ENTER to start a new line.

Cut, Copy, and Paste

These keystrokes will enable you to move text freely between any two Windows applications. Practice these and remember them; they will be a boon to your productivity in using Windows on the Internet. They use the universal Windows clipboard to move and copy text and graphics between any two locations within Windows.

Objective: Learn to use keystrokes for Cut, Copy, and Paste.

❏ Select the copyright line.

❏ Press CTRL+C to copy these words into the clipboard.

❏ Use ALT+TAB to return to Program Manager.

❏ Double-click NOTEPAD. (This could be any Windows application, from e-mail to WordPerfect to an HTML editor.)

❏ Press CTRL+V.

This will paste the copyright line into Notepad. Using Paste does not affect the clipboard contents. You can repeatedly paste the same text until you change the clipboard contents with Cut or Copy. For example . . .

❏ Press CTRL+V two more times to make sure the clipboard is preserved.

❏ Use ALT+TAB to return to WordPad.

❏ Select an entire paragraph of text.

❏ Press CTRL+X to cut it from the document.

❏ Move your insertion point to another spot in the document.

❏ Press CTRL+V to paste the paragraph to the new spot.

Using CUT, COPY, and PASTE in conjunction with application switching (such as ALT+TAB) is the key to working quickly, easily, and powerfully on the Internet with Windows. For example, transferring text from your Web browser to your word processor will be a snap. Simply use your mouse to select the desired text right on the Web page, press CTRL+C to copy it to your clipboard, press ALT+TAB to jump to your word processor, press CTRL+V to paste the text into a document, then press ALT+TAB again to return to the Internet for more text. Of course, you can reverse the process to transfer information from your word processor to an Internet application.

The next two lessons are on Netscape Navigator and the Eudora for Windows mail application. Both Netscape and Internet mail programs can stifle your productivity by making you write down and retype lots of annoying little text strings. Or, you can cruise the information super-highway with your Windows wide open.

Saving URLs

Here's an optional hands-on exercise that will prevent you from losing track of important information sites around the Internet. You will create a new icon for your Primary folder that will use the Windows WordPad to save a file of important URLS, along with a brief note on each. You then will be able to get to your URL list merely by double-clicking on this new icon, which always will be available in your Primary folder.

Objective: Create an icon that provides instant access to important Internet URLs.

❑ Open your Primary folder.

❑ Click FILE, NEW, SHORTCUT to create a new icon in **Primary**.

❑ Type **write.exe   c:\internet.wri** and press ENTER.

❑ Type **URLs** and press ENTER.

You now have created an icon that will instantly open a file containing all your URLs, but the file does not yet exist. The first time you activate this icon you'll get an error message, so let's create the file now.

❑ Double-click your new URLS icon.

A dialog box will warn you that the file does not exist, but the file will pop up instantly after this exercise.

❑ Click OK.

❑ Click FILE, SAVE to save the file.

❑ Type `c:\internet.wri` and press ENTER.

The file now exists, so you can exit.

From now on, whenever you discover a valuable URL on the Internet, highlight it, press CTRL+C to copy it to the clipboard, then use ALT+TAB to switch to your Primary folder or use the Taskbar to open the Primary folder. Then double-click your URLs icon, then use CTRL+V to paste in the URL. You then can use ALT+TAB to go back to your Internet application and copy some text to paste in here for a brief reminder, or you can type it in from scratch. Keep each URL on a separate line with the descriptive paragraph immediately under it. The FIND feature (EDIT, FIND or CTRL+F) will enable you to quickly locate URLs by searching for key words in the description that you wrote.

New Techniques for Windows 95

Windows 95 has many new features for managing files and folders. For example, you can place the URL file itself on your desktop and then double-click it to activate WordPad. And you could maintain on your desktop several URL files to organize your URLs into categories.

If you access the Internet from more than one computer, you might want to check out the new Windows 95 Briefcase feature to use for your URLs. Briefcase can store all of your URLs and enable you to easily copy them to a notebook or to a floppy disk. And, if you update any of your URL files while you're using your notebook, Briefcase can synchronize the two separate collections of files so your desktop computer will be updated with the changes.

The techniques presented in this chapter are, of course, not the only ways to save URLs. Windows 95 is rich in powerful features that can help you organize files. You might discover some on your own or you might learn them from other users. Ask around, read other books, read the Windows 95 help files or a manual, and be open to using new techniques and features.

You also will find that Internet browsers have a built-in bookmark feature that stores your best URLs. This bookmark list might quickly become full, or you might find URLS you want to remember that do not merit a bookmark slot. That's when you'll appreciate your URLs file.

Wrap-up

Here's the final hands-on exercise to close all the Windows you've opened and clean up your desktop.

Objective: Close all the extra open applications.

❑ Activate the Taskbar and right-click CALCULATOR.

❑ Click CLOSE.

❑ Activate the Taskbar and right-click WORDPAD.

❑ Click CLOSE and don't save the changes we made.

Continue to close all open applications you no longer need to use now. Or, if you're through for now, you can click simply exit.

Moving On

Congratulations on sticking with us through this long lesson! It seemed like a lot of work, didn't it? You soon are going to see, however, a payoff for that work when you begin browsing the Web in the next chapter. The techniques you've learned here will serve you for many years as you trek through the vast reaches of cyberspace. Now that you've completed the Windows lessons, let's move on to the next chapter to learn about the vehicle that will transport you through cyberspace: the Netscape Navigator.

CHAPTER 8

Browsers
Your Intranet Needs a Standard

Your Intranet will be more successful if you standardize on one Web browser for all users. This won't be difficult because the browser industry has evolved into a two-tier market. The first tier contains Netscape and the Microsoft Internet Explorer. The second tier is all the others. Both top-tier applications are rich with powerful features, such as Java, plug-ins, and ActiveX support.

The second tier includes a perplexing array of low-end (free) browsers, "conglomerated" Internet suites, and browser-enabled application software. The next iteration of Lotus Notes (Notes 5) might turn into a major browser player for large organizations committed to deploying Notes, but does not challenge the top tier today. Stick with the top tier.

To make things a little harder, although we recommend a single browser for all users, some Internet sites are offering dual paths, each optimized for either Netscape or Microsoft Explorer. If you can't decide which browser to feature, the same duality also is an option for your Intranet. However, while the dual-path might make sense for pages being published on external servers, it is madness for Intranet publishing.

A dual-path Intranet is a time-wasting drain on resources, yet we still find some technical people who express interest in this approach. Management should squash such ideas like bugs.

The purpose of your Intranet is to easily generate and distribute content. A dual-path system won't contribute anything to information distribution, but will contribute a lot toward increasing user confusion and will increase resulting workload and update problems. Believe us, you'll have enough trouble keeping the content updated even when it only has to be done once.

So, which browser do you choose? Unless your organization is heavily invested in Microsoft development work, we recommend that you stick with the Netscape standard. Because about 75 percent of all Internet Web traffic is using Netscape, we've chosen it for the main focus of this chapter. As of the fall of 1996, Microsoft Explorer commanded about 10 percent of Web traffic, but although we expect that percentage to grow and other browsers to fade, Netscape still has the lead. Ultimately, whatever you choose, as we've said several times already, the most important task is to pick a single browser and stick with it.

Reasons to Standardize on One Intranet Browser

If you choose Netscape, even though it's far and away the leader, you still might have a significant group of users who want something else.

Here are some factors you can present to them or to management to help bolster your single browser decision.

Common Training   As simple as browsers are to use, the top browsers have many advanced features that will require several hours of training and more hours of practice to be fully exploited. You'll have your hands full enough just running classes for one browser; you'll really hate trying to set up a dual training track.

Streamlined Technical Support   When someone calls with a problem, your first question won't have to be, "Well, which browser are you using . . . Oh, well, our Explorer expert is out today, I can only help you with Netscape." Plus, you'll want to know that the problems you iron out for one browser won't keep surfacing in the other. And, you'll have to maintain only one set of bug reports and fixes.

Consistent Appearance   Web-content producers can create content that they know everyone will be able to use on all workstations. Pages produced for each browser will appear slightly or sometimes very different. If everyone uses a common browser, authors can be confident that other users will see what they see when viewing their web pages. The alternative is to advise authors to try their page with several different browsers, but that's a time-wasting process.

Universal Plug-In Support   Plug-ins and helper applications are changing so rapidly today that keeping up with a single browser already is a losing battle. You'll never have everyone up-to-date. Trying to track the technology updates on two browsers will be worse than twice as bad.

Simplified Licensing and Upgrades   Site licenses are often cheaper when you license larger numbers of workstations. And, when your organization moves to a browser upgrade or to other Intranet technology in the future, you'll have to worry about only one set of conversion problems, and you can cut one licensing deal instead of many.

The Great Debate

Netscape's majority share of the browser market shows no signs of disappearing. As the market leader, it's certainly an excellent investment for corporate users. Microsoft's Internet Explorer uses a different technology for extending its functions, called *ActiveX components*, but Explorer is beginning to support Netscape-style plug-ins even as plug-ins for Netscape, such as the OLE control plug-in by Ncompass, are moving to provide ActiveX support.

Are we saying to close the door on the Microsoft Explorer and never look back? Not at all. No one in the PC industry has succeeded by ignoring Microsoft. You can like them or not, but the bottom line is that they produce quality products and constantly improve. Thus, while Netscape is the leader today, we recommend tracking industry developments and keeping an open mind. So before we move on and concentrate on Netscape, here are a few factors to consider about the Microsoft Explorer.

Internet Explorer

The main problem with Microsoft Internet Explorer is that it renders pages differently than Netscape. Sites that look balanced and well-planned in Netscape might look somewhat askew in Explorer. Of course the reverse is true, but not to the same degree. And more important, very few sites are designed specifically for Explorer although some are offering visitors a choice of selecting pages optimized for either Netscape or Explorer.

One of Explorer's chief strengths is that its user interface is a seamless extension of the Windows 95 interface. For example, the bookmark feature in Explorer uses the same folders as everything else in Windows 95, so there's nothing new to learn. The Explorer bookmark folder is more powerful and easier to use than Netscape's bookmark feature. However, Netscape probably will upgrade their bookmarks to use the Windows 95 folders and might have done so by the time you read this.

Other Browser Options

What do you do with users who haven't been upgraded to Windows or Macintosh PCs? The cold truth is that it's time for these folks to move forward. The new interface introduced with Windows 95 has been mastered by tens of millions of users and has proven to be a reliable, user-friendly environment.

Any DOS-loving hangers-on in your organization should be made aware of the enormous productivity-enhancing aspects of the Windows environment. They're missing too much to hang back.

And, anyone reluctant to switch to Windows because they claim to be too busy to learn a new system is missing the point. The busier a person's schedule, the more they need to move to Windows. Only the most casual computer user can afford to remain in a non-GUI environment. If, however, you do find a few senior workers who won't even look at Windows, then look at the Lynx browser for them.

Lynx is a character-mode Web browser that runs on both Unix and DOS systems. Navigating Web pages is done with the cursor control keys and a few keyboard controls. Of course, graphics won't be displayed and text formatting is very primitive, so these folks might find that an Intranet serves only a limited purpose. Here is some contact information in case you need to accommodate users who haven't yet gone with the mainstream flow:

- *Lynx* can be used to access information on the Web or to build information systems intended primarily for local access. Current versions of Lynx run on UNIX and VMS. For more information visit **www.cc.ukans.edu/lynx_help/Lynx_users_guide.html**.

- *DOSLynx* is intended for instructional and research educational use. Licensing for noneducational use had not been established when we wrote this book, but you can contact them on the hypertext page at **ftp://ftp2.cc.ukans.edu/pub/WWW/DosLynx/readme.htm**. This product runs even on 8086 PCs with monochrome monitors, and it includes a built-in TCP/IP stack (Waterloo TCP/IP).

- *Line Mode Browser (WWW)* is a character-based Web browser developed for use on terminals. It can be run in interactive mode, noninteractive mode, or as a proxy client, and it gives a variety of possibilities for data format conversion and filtering, among other things. Its home page is **www.w3.organization/hypertext/WWW/LineMode**.

- *Chimera* is a World Wide Web browser for UNIX-based machines running the X window system; it has a Web page at **www.unlv.edu/chimera**. The source for Chimera can be retrieved directly at **ftp.cs.unlv.edu**.

Netscape Navigator

Netscape's chief strength is in its extension to the basic HTML standards. Web page designers can use these extensions to create a wider variety of designs and, blessedly, spare us from looking at an endless stream of look-alike sites.

Netscape has a strong, built-in e-mail feature, though it lacks the power of a dedicated Internet e-mail application such as Eudora (more on this in the next chapter). But Netscape mail has other trade-offs. For example, Netscape mail uses its own, proprietary address book. Windows 95 enables you to create a single address book that can be used across applications, such as Internet Explorer, e-mail, and faxing. That spares you from making double entries, as would be necessary if you used Netscape's e-mail.

The e-mail features in both Netscape and Explorer might leave your users wanting a dedicated package, such as Eudora. One day, most likely, both browsers will be good enough to eliminate the need for a standalone e-mail application, but consider for now that they are works-in-progress. Now let's get an updated copy of Netscape and move into the hands-on training.

Getting the Latest Netscape

If you don't have Netscape—or if you'd just like to get the latest version—you can download a free trial version from the Internet. You can purchase the commercial version of the Netscape Web browser directly from Netscape by calling them at 416-528-2555, faxing them at 416-528-4140, e-mailing them at `sales@netscape.com`, or by visiting their online store on the Web at `http://home.netscape.com`. Find the link that lets you download the latest version of Netscape.

You can use the URL listed here as a starting point for discovering all of the Netscape products available today. Usually they have Beta test versions of the next generation that you might be tempted to try. Perhaps one or two people in your organization could use the latest

Beta version, but mainstream users should stick with a registered copy of the latest official release. That's not because there ever has been any significant problems with the Beta versions, but the Beta versions can be annoying to use because they expire after only a few weeks. Using beta copies forces users into a routine of regular downloads and updates.

Creating Some On-Screen Elbowroom

Most Web pages are too large to fit into the Netscape main screen all at once, but everyone ought to be able to see as much as possible. In this first Netscape exercise, we will make sure that you know how to maximize the total Netscape viewing area by eliminating some buttons that unnecessarily clutter the screen. We also have included a listing of keystroke equivalents that replace the buttons once they are hidden from view.

Objective: Maximize your Netscape viewing area.

❑ Start Netscape with an Internet connection.

❑ Press CTRL+L, type **home.netscape.com** and press ENTER.

Notice how this document appears on-screen; especially note how little of the document you can see at one time. Scroll through this document using your UP ARROW or your DOWN ARROW keys, or your mouse. Now let's improve your view.

❑ Double-click the title bar to maximize Netscape on the screen.

If your view already looks like the screen shown in Fig. 8-1, you can skip the next two steps.

❑ If not, click OPTIONS then uncheck SHOW TOOLBAR.

❑ Click OPTIONS, then uncheck SHOW DIRECTORY BUTTONS.

Once these two button bars are eliminated (see Fig. 8-1), users will enjoy the increased viewing area. The toolbar we just eliminated is pretty much a waste of screen space. The buttons on both of them either have keystroke equivalents, right mouse button equivalents, or are used so seldom that they do not merit full-time screen space. The directory buttons, of course, are a complete waste of space in an Intranet environment.

Of course, you can eliminate the location bar too, but that's a crucial navigation tool that most users will prefer to keep. The next table lists simple keystroke and right-mouse-button replacements for the buttons that were just hidden.

Navigating a Downloaded Web Document

Your fellow workers will devote an ever-increasing portion of their day to browsing through documents in Netscape. We've included here some tips and tricks that can result in a big pay-off in productivity savings. You can try the exercises yourself and then integrate them into Netscape, Internet, or Intranet training classes.

Since Web pages are no more than documents, let's review some shortcuts to moving around within an opened document, because everyone

Figure 8-1

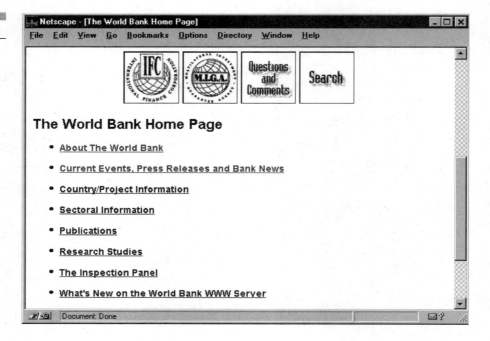

TABLE 8.1	Buttons	Equivalent
Netscape Surfing Keystrokes	**Toolbar button**	
	Back	ALT+LEFT ARROW or right mouse, BACK
	Forward	ALT+RIGHT ARROW or right mouse, FORWARD
	Home	Click GO, HOME
	Reload	CTRL+R or VIEW, RELOAD
	Open location	CTRL+L or FILE, OPEN LOCATION...
	Open file	CTRL+O or FILE, OPEN FILE...
	Print	CTRL+P or FILE, PRINT...
	Find	CTRL+F or EDIT, FIND...
	Save	CTRL+S or FILE, SAVE AS...
	Stop	ESCAPE or GO, STOP LOADING
	Directory button	
	What's new!	Click DIRECTORY, WHAT'S NEW!
	What's cool!	Click DIRECTORY, WHAT'S COOL!
	Handbook	Click HELP, HANDBOOK
	Net search	Click DIRECTORY, INTERNET SEARCH
	Net directory	Click DIRECTORY, INTERNET DIRECTORY

needs to be as efficient at surfing individual documents as they are at surfing the entire Web. The example you'll load first is a long Web document that defines the commonly used Internet terms. Later, we'll include a lesson to show you how to save this document and turn it into an accessible reference source.

Objective: Learn quick-surfing shortcuts.

❏ Start Netscape with an Internet connection.

❏ Double-click in the LOCATION text entry box.

❏ Type **www.marketing-coach.com/mh-guide** and press ENTER.

❏ Click on GLOSSARY.

This is an online glossary from our first McGraw-Hill Internet book. You can use this document to teach some quick browsing methods.

❑ Press DOWN ARROW to scroll down through this document.

❑ Press UP ARROW to scroll up through this document.

❑ Use your mouse on the scroll bar on the right of the screen.

Use the arrows at the top or the bottom to scroll up or down. Grab the elevator button (square box) on the scroll bar and drag it up or down to more quickly scroll long distances.

❑ Press CTRL+END to jump to the bottom of this document.

❑ Press CTRL+HOME to jump to the top of this document.

❑ Press PG DN a couple of times.

❑ Press PG UP a couple of times.

Remember these keystrokes throughout all your Web surfing. When your computer is pushing the limits, using the mouse places a strain on your Windows resources. If the mouse acts sluggish or skittery, try using these keystrokes instead.

Finding the Information You Need

You want to make sure that your users can take the power of Netscape outside the boundaries of your Intranet. The Web has an array of fast, powerful, and comprehensive search engines that will help your Intranet users locate information they can't find via an Intranet.

You probably won't be able to keep track of all the search engines that are available on the Web, because new services constantly emerge. We have, however, profiled two of them here because they both are highly popular, are very powerful, and are representative of basic Web search techniques. Once these two are mastered, learning the others will be a snap. Otherwise there are just two reasons to try alternative search engines: (1) the others might better suit individual users than the two profiled in these exercises, and (2) the services profiled here might be too busy.

You might also want to make an array of search engines available to your users. Perhaps the organization's home page will include a list of search engine links. Or, you could include them on a default Bookmark List and put them under a folder called **Search Resources**. However er you present them to users, you want to make sure that everyone on your Intranet can get quick answers to their research demands. The following hands-on lessons can be used to help users master the concepts.

Lycos

Lycos is a creation of Carnegie-Mellon University in Pittsburgh (see Fig. 8-2). It's oriented toward keyword searches and offers several search options. This engine is fast and comprehensive, though at times, you might believe that it's slow. Just remember, you are sharing this service with millions of people around the world. Consider the wonder that it works at all!

Let's run through an exercise to demonstrate how to use Lycos to look up a specific topic.

Objective: Learn to search the Web with Lycos.

❑ Press CTRL+L, type **www.lycos.com** and press ENTER.

Netscape no longer requires that cumbersome **http://**, so get in the habit of omitting it.

❑ Click ENHANCE YOUR SEARCH to see search options.

Figure 8-2

❑ Click in QUERY and type `hot air balloon`.

❑ Double-click in MIN TERMS and type **3**.

This means that Lycos will give a higher score to documents that contain all three terms you entered. It also will show documents that contain any two terms or any single term, but the weighting will favor documents with all three terms.

❑ Double-click in MAX-HITS and type **25**.

❑ Click START SEARCH and wait.

In April, 1996, Lycos reported, "Found 37660 documents matching at least one search term. Printing only the first 25 of 170 documents with at least scores of 0.010 and matching 3 search terms." Browse through the listing you received and see your results.

❑ Press CTRL+END to jump to the bottom of this lengthy page.

❑ Click the right mouse button and click BACK.

You could click BACK TO THE LYCOS HOME PAGE but you didn't get here from the home page, so we only needed to go back one page. Note that you also could click on NEXT 25 HITS to continue displaying more of the listings that matched all three terms. Try some other searches on topics that interest you.

❑ Reset the MIN TERMS text-entry box, if necessary.

You can read more about using Lycos by clicking on some of the links on Lycos' home page. And, you can get details on the searching mechanism itself by clicking on SEARCH LANGUAGE HELP on the search form page.

The Best Search Page of All

These lessons on Yahoo! and Lycos give users specific searching steps, but you'll want them to have more searching tools available than just these two. You could spend a couple days researching the best Web search engines and build a tailored page on your Intranet for all of the good links you find.

Or, you can take the simple route and include the most comprehensive compilation of search engines that we've found: `www.search.com` If you make available this link on your organization's home page, you'll probably never have to field any requests from users for more searching tools. `Search.com` includes all the most popular search engines, plus collections of URLs sorted out by major category and a vast array of Internet directory services that can help pinpoint other organizations and even individuals. It's the only search URL you'll need to provide.

Yahoo!

Yahoo! is one of the earliest Web search engines (see Fig. 8-3). Yahoo's primary organization is topic-based. Instead of looking for your information by a keyword search, you can scan broad categories to find things that catch your eye. Yahoo! also includes a keyword search, but it's so similar to Lycos that we will just use its topic-based search function here.

Objective: Learn to search the Web with Yahoo!.

❏ Press CTRL+L, type **www.yahoo.com**, and press ENTER.

This page offers more options than Lycos does, but it still includes a keyword-search, text-entry box. You can click on OPTIONS to tailor your search more precisely. For now, though, let us explore some of the other search methods that Yahoo! offers.

Figure 8-3

❑ Click on any major topic or subtopic and follow the thread.

For example, click on BUSINESS AND ECONOMY, then click on MARKETING, then browse the list.

❑ Click on the YAHOO! graphic to return to the home page.

❑ Click on POPULAR to see the 50 most popular Yahoo sites.

Check out some of them if you want to.

❑ Click on the YAHOO! graphic to return to the home page.

❑ Click on HEADLINES to see news categories.

❑ Click on a news category to see related headlines.

Check out some that interest you.

❑ Click on the YAHOO! graphic to return to the home page.

❑ Click on NEW to see the latest additions to Yahoo!

Note that Yahoo! is growing by hundreds of links per day.

❑ Click on the YAHOO! graphic to return to the home page.

❑ Click on COOL to see the Yahoo! *COOL Links.*

On this page you'll find a dazzling array of unrelated links. Try a few and have some fun!

❑ Click on the YAHOO! graphic to return to the home page.

Remember, if you can't see this graphic, press CTRL+HOME to return to the top of the current page.

❑ Click on RANDOM.

This is for those days when you just can't decide what to read. Sit back and leave the driving to Yahoo!

❑ Click on the YAHOO! graphic to return to the home page.

❑ Click on INFO to get help with Yahoo.

Be sure to check out YAHOO HELP—QUICK TIPS ON USING YAHOO so you'll do even better on searches when you really need to find something specific and find it fast.

❑ Click on the YAHOO! graphic to return to the home page.

If the home page you've created for your organization is not yet indexed on Yahoo, be sure to click on ADD URL so you can enter your contact information. Expect to be able to find your page listed here in a week or so after adding your URL. Be sure that users understand that the pages they index with a search engine must be publicly available pages; it would be a major waste to have anyone reference Intranet pages in a search index.

Remember, also, that there are many other good search engines in Appendix B, "Continuing Education," as well as on the page we've been using for our Web exercises.

Marking Cyberspace Trails

The power of these amazing search engines can lead users to wander off into cyberspace and get lost. Fortunately, the Netscape folks experienced this lost feeling enough times that they created some tools for marking a trail through cyberspace. Let's see how Netscape can help users quickly return to screens they've seen before.

Back and Forward

The simplest trail-marking features are BACK and FORWARD. Netscape includes three methods to activate these two features, but we'll include only two because one method is the Toolbar buttons that you removed earlier. No need to waste screen space when you have these convenient alternatives.

Objective: Use Netscape Back and Forward features.

❑ Click the right mouse button anywhere on the current Web page.
❑ Click BACK.
❑ Click the right mouse button anywhere on the current Web page.
❑ Click FORWARD.
Press ALT+LEFT ARROW three times.
Press ALT+RIGHT ARROW three times.

View History

If the document to which you want to return is a long way back, these might become tedious navigation tools, although you can jump back very rapidly using the ALT+LEFT ARROW keystroke. Still, there are more direct routes back to pages you have previously viewed. Let's practice using them now.

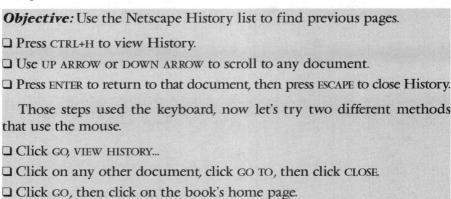

Objective: Use the Netscape History list to find previous pages.

❑ Press CTRL+H to view History.

❑ Use UP ARROW or DOWN ARROW to scroll to any document.

❑ Press ENTER to return to that document, then press ESCAPE to close History.

Those steps used the keyboard, now let's try two different methods that use the mouse.

❑ Click GO, VIEW HISTORY...

❑ Click on any other document, click GO TO, then click CLOSE.

❑ Click GO, then click on the book's home page.

If you activated this menu with ALT+G, you might prefer to make your selection by pressing the underlined number of the document you want to see. The LOCATION text entry box in Netscape includes a history list. Use your mouse to click on the drop-arrow at the end of LOCATION and then click on any link to which you want to return. With all of these techniques at your fingertips, you should never lose track of an interesting site or valuable information.

Netscape Caching

When you use the commands you just learned, you might notice that the screens load more quickly than they did originally. That's because Netscape stores downloaded screens (called *caching* in computer talk) so that it doesn't have to download them from the Internet again if you decide to return. The larger the cache size, the more screens Netscape can hold and the faster your system will respond to BACK and FORWARD. Netscape has two caches, one in RAM memory and another on your hard drive or network that it uses once the RAM cache is full.

The default cache sizes that are set in Netscape are compromises to accommodate computers that have little free memory. Hard disk prices have dropped so dramatically that you might now have more free disk space *after* installing all of your applications than you used to have when your hard drive was empty. RAM memory remains relatively expensive, so it's not likely you have a lot of free RAM going to waste. You can increase both cache sizes to improve speed by following these steps:

Objective: Increase Netscape's cache size.

❑ Click OPTIONS, NETWORK PREFERENCES...

❑ Click on the CACHE tab (see Fig. 8-4).

❑ Double-click in the MEMORY CACHE text-entry box.

If you have 16 Mbytes of RAM you can try setting this to 4000 kbytes (4 Mbytes). If you run a lot of other applications at the same time, you might have to live with a smaller Netscape memory cache, perhaps two megabytes. Whatever your computer's memory cache, you'll have to balance this setting against other memory demands.

❑ Double-click in the DISK CACHE text entry box.

❑ Type **32000** and click OK.

The version of Netscape used for this book accepted a maximum disk cache of 32 Mbytes. You can try more on your system if you like— perhaps they've updated this feature—but when I set mine above 32,000 kbytes Netscape changed the setting to zero (0). If you attempt to set your disk cache greater than 32,000 be sure to return and see if Netscape accepted the higher setting.

❑ Click OPTIONS, SAVE OPTIONS.

Switching Applications

What if you need another application while you're surfing? Remember that Windows has full multitasking ability. That means that it can perform more than one function at a time. Here are two techniques to keep in mind when you're surfing the Net.

You can switch to other open Windows applications by cycling through them with the ALT+TAB key or by clicking on the Taskbar to see your current applications. This is particularly valuable when you hit during peak hours a Website that uses extensive graphics. You can ALT+TAB to another application and get a little work done while Netscape continues to download. For example, you could jump to Eudora and compose an e-mail message. It's not much, but at least you can save a little time instead of watching the hourglass.

You can open multiple Netscape Windows, although this certainly is not a solution to long download times. But it does permit you to see two Web pages at once, or three Web pages, or more! When you create multiple Netscape sessions each occurrence is a separate Windows task that

Figure 8-4

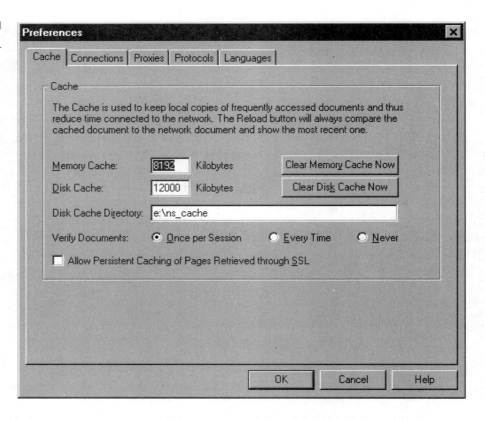

will appear on the Taskbar and to which you can switch using ALT+TAB. Follow these steps to open an additional Netscape window (see Fig. 8-5).

Objective: Learn to open multiple Netscape windows.

❑ Click FILE, NEW WEB BROWSER or press CTRL+N.

This opens a new Netscape window that loads your default home page. You might be able to see the first session in the background. You can navigate in either one now, setting them both to different URLs. If you can see both of them you can use your mouse to switch back and forth. It's probably best, however, to run them separately, maximized, so let's do that now and learn how to switch between them when they're maximized.

❑ Double-click in the title bar of the new Netscape window.

Do this *only* if the current Netscape window is not already maximized.

❑ Activate the Taskbar to see both of them.

The icons will be identical, but you'll see the title of the current page in each session in square brackets after NETSCAPE.

❏ Click on the first Netscape session you had open.

❏ Press ALT+TAB once to return to the new Netscape window.

Note that this menu also lists in square brackets the name of each window's current document.

❏ Press ALT+TAB once again to return to the first window.

❏ Press ALT+TAB once to return to the new Netscape window.

Of course you don't have to run these windows maximized. You might want to use the RESTORE command (the middle icon in the upper-right corner) and then size them so that you can see both Web pages at the same time, perhaps to compare two Websites.

❏ Click FILE, CLOSE to close the new Web browser.

Notice that CLOSE closes only the current window and that you still could select EXIT to quit Netscape. But when you open multiple windows you use this command to close just this window. Closing one will not

Figure 8-5

terminate your Internet connection, because you still have the first Netscape window open. Be sure you still have the glossary document loaded.

Use the Netscape FIND Command

Many of the hypertext Web pages that you'll view include jumps to bookmarks within the same document. You'll be able to tell if you've jumped to another spot within the same document because the URL will not change except for the very end, onto which will be appended a pound sign (#) and the bookmark name.

But you won't always find the information you want by using hypertext jumps. Sometimes you'll need to search the full text of the current Web document. Netscape has a Find feature that we'll practice now. For this exercise, let's say you want to look up the definition of the acronym *ISDN*.

Objective: Learn to use the Netscape FIND feature.

❏ Press CTRL+H and go to the glossary.

❏ Press CTRL+F or click on EDIT, FIND.

❏ Type **ISDN** and press ENTER to jump to that phrase.

This finds text only within this specific document. This is not searching the Web itself. It's not even searching other documents that are on the same Website. This feature finds text only within your current Web document.

Using the Information You Find

Finding an important business lead, tip, or idea can bring value to your organization. Finding some research material you've been seeking can be a huge relief. Discovering exciting information on the Web that you never knew existed is exhilarating. But once you find something, you need to know how to transfer it into your system in a useful format. There are numerous options, and you probably will use them all depending on the information you've found and on how you plan to use it later.

Copying and Pasting Web Pages

Probably the quickest, simplest, and most overlooked option for transferring Web text is with the Windows clipboard and the COPY and PASTE commands. If you can see the information you usually can paste it into your word processor. After the transfer, you can reshape and reformat the text, embellish it with nice fonts, and print it as part of a larger document.

Objective: Learn to transfer Web text into your word processor.

❏ Find your word processor icon and start the program.

❏ Use ALT+TAB to cycle back to Netscape.

❏ Drag your mouse to highlight the ISDN listing.

❏ Press CTRL+C to copy it to the Windows clipboard.

❏ Use ALT+TAB to cycle to your word processor.

❏ Press CTRL+V to paste the copied text into a blank document.

You now could go back to Netscape and grab more text from any Web document in the world!

You won't be able to grab all of the text you read on the Web, because some text actually is part of a graphic image. In those cases, you won't be able to grab the text you want by simply dragging your mouse over it. You'll know it's not regular text characters because, as you drag your mouse, the text will not appear highlighted.

NOTE: *Netscape has a command that will automatically select all of the text on a Web page. You can press CTRL+A or click edit, select all. Then use the normal Windows command to copy the selected text to the clipboard.*

Printing in Netscape

If users only need to read a hypertext document and don't need to use it in a word processor, they can print the document directly in Netscape. This is a quick way to get a hard copy of Internet information, but it is, of course, completely inflexible because it can't be reformatted.

When a document is printed directly, it shows all the graphics as they appear on the screen. And, Netscape offers optional embellishments for printed Web pages that include headers and footers with name, date, and URL. We'll show you these printing setup options later.

Printing a Web document is perfect for information such as airline schedules, data tables, phone or address listings, anytime a quick printout is needed, or whenever the graphics images are needed along with the text.

Objective: Learn to print a Web document.

❑ Click FILE, PRINT PREVIEW then use ZOOM IN and ZOOM OUT.

Zoom in to better see the header and footer on each page. Use TWO PAGE and ONE PAGE to change views, and use NEXT PAGE and PREV PAGE to turn document pages. You can print from the preview screen by clicking on the PRINT... button, but instead let's return to the regular browsing screen and choose some page setup options.

❑ Click CLOSE.

❑ Click FILE, PAGE SETUP... (see Fig. 8-6).

The best settings for PAGE OPTIONS, at the top-left, will depend on the printer you're using, so we'll let you experiment with those. The same applies to the MARGINS settings.

❑ Uncheck DOCUMENT TITLE if you want to remove the title from the header of each page.

❑ Uncheck DOCUMENT LOCATION (URL) if you want to remove the URL from the header of each page.

❑ Click PAGE NUMBER, PAGE TOTAL, and DATE PRINTED as desired for the information you want included in the footer of each page.

❑ Click FILE, PRINT... then select options as desired.

❑ Click OK to print a URL Summary.

If you don't have a printer ready right now, you can click CANCEL to end this exercise without printing.

Saving Web Documents

Netscape will save hypertext documents, but if users aren't careful the documents will be saved with all of the hypertext markup language (HTML) codes. If that happens, the extraneous codes will need to be manually stripped to get down to only the text. In case that happens, we've

Figure 8-6

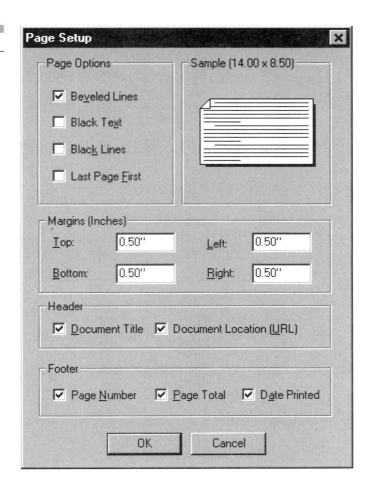

provided a WordPerfect for Windows macro that will strip a WordPerfect document of all HTML codes (see "Cleaning HTML Codes from Saved Web Documents" below). An even better option, however, is to make sure that users know how to make Netscape clean the HTML codes from hypertext documents when it saves them, as shown in the next exercise.

Objective: Learn to save a Web document.

❑ Click FILE, SAVE AS... or press CTRL+S.

Netscape creates a name for you that's extracted from the URL of the Web document, then it appends the extension **htm**, which is DOS syntax for hypertext markup language (HTML). You can, of course, change the name as desired.

Figure 8-7

❏ Click on the SAVE FILE AS TYPE drop list.

❏ Change to `Plain Text (*.txt)` (see Fig. 8-7).

You don't have to actually use the `txt` extension; the document will be saved as plain text even if you keep the `htm` extension, as long as the file type has been set correctly with this drop list.

❏ Use the DRIVES and DIRECTORIES windows to set the desired path.

You can click the NETWORK button to access your available network drives. Put this document in a directory that you commonly use for word processing, because you'll open it later in this exercise. Please write down or remember the directory.

❏ Click OK to save the document.

❏ Use ALT+TAB to switch to your word processor. Or, if your word processor is not running, start it now.

❏ Click FILE, OPEN... or press CTRL+O.

Navigate to the saved Web document and double-click on it to open it and display the conversion dialog box.

For WordPerfect for Windows only (see Fig. 8-8):

❏ Click the drop-list arrow to get a list of formats.

❏ Select ANSI (WINDOWS) TEXT CR/LF TO SRT and click OK.

❏ Click FILE, SAVE or press CTRL+S, then click OK.

For Microsoft Word for Windows:

❏ Click FILE, SAVE or press CTRL+S.

At this point, the document you had in Netscape now has been saved in the format of your word processor. If you didn't switch to plain text you'll see a lot of HTML codes. You can use the macro to remove them, or you can return to Netscape and save the document again in the plain-text format.

Cleaning HTML Codes from Saved Web Documents

If you don't switch Netscape into the correct saving mode, or if someone sends you an HTML document, cleaning out the HTML codes will be an agonizing task. But if you don't clean out the HTML codes you won't have easy access to the plain text. So, to make your HTML documents more useful, we've written a macro for WordPerfect for Windows 6.0/6.1 that automates this tedious task and will clean an HTML document in seconds.

Of course, before you use such a document, consider carefully the document's copyright. Sometimes all of a document's copyright information is buried inside HTML codes. Remember, documents placed on the Web do not lose their copyright. The safest course is for everyone to be up-front about text they use by e-mailing the copyright holder for reprint permission. Most people are glad to grant permission, especially if their URL will be cited in the document in which their text is used.

Figure 8-8

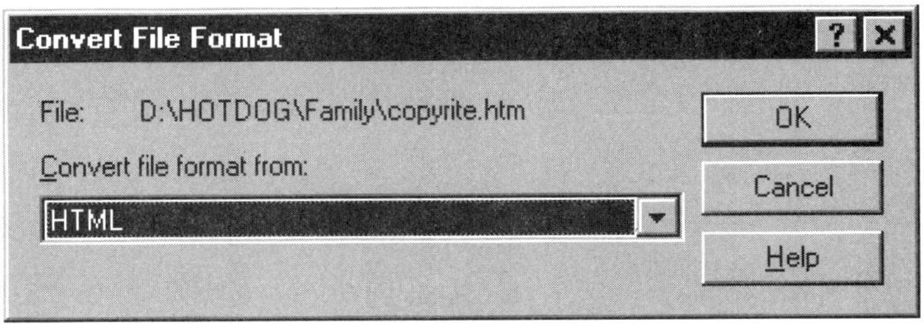

Convert File Format

File: D:\HOTDOG\Family\copyrite.htm

Convert file format from:

HTML

OK

Cancel

Help

Saving Images

The last method you have for extracting Internet information into usable formats is to save graphics files. Netscape makes this very easy. All you have to do is click your right mouse button on any Web page graphic and choose the correct save option.

Objective: Learn to save a Web page graphic image.

❑ Press CTRL+H and return to any previously viewed home page.

❑ Click the right mouse button over any graphic image (see Fig. 8-9).

❑ Click SAVE THIS IMAGE AS...

❑ Select a directory in which to save it.

❑ Click OK.

The image has been saved in the Graphics Interchange Format (compressed graphic images). When this book was written, neither Microsoft Word nor WordPerfect for Windows could handle GIF or JPEG files directly. Since the Internet is strewn with millions of images in these two formats, we hope that both will have been updated to handle GIFs, JPEGs, or both by the time you read this. If not, then be sure you provide users with a graphics application or a graphics conversion application that will handle GIF and JPEG images.

Right Mouse Button Bonuses

When you used the right mouse button in the last exercise, you might have noticed that the menu offered several other shortcuts. We'll run through some of them now, in case you missed them or didn't save a graphic. To see these commands actually function you'll need a Web page that has a graphic image. Continue to use the book's home page.

Netscape also uses the right mouse button to give you an easy method to copy the URL of a hypertext link into your Windows clipboard. You then might use ALT+TAB to cycle to your word processor or to your reserved URL storage file (see Chap. 7) and paste in the URL. As you've seen, some URLs are a real mess to retype, so this method might save a lot of time, aggravation, and mistakes.

Figure 8-9

Objective: Save a link location to the Windows clipboard.

❑ Jump to **www.marketing-coach/mh-guide/glossary**.

❑ Place the mouse over the **Book Home** link, but don't click.

Read the link's URL on the status line at the bottom of the screen. You don't want to type that, do you? Remember, many Web addresses are case-sensitive, so you will have to get all the characters exactly right if you attempt to retype them.

❑ Click the right mouse button and click COPY THIS LINK LOCATION.

The URL is now in the Windows clipboard. If you wanted to paste it into another Windows application you now would use ALT+TAB to switch applications, then you would press CTRL+V to paste it.

Bookmarks

The Bookmarks tool is among the most powerful and important tools in Netscape. Bookmarks creates a permanent file that saves the URL of any Internet document and assigns it a plain-language name. A Bookmarks list can be popped up any time to provide a quick jump to favorite sites, both Internet sites and Intranet sites.

We'll demonstrate four different Bookmark features: (1) adding Bookmarks, (2) editing Bookmarks, (3) modifying and arranging the Bookmarks List itself, and (4) turning the Bookmarks List into your own personal home page.

Adding Bookmarks

There are two ways to add personal Bookmarks in Netscape. The first is so easy you don't even need a hands-on exercise to learn it. Whenever you see a site for which you want easy access, simply press CTRL+D for the ADD BOOKMARK command. To use the mouse you would click BOOKMARKS, ADD BOOKMARK. The current URL is added to the Bookmark list under the main folder unless you've specified another folder as a default. We'll demonstrate later how to move Bookmarks to any category.

You also can add Bookmarks directly to the list (see Fig. 8-10). This has the advantage of enabling users to enter Bookmarks for sites they've yet to visit, or to add Bookmarks to a selected category. You might want to use this technique to set up some important Bookmarks for all users in advance. Let's try it now.

Objective: Add a Bookmark directly to the listing.

❑ Press CTRL+B or click BOOKMARKS, GO TO BOOKMARKS...

❑ Click on the top folder on the list.

❑ Click ITEM, INSERT FOLDER...

❑ Type PRACTICE and click OK.

This creates a new folder under the main folder.

❑ Click on the folder **Practice**.

❑ Click ITEM, INSERT BOOKMARK...

❑ Type **Internet Glossary** and press TAB to jump to LOCATION (URL).

❑ Type **http://www.marketing-coach.com/mh-guide/glossary.htm** and click OK.

❑ Click on the folder **Practice**.

❑ Click ITEM, INSERT BOOKMARK...

❑ Type **Lycos** and press TAB to jump to LOCATION (URL).

❑ Type **http://www.lycos.com** and click OK.

❑ Click ITEM, INSERT BOOKMARK...

❑ Type **Yellow Pages** and press TAB to jump to LOCATION (URL).

❑ Type **http://www.yellow.com** and click OK.

❑ Click on the top folder on the list.

❑ Click ITEM, INSERT FOLDER...

❑ Type **Internet Resources** and click OK.

Figure 8-10

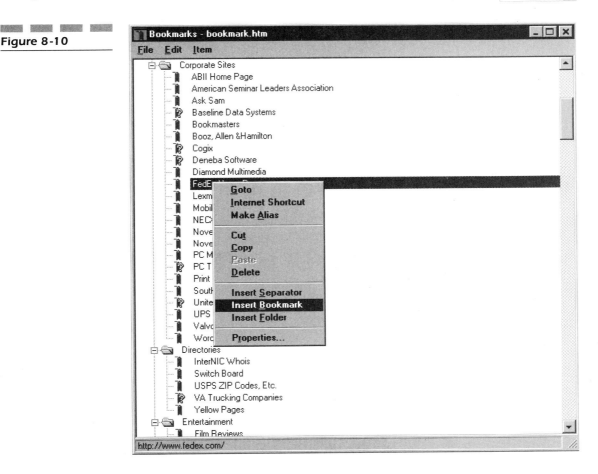

This creates another new folder.

❏ Click on the top folder on the list.

❏ Click ITEM, INSERT HEADER...

❏ Type **Directories** and click OK.

You can continue the lesson now by adding folders for other common categories. Additional headings that you could create include Search Resources, Reference Resources, Corporations, Universities, and Miscellaneous.

Now that you've set up all of these folders, here are two more exercises that will let you check out your Bookmarks and sort your Bookmarks for quicker reference.

Objective: Check Bookmark URLs.

❑ Click BOOKMARKS, GO TO BOOKMARKS.

❑ Click FILE, WHAT'S NEW? (see Fig. 8-11).

❑ Click START CHECKING to have Netscape verify your Bookmarks.

If you only want to check out some of your Bookmarks, select the ones you want to check before starting the check. To do that, hold down either CTRL key as you click so you can select multiple links.

Netscape can also sort the current Bookmarks to make the listings easier to scan. Follow the steps in the next exercise to learn how.

Objective: Learn how to sort Bookmarks.

❑ Click on the top folder.

❑ Click ITEM, SORT BOOKMARKS.

If this command is disabled, you're not on the top folder. If that's true, scroll through the list and highlight the top folder, then repeat the command.

To place a new Bookmark in a category other than the default, it first must be added to the list under the default folder. Then you can open the

Figure 8-11

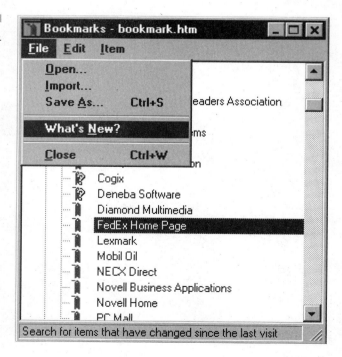

Bookmark List by pressing CTRL+B, at which point the new Bookmark can be dragged and dropped onto the desired category. But the default category can be changed at any time. Follow these steps to learn how.

Objective: Learn to specify a default Bookmark category.

❑ Click on the folder of the category you want to be the default.

❑ Click ITEM, SET TO NEW BOOKMARKS FOLDER.

For example, a folder called **New** could be created and made to be the default. That way all new bookmarks go there, so they can easily be moved later to their proper folder(s).

❑ Press ALT+F4 to return to Netscape.

Editing Existing Bookmarks

Sometimes URLs in Bookmarks will change, or a user will want to add some new information about a Bookmark site to its description. Fortunately, Netscape makes these tasks simple because Bookmark editing is a snap.

There's a bonus associated with this procedure. When a Bookmark is edited, the last date it was visited is updated. Sometimes, then, you might want to start this process just to see that information even if you do not need to edit the link information.

Objective: Learn to edit a Bookmark.

❑ Click on any existing Bookmark.

❑ Click the right mouse button, click PROPERTIES.

❑ Make any necessary changes, then click OK.

Note the two dates near the bottom of the dialog box.

Modifying Bookmarks

The order of the folders and the document references under each folder can be rearranged at any time simply by dragging any entry either to a new folder or to a new location under the same folder.

Objective: Modify the bookmark listing.

❑ Drag and drop `Internet Glossary` onto the `Internet Resources` folder.

❑ Click on `Internet Resources`.

❑ Click ITEM, INSERT BOOKMARK.

❑ Type `Yahoo`, then press TAB.

❑ Type `http://www.yahoo.com`, then press ENTER.

❑ Drag and drop `Yellow Pages` onto the `Directories` folder.

❑ Click on the folder `Practice` and delete it by pressing DELETE or by clicking on EDIT, DELETE.

Now that you've rearranged everything, let's sort your Bookmarks.

❑ Click on the top folder.

❑ Click ITEM, SORT BOOKMARKS.

❑ Click the exit button or press ALT+F4 to exit the Netscape Bookmarks window.

There are several ways to use a Bookmark List to surf the Internet. Here's a summary:

■ Press CTRL+B and double-click the item on the list.

■ Click BOOKMARKS, GO TO BOOKMARKS..., and double-click the item on the list.

■ Click BOOKMARKS and click on the drop-down menu or submenu of Bookmarks.

■ Press ALT+B, then use DOWN ARROW to highlight the link you want, then press ENTER.

Selecting the Menu Folder While you were editing Bookmarks, you might have found a feature that lets you control which folder Netscape uses to build the drop-down menu mentioned in the last bullet above. We'll give you a hands-on exercise that will illustrate how to use this feature.

Objective: Learn to set the drop-menu folder.

❑ Press ALT+B and stop.

This keystroke has activated the Bookmarks drop menu. Note that, by default, this menu begins with your main folder. The only folders you see here are the ones directly off this main folder. If an entry here has links under it you'll see a triangle next to its name, and you can see the links by highlighting their parent folder. Let's do that.

❑ Press DOWN ARROW until you highlight `Internet Resources.`

You now can see the links under this folder.

❏ Press G to GO TO BOOKMARKS.

❏ Click on the **Internet Resources** folder.

❏ Click ITEM, SET TO BOOKMARK MENU FOLDER.

❏ Press ALT+F4 to close the Bookmark window.

❏ Press ALT+B to see the Bookmark drop menu.

Now the only items you see on this menu are the ones under the **Internet Resources** folder. This feature might not make a lot of sense right now, with so few links and folders, but when you have hundreds of links you might want to change the menu folder for a while to more easily activate links in a focused category. But you eventually will want to restore your main folder as the menu folder. Let's do that now to finish this exercise.

❏ Press G to GO TO BOOKMARKS.

❏ Click on the main folder at the top of the list.

❏ Click ITEM, SET TO BOOKMARK MENU FOLDER.

❏ Press ALT+F4 to close the Bookmark window.

❏ Press ALT+B to see the Bookmark drop menu.

Note that the entire list is again visible.

Saving Bookmarks   A Bookmark file can become a highly valuable business asset, because it can contain links to crucial business contacts from around the world. Netscape keeps this valuable resource in its program directory. Many users do not regularly run a backup of their program directories. If your Netscape program directory isn't backed up frequently, then some priceless contacts could be lost.

Establish a procedure that will help users periodically copy their bookmark files to a floppy or to a directory on the network that is included in regular backup sessions. Don't trust this to chance. Netscape bookmark files might be among your organization's most treasured business resources; protect them all.

Bookmark Summary   Bookmarks are an important feature of Netscape because they will speed all users' work by enabling them to save any URL they find on the Internet. Please note that Bookmarks are not limited to saving URLs of Web documents. Bookmarks can save the URL of anything on the Internet or your own Intranet, including FTP sites, Gopher sites, and newsgroups.

Creating Your Own Home Page

When Netscape starts, it automatically loads a default home page. This home page can be any site on the Internet, any hypertext document on an Intranet, and even any file on a local drive. Most likely, you'll want to set up an Intranet page as the default home page for all users. This page will have links to the most frequently used places that your users might access.

We suggest that you avoid making this page a work of art and focus your efforts on creating an Intranet home page that is rich in links to valuable and productive resources—both on an Intranet and on the Internet. The next hands-on exercise shows how to designate a new home page.

Objective: Set up a file as the default home page.

❑ Click OPTIONS, PREFERENCES...

❑ Click on the STYLES tab.

❑ Click START WITH:, HOME PAGE LOCATION:

❑ Click in the text entry box immediately below this button.

❑ Type `file:///bookmark.htm` and click OK.

Of course, this is only a sample. But many users will appreciate having their Netscape start by opening their Bookmark file. An important thing to note is that you must include *three* slashes after the colon if you specify a filename instead of an Internet resource (see Fig. 8-12).

If you set up users to have their Bookmarks load as the default home page, then every time Netscape starts it will display the Bookmarks in hypertext. The folders will show up as bold headings and each entry will show up as a hypertext jump. If the cursor is placed, without clicking the mouse, over a highlighted jump, the URL can be read in the status bar at the bottom of the screen. Any manually entered descriptions on the Bookmark List will show up as regular text under their associated hypertext jump entries.

Netscape Plug-Ins

The Internet changes too rapidly to pin it down in a book, and among the fastest changing things about the Internet is Netscape itself. We won't

Figure 8-12

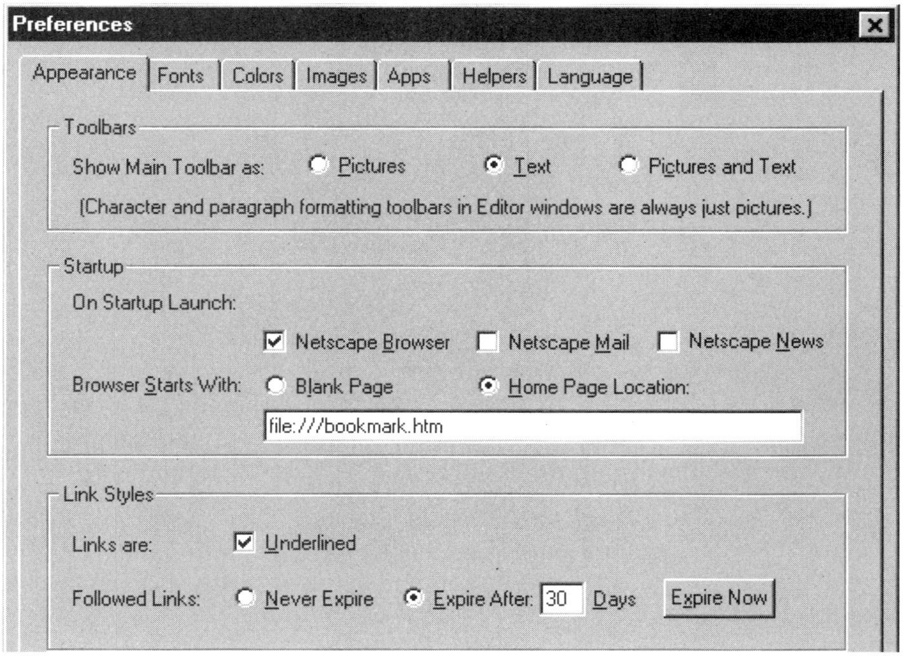

Preferences ✕

| Appearance | Fonts | Colors | Images | Apps | Helpers | Language |

┌─ Toolbars ───┐
  Show Main Toolbar as: ○ Pictures   ● Text   ○ Pictures and Text

  (Character and paragraph formatting toolbars in Editor windows are always just pictures.)
└──┘

┌─ Startup ──┐
  On Startup Launch:

      ☑ Netscape Browser   ☐ Netscape Mail   ☐ Netscape News

  Browser Starts With: ○ Blank Page   ● Home Page Location:
                        file:///bookmark.htm
└──┘

┌─ Link Styles ──┐
  Links are: ☑ Underlined

  Followed Links: ○ Never Expire ● Expire After: 30 Days   [Expire Now]
└──┘

even attempt to convince you that this book is the final word on any of the remaining topics in this chapter, because there probably never will be any final word. As in music, television, and movies, there always will be new releases.

Nonetheless, some exciting developments are hot for now and will remain hot for the next couple of years. So, we'll introduce you to them and help you understand them. You will, however, need to use the Internet to stay abreast of these rapidly changing technologies.

First, what in the world is a *Netscape Plug-In?* A plug-in is a module of programming code that lets Internet developers create add-on applications for Netscape that extend Netscape's capabilities. Plug-ins appear to users simply as specialized functions within Netscape and don't require a lot of technical knowledge to use.

Second, how do Netscape plug-ins work? When Netscape Navigator starts up, it checks for installed plug-in modules. The opening Netscape screen briefly displays information about loading plug-ins, but otherwise it loads as if there were no plug-ins installed. Later, if Netscape encounters a hypertext document that includes special coding (an embedded MIME type or custom file) that requires the use of a plug-in, then the required module is loaded automatically. The plug-in is discarded when the associated hypertext document is closed.

This process is invisible to users once the plug-ins have been installed. If, however, a Web page is loaded that needs a non-installed plug-in, the user may be directed through the process of downloading the plug-in and installing it in Netscape. This usually is a straightforward process that includes simple, on-screen guidance.

With any plug-ins, however, the user will have to decide whether or not it's worth the time and disk space in exchange for the added functions. A plug-in easily could be a megabyte or more in size. Often plug-ins just boost the "gee whiz" aspect of the site and contribute nothing toward the delivery of information, so they should be evaluated carefully.

Third, what can Netscape plug-ins do? The limits are as large as cyberspace itself. No one can predict what's coming any more than Alexander Graham Bell could have predicted that phone lines would one day deliver information via the Internet.

Netscape

To find sites for downloading add-on application software specific to your platform, start Netscape and click on HELP, FREQUENTLY ASKED QUESTIONS, then click SYSTEM REQUIREMENTS. You soon will have most of the popular plug-ins and helper applications. Once you've installed them, you'll be able to enjoy the enhanced capability of your Netscape browser. Many of the plug-ins are implemented through Java-based programming code that interfaces with the special features of the plug-in. Let's learn a little more about Java and JavaScript.

Java and JavaScript

Netscape includes a built-in scripting language called JavaScript. JavaScript is based on the Java programming language developed by Sun Microsystems. Java gives dynamic programming capability to previously static Web documents. Java supports programming for the Internet in the form of platform-independent Java applets. Applets are mini-applications that function within a larger, parent application—Netscape, for example.

Figure 8-13

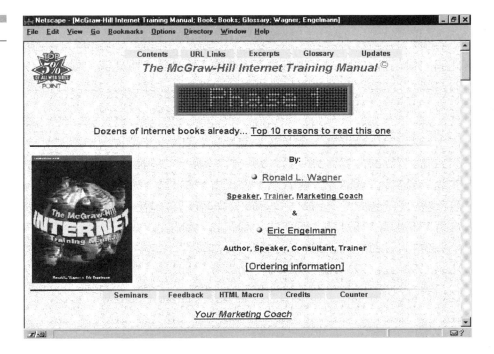

The home page of our Internet book, *The McGraw-Hill Internet Training Manual* features a Java applet (see Fig. 8-13). It's an LED display screen that scrolls a continuous message that outlines the book's major features.

JavaScript supports most of the full power of Java but reduces some of Java's strict programming demands. JavaScript is embedded in HTML documents and requires no special action from users to run the script. Thus, Netscape's JavaScript gives Web programmers the ability to create real-time action, animation, and interactivity.

Unlike a plug-in, a JavaScript function or a Java applet will run because the capability is programmed into Netscape Navigator 2.0 and later versions; users don't have to download anything. Now let's look at some popular Netscape plug-ins.

Shockwave

Shockwave for Director delivers high-impact, interactive multimedia productions by bringing optimized Director productions, with interactive graphics, sounds and animation, to the Internet. With support for

Figure 8-14

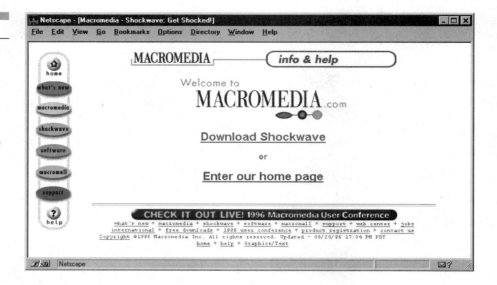

streaming and caching movies, Shockwave for Director sets a new level of interactive performance (see Fig. 8-14).

The Shockwave technology has been adopted by Netscape and many other companies for integration into their Internet browsers, authoring tools, and related products. With Netscape Navigator, users can download Director multimedia movies as quickly as a simple digitized image. Because Director is embedded into Netscape, Director movies run seamlessly at full power.

Crescendo

We call the World Wide Web a multimedia environment, but in most cases that's a misnomer because few Websites include sound. They often have stunning graphics, pretty colors, and some even feature animation. But click on almost any Web page out there and you will encounter stone-cold silence. Can you imagine the feel and texture of a Website that had its own background music? Its own theme song? In the not too distant future, Website background music will be expected just as much as it is in movies and television. Then we'll have true multimedia.

Crescendo is a Netscape plug-in that delivers the gift of background music. As you surf the Web, you soon might be listening to background music on many sites. And that might be most of them before long.

If you're responsible for creating your organization's Website, you can use Crescendo yourself and give your visitors a treat. A theme song will help them remember your site, and some well-chosen background music might keep them browsing longer. Of course, as with any plug-in, remember that first-time visitors who don't have Crescendo on their systems will not hear your music unless they complete the necessary download and installation steps.

What's Next?

The only safe prediction about Netscape plug-ins is that there will be more of them, and you won't be able to keep up with them by reading Internet books. So how will you keep track? The answer depends on whether you're a Web consumer or a Web producer.

If you're a Web consumer, you don't have to worry much about new developments in Netscape plug-ins. Many will come and go without your ever hearing of them. When you encounter a Website that requires a plug-in you don't have, you'll be alerted and directed to download and install the required plug-in. The procedure will be similar for all of them. But before you download any plug-in, take a moment to consider whether your business will be advanced by the time and disk space you'll need to install it.

If you're a Web producer, you can't rely on learning about plug-ins by accidentally coming across them while you surf the Net. To keep up-to-date, you can regularly check the Netscape home page for new plug-ins. And you can regularly check the major Web search engines, such as Yahoo! and Lycos, by searching for the keywords `Netscape plug-ins`.

CHAPTER 9

Intranet Mail
and
News

This chapter covers two separate Intranet functions, mail and newsgroups. *Electronic mail* (e-mail) is the most commonly used feature of the Internet, and its usage is growing daily. Mail most likely will be the most commonly used tool on your Intranet as well.

Newsgroups today carry public discussions on more than 28,000 topics, and that number, too, is growing daily. Your Intranet will connect to the public newsgroups and, perhaps, to several of your organization's own private newsgroups.

The main focus of this chapter is to give you tips and exercises to help you smoothly integrate Netscape mail and Netscape newsgroups into your Intranet. Both of these Netscape features are adequate to satisfy the needs of most of your users, they are included at no extra cost, and they don't require additional disk space or installation. We'll also give you an overview of some competing applications so you can decide if Netscape will do the trick, or if you need to invest in one of the stand-alone applications.

Electronic Mail

You'll find a confusing array of e-mail applications on the market, but we suggest you evaluate all of them based on your *needs* rather than on advertising hype. To simplify your selection, we'll narrow down the list of possibilities to three options and point out the pros and cons of each:

1. Microsoft Exchange
2. Eudora Pro
3. Netscape Mail

This might seem like an oversimplification, but because these packages probably will fulfull the needs of your users, why consider more? Besides, each of these is a mainstream application and will keep you in synch with the majority of other organizations. You don't want to be out on a limb alone, using some peculiar mail application. Choosing a commonly used mail application will help with training costs, too, because many newly hired employees will have used your application already.

Microsoft Exchange

Microsoft Exchange has two main advantages; it's free with Windows 95 and it integrates smoothly with Windows 95. (You can expect it to be a standard in Windows NT as well.) It also permits users to include different font faces, sizes, colors, and advanced text formatting. But only other Microsoft Exchange users will see those special effects because other e-mail applications ignore the formatting information.

The first release of Exchange did not even provide for using an automatic signature file, a glaring omission that says Microsoft is not yet serious about having this application be used as a professional e-mail tool. Count on improvements in future releases, but until then this is the least useful e-mail option of the three. Still, if you're implementing an Intranet for a very small organization on a Windows 95 network, you should consider standardizing on the Microsoft Exchange now and waiting for the upgrades that are sure to follow.

Eudora Pro

Eudora Pro by Qualcomm is the best Internet e-mail application available. Eudora Pro easily can fulfill all of your Intranet communication needs; it is rich with advanced features and will fully support your most demanding, professional users. For example, Eudora Pro can filter incoming messages according to user-specified rules and can then transfer messages to designated folders. Both Microsoft Exchange and Netscape Mail permit you to drag-and-drop messages into different folders, but neither has Eudora Pro's rules-based, automatic sorting that might eliminate the need to drag-and-drop.

The main disadvantage of Eudora Pro is that it's not free, though it is reasonably priced. You can download a shareware version of Eudora but its features are limited and you might as well stick with Netscape mail.

The Pro version can be worth the additional investment for users who need to conduct extensive business communication via e-mail. Eudora Pro's advanced features can be a boon to your business. We suggest you use the trial period Qualcomm offers for its Pro version so you can evaluate the added features. Consider testing it with a select group of users as you evaluate the trade-offs versus the cost increase.

More on Eudora Pro

We've not focused on Eudora Pro in this book, but you can find extensive hands-on lessons for Eudora Pro in another book written by us: *The McGraw-Hill Internet Training Manual* (**www.marketing coach.com/mh-guide**). This book dedicates an entire chapter to Eudora Pro and shows how to set up Eudora's advanced features, such as filters and multiple signature files. Here's a quick summary of Eudora's advantages over Netscape Mail.

- Eudora Pro's support for LAN connectivity makes it scalable from individual users to corporate networks.
- Eudora Pro supports the three major industry standard attachment formats, a necessity for cross-platform communications.
- Eudora Pro provides support for a wide variety of platforms, allowing it to exist in heterogenous platforms and to bridge the gap between all PC computing environments.
- Netscape's message management functionality is also minimal; there is no filtering or ability to save a message to a text file. The Netscape product is an add-on to the WWW browser, designed for browser users with casual e-mail needs.

You can purchase Eudora Pro at its retail price directly from its manufacturer, Qualcomm, by calling them at 800-2-EUDORA, or by e-mailing them at **quest-rep@qualcomm.com**. If you call, however, even they will suggest that you buy Eudora Pro at a local store, because the store can offer a large price discount. Qualcomm doesn't want you to pay retail.

You can also subscribe to Qualcomm's newsletter to stay abreast of the latest changes to Eudora Pro. Send an e-mail message to **majordomo@qualcomm.com**, leave the subject line blank, and enter only the text **subscribe quest_news** in the body.

They also have an unmoderated newsgroup that discusses Eudora, as well as general tips and ideas on using Internet e-mail. Send an e-mail message to **majordomo@qualcomm.com**, leave the subject line blank, and enter only the text **windows-eudora-forum** in the body.

After you've tested Eudora Pro, you might decide to provide it to only a limited group of power users. Thus, Eudora Pro would be used to satisfy the special needs of your aggressive users while you would let the majority use Netscape mail.

Why You Might Not Need Another Mail Package

In terms of features, the Netscape mail application lies somewhere between Microsoft Exchange and Eudora Pro. Netscape mail is not the most powerful mail application in the world, but it has the basic features needed for business usage and might provide all the e-mail power your Intranet will need. Its familiar Netscape interface can produce significant productivity and cost benefits.

Also, you will save training costs because many users will need no training and can get online quickly. And, even if some users do need training, the classes can be short sessions, perhaps half-day classes at most.

Netscape mail offers another significant benefit over other packages, because it's built into Netscape. Obviously, this saves on acquisition costs, but it also spares you the administrative hassles of installing an additional application and tracking its upgrades, bug reports, and patches. It also gives Netscape mail the unique advantage of seamless integration with the Netscape Web browser. This integration means that, while users are surfing the Net or your Intranet, they can check e-mail by clicking on an icon (see Fig. 9-1). This tightly integrated, mail-checking feature might save hours of productivity all by itself over the years.

Netscape mail has another edge on the competition because of its ability to handle HTML documents. Recipients who use Netscape mail will see the HTML pages in familiar Web page format. Sending e-mail in the form of HTML files can offer an exciting boost to productivity, because HTML messages can convey much more than plain-text messages. And, imagine how differently your users will feel about e-mail messages that look like a Web page.

Let us switch now to some hands-on exercises on setting up Netscape mail and tailoring its options. And remember, you are free to use these lessons in your organization's training material.

Setting Up Netscape Electronic Mail

Another Netscape advantage over standalone mail applications is that some of the setup work might have been done when you installed Netscape. So some tasks won't need to be duplicated as they would in a

Figure 9-1

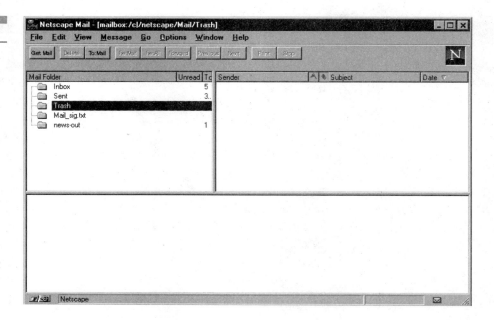

separate application, and the settings that will need to be changed will use familiar dialog boxes.

The next exercise will guide you through Netscape mail setup. Before you begin, be sure you have on hand all the necessary technical mail information. You might need to check with your Internet service provider if you don't already have the information, but setup is actually quite simple once you have the required information.

Objective: Learn to set up Netscape mail.

❑ Start Netscape.

❑ Click OPTIONS, MAIL AND NEWS PREFERENCES...

❑ Click on the SERVERS tab (see Fig. 9-2).

❑ Click in OUTGOING MAIL (SMTP) SERVER.

❑ Enter your SMTP Mail Server information.

Part of this will contain your domain name; for example, `mail.yourdomain.com` is typical.

❑ Click in INCOMING MAIL (POP) SERVER.

❑ Enter your POP Mail Server name.

❑ Click in POP USER NAME.

❑ Enter your basic e-mail name.

This will be the part of your e-mail address that precedes the @ symbol.

❑ Click in MAIL DIRECTORY.

❑ Enter the drive and path for your mail folders.

Be sure that you select a drive and path that gets backed-up regularly. Your Netscape e-mail folders will eventually contain crucial business information and contacts. Most users save mail under the default Netscape directory and forget to ever back up the files. That could be a costly oversight.

❑ Check NONE after MAXIMUM MESSAGE SIZE.

You don't want to specify a maximum message size unless you know of some limitation that mandates a specific setting.

❑ Click on REMOVED FROM THE SERVER.

Figure 9-2

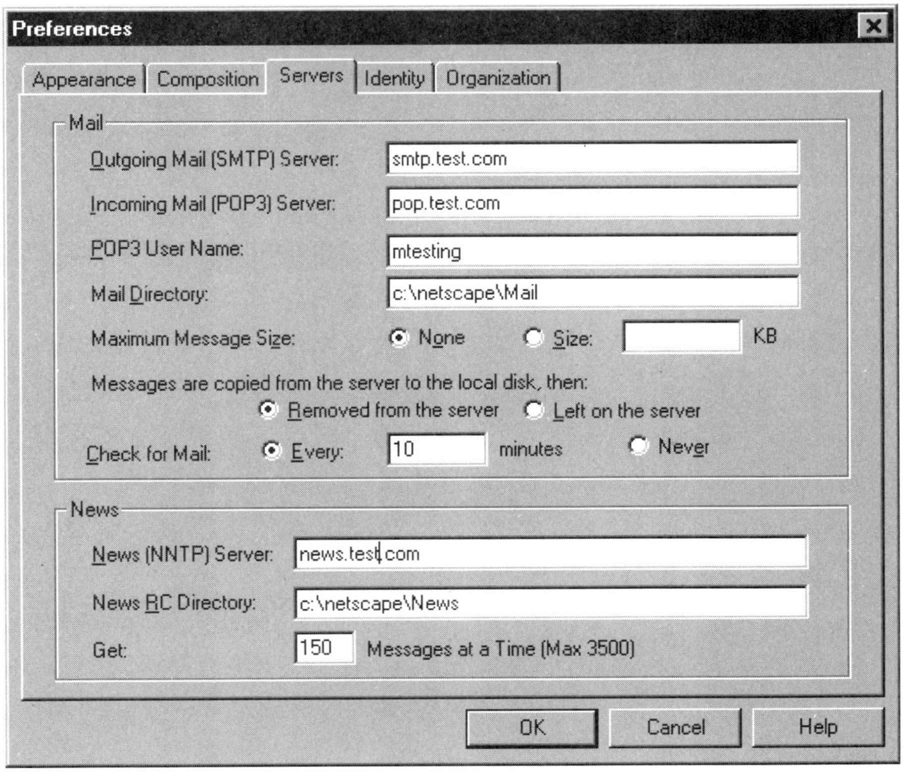

This will delete your e-mail messages from your mail server after they are downloaded. Don't select the option to leave them on your mail server without checking your mail administrator's opinion.

❑ Click on a CHECK FOR MAIL option.

If you check NEVER, then you will have to check manually for e-mail. Checking EVERY and specifying a time will alert Netscape to automatically check mail for you while you're browsing.

❑ Click on the APPEARANCE tab.

❑ Check a WHEN SENDING AND RECEIVING ELECTRONIC MAIL option.

If you're using Windows 95 you can tell Netscape to use the Exchange client for your mail and news. If you select the Exchange option you won't need to complete any of the hands-on exercises after we've finished this setup exercise. The default is to let Netscape handle your mail and news.

❑ Select the remaining appearance options as desired.

❑ Click the COMPOSITION tab.

❑ Check the MIME COMPLIANT option.

If your recipients get scrambled messages then come back here and check the 8-bit option. These days, however, you can pretty much count on people having MIME compliant e-mail.

❑ Select an option for your outgoing messages.

A copy of all messages can be e-mailed to store them on another system. Most likely, however, you will configure this to store messages on a backed-up network drive. If so, use the same directory here that you specified earlier for your mail files.

❑ Check AUTOMATICALLY QUOTE ORIGINAL MESSAGE WHEN REPLYING.

This will include the entire original message in your reply messages. It will place a bracket symbol (< or >) in front of each of the original lines. This is a valuable option because it will greatly speed the accuracy and increase the understanding of replies that users send.

❑ Click the IDENTITY tab.

❑ Click in YOUR NAME and enter your real name.

❑ Click in YOUR EMAIL and enter your e-mail address.

❑ Click in REPLY-TO-ADDRESS.

Enter either the same e-mail address you entered in the box above or another e-mail address, if desired.

❑ Click in YOUR ORGANIZATION.

This is optional. Enter the real name of your organization.

❑ Click in SIGNATURE FILE (see Fig. 9-3).

Enter a path and file name for an ASCII file that will be used for an automatic signature blcok. For example, the path might be **C:\NETSCAPE**. For the file name, use **MAIL-SIG.TXT**. We'll use this name after this setup exercise when we illustrate how to create a signature file.

❑ Click OK.

❑ Click OPTIONS, SAVE OPTIONS.

Figure 9-3

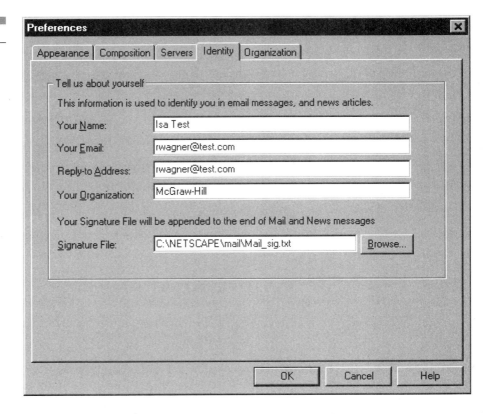

Creating a Signature File

Now that a signature file has been specified in the setup phase, the actual signature file must be created and saved in the correct directory. We've included a sample that will help with the design (see Fig. 9-4). A signature file is just a simple ASCII text file, so you should easily be able to outline these steps for your users so that each one can create his or her own signature file with the Windows 95 Notepad.

Objective: Learn how to create a Netscape mail signature file.

❑ Activate the START button.

❑ Click PROGRAMS, ACCESSORIES, NOTEPAD.

❑ Create your signature.

    Be kind to your readers. Remember that everyone to whom you send e-mail will see these lines at the end of EVERY one of your messages. Keep your signature file short.

❑ Press ALT+F4 or click FILE, EXIT.

❑ Press ENTER or click YES to save the file.

❑ Select the directory you specified in setup.

❑ Enter the filename `mail-sig.txt` and press ENTER or click OK.

    Netscape mail uses this one signature file on every message. The signature block will be appended to the end of all new messages during the composition phase and can be edited on-the-fly if desired. Eudora Pro, by contrast, lets users save two different signature files. Then, on each message, users can select either signature or select NONE if they don't want a signature file. But the signature block does not appear in front of the user during the composition phase and thus cannot be edited on-the-fly.

Electronic Mail Messages

The next set of exercises will show you how to create and send e-mail messages using Netscape mail. It covers the basics that users will need to send original e-mail messages, and to reply to, forward, and delete messages. More detailed help on Netscape e-mail is available from the Netscape home page.

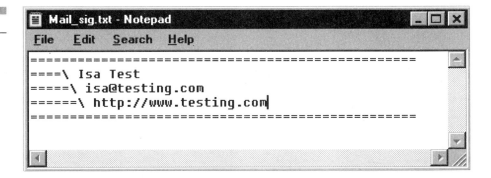

Figure 9-4

Netscape Address Book

Once the Netscape mail setup has been completed, sending e-mail messages is a simple procedure. Netscape mail includes an address book that lets users store e-mail addresses, as well as other contact information. So, before we start the lesson on using Netscape mail, let's set up the Netscape address book and enter some frequently used e-mail addresses (see Fig. 9-5).

Objective: Learn to use the Netscape address book.

❑ Click WINDOW, ADDRESS BOOK.

❑ Click ITEM, ADD USER.

❑ Enter a Nickname, using lowercase text only.

❑ Click in NAME or press TAB.

❑ Enter the person's real name, using the form last name, first name.

❑ Click in E-MAIL ADDRESS or press TAB.

❑ Enter the person's e-mail address.

❑ Click in DESCRIPTION or press TAB.

This is a good place for other contact information such as phone number, fax number, company, and snail mail address.

❑ Click OK.

Be sure to choose the directory in which all address books are stored carefully; these files will include crucial business information. Make sure users specify a directory that will be backed up. If necessary, they can use the FILE, SAVE AS command to copy the **address.htm** file to a directory that gets backed up.

Figure 9-5

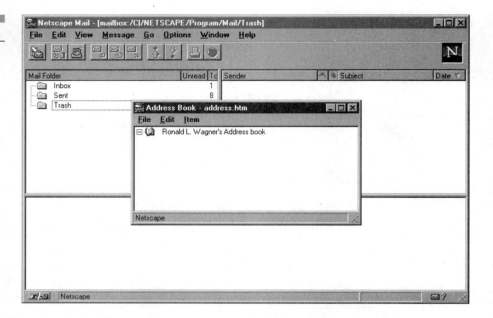

Mailing Documents

Netscape stores the messages it sends in a folder called **Sent**. We'll cover Netscape mail folder management at the end of this e-mail lesson. Remember, Netscape mail offers no automatic filters, so users will have to manually drag-and-drop messages between folders if they want messages sorted by category.

Users can start an e-mail message within Netscape in several ways. From within Netscape, users can press CTRL+M or they can open the Netscape Mail window and click on the TO: MAIL button. Also, users often will encounter Web page links that let them send messages with a mouse click. When they click on such a link, they will get the normal Netscape e-mail window.

Objective: Learn to send a message with Netscape mail.

❑ Click FILE, NEW MAIL MESSAGE or press CTRL+M.

❑ Enter an e-mail address (use your own for practice).

Or, click on the MAIL TO button to go to the Netscape address book. Highlight the recipient's name, click TO, then click OK. The e-mail address information is entered for you.

❑ Click in SUBJECT or press TAB twice.

❑ Enter text for a subject.

❑ Click in the message window or press TAB.

❑ Type a message.

❑ Click on the SEND button, or click FILE, SEND NOW or press CTRL+ENTER to send the message.

The message, the recipient, and the date and time will be saved in the **Sent** folder in your Netscape Mail window. You should be back in Netscape now, so let's verify that information.

❑ Click WINDOW, NETSCAPE MAIL.

❑ Click on the SENT folder under the MAIL FOLDER column on the left.

By default, each message is arranged in descending order, by date. The next few steps show how to change the sort order, which will be very helpful as users accumulate a long list of sent messages. Since we've sent only one message so far, these steps won't show much but they'll demonstrate the principle.

❑ Click VIEW, SORT, then choose a sort option.

❑ Click VIEW, SORT, ASCENDING to reverse the current sort option.

❑ To view a message, click on it in the right window.

By default, a shortened form of the message header appears. This option shows plenty of information for most messages. If a message has had transmission difficulty, then more of its header information can be displayed. The next step will change the header display option to help with troubleshooting.

❑ Click OPTIONS, SHOW ALL HEADERS.

The other menu items are optional in most cases, so now all the basics for sending e-mail messages are displayed. Netscape help can be read for information on the more advanced features.

Attaching Files

Often, users will need to send a file along with an e-mail message. The Netscape file attachment feature is a fabulous tool for long-distance collaboration; it enables users to attach any type of file. That includes word processing documents, spreadsheets, graphics, programs, software drivers, and databases. Netscape will send files such as these without altering even a single byte. Recipients then receive exactly the same file stored on your local system.

To ensure that users have something to send during this exercise, we will use the current Netscape Bookmark file. This is a good exercise because many people swap Bookmark files to share links they've found.

Objective: Learn to attach a file to an e-mail message.

❑ Click TO: MAIL or press CTRL+M to start a new message now.

❑ Enter yourself as the recipient.

❑ Enter `Test Attachment 1` as the subject.

❑ Enter `>hands-on attachment test` in the message window.

❑ Click ATTACHMENT, then click ATTACH FILE.

Use the ENTER FILE TO ATTACH dialog box to navigate to the Netscape bookmark file, which should be in the current directory now. If it's not, navigate to the default Netscape directory. The file you want to send is named `bookmark.htm`.

Highlight the file you wish to send.

❑ Click OPEN, click OK.

The selected file is now attached to this message and will ride along with the message across cyberspace. The steps above can be repeated so that a list of files can be attached to one message. Normally, though, the list will have but one file.

❑ Click SEND to send the message and attachment list.

Large files can be attached to messages, but generally there's a limit on total message size of two megabytes on Internet mail. This limitation varies, and some systems have a much lower tolerance of large e-mail messages. Check with your Internet service provider to find out about any limitations their system might impose.

Be sure your users know of any limitations on attachment file size. Otherwise, some users might plan a critical project on the assumption that they'll be able to transfer all the files between offices. If they know the limitations in advance they can make sure they break down the project into sendable file sizes.

Managing Netscape Mail Folders

Netscape lets users create lists of folders so that they can organize their messages, both incoming and outgoing. Once the needed folders have been created, messages can be dragged-and-dropped between folders.

This next exercise assumes you still have open the Netscape mail window that we used earlier. Here's our last Netscape e-mail exercise.

Objective: Learn to manage Netscape mail folders.

❑ Click FILE, NEW FOLDER.

❑ Type PERSONAL, then click OK or press ENTER.

❑ Click FILE, NEW FOLDER.

❑ Type TESTING, then click OK or press ENTER.

Now we'll illustrate how to delete folders.

❑ Click on TESTING. Keep the mouse inside the left window.

❑ Click the right mouse button, then click DELETE FOLDER.

Folders that contain messages cannot be deleted—the folder will have to be emptied first.

Netscape Newsgroups

The Netscape newsgroup reader simplifies and streamlines access to the Usenet by integrating the newsgroup function into the Netscape Web browser. Today, while most Internet users use a standalone application to handle their e-mail, standalone newsgroup readers are fading fast and Netscape might soon be the standard.

Newsgroups are electronic *community bulletin boards* that each serve as "info central" for individual topics. Messages are *posted* in the open, and anyone who looks at the newsgroup will see all the messages that have been posted by the group's users.

Your Internet service provider includes a news server that actually holds messages from all the newsgroups that they receive. Your provider might offer fewer than half the total number of public newsgroups. Or, your organization might contract for its own direct Usenet feed. Having a direct feed gives an organization the ability to tailor its selection of newsgroups and eliminate many of the nonbusiness newsgroups.

How Many Newsgroups Are There?

How many can you stand?

When we researched this book we found more than 15,000 public newsgroups. But less than a year earlier we reported 11,000 in another

Internet book. Today? Well, there's no way to tell—and what we've referenced here includes just the *public* newsgroups. It literally would be impossible to count the private newsgroups because they can't be seen by outsiders.

Your Internet service might not make available all newsgroups. For example, we found one Internet service provider that offered 5450 newsgroups; another provider might offer more or fewer. If you contract for your own you will need a *Network News Transfer Protocol* (NNTP) server.

Since so many thousands of newgroups exist, the Netscape newsreader enables you to select, from the master list of all the groups it finds on your news server, only those newsgroups that you choose to see. This process is called *subscribing*, although your system maintains full access even to the newsgroups to which you are not subscribed. Subscribing and unsubscribing to newsgroups uses an internal process that is handled by Netscape.

A user who wants to see an additional group at any time can subscribe and instantly see the group's postings. Subscribing simply means that Netscape automatically checks that newsgroup for new messages when the news reader is started. Similarly, if a user unsubscribes to a group, Netscape merely stops displaying that newsgroup's postings, yet it remains available for resubscription. We'll cover subscribing and unsubscribing later; first we will show you how to read newsgroup messages.

Reading

Before you can read newsgroups you have to download the list of those that your organization's news server provides. We'll give you a hands-on exercise later that will download the list, and then another that will illustrate how to read messages.

The Netscape news module has three frames. The top left frame displays newsgroup names. When Netscape news is first started, this list will be very short and will contain only the names that Netscape provides as a default.

To the right of the list frame is a frame that lists the headers of the messages within the newsgroup that's highlighted in the left frame. The bottom frame shows the text of the individual message that is highlighted in the upper-right frame.

Popular Usenet newsgroups

To further complicate the newsgroup counting game, many newsgroups that show up in the list in the left window will be empty. During a trial run, while randomly browsing unsubscribed newsgroups, we found that about one newsgroup in three was empty. Nonetheless, thousands of others are active. Table 9.1 lists a few of the major categories:

Each original article is listed against the left side of the right frame (see Fig. 9-6). Indented articles that appear under an article are related articles that represent replies to the original. If someone replies to a reply, that article will be shown indented yet another level, and so forth. This hierarchical listing system creates a *thread*, sort of a focused, on-going conversation. Threads help users track a focused conversation as if they were eavesdropping on it.

TABLE 9.1

Usenet Newsgroup Categories

Category	Topics
alt	Alternative topics, few of which are business-oriented˙
bionet	Professional biologists
biz	Business discussions, advertisements, and postings of new products and services
clari	ClariNet news services†
comp	Computer-related topics
k12	Kindergarten through twelfth-grade teachers
misc	Miscellaneous topics, but none as far out as alt.
news	Usenet is so big it actually has its own group for news about itself.
rec	Recreational topics‡
relcom	Former Soviet Union
sci	Science topics
soc	Social topics with an international flavor and religious topics
talk	Not enough talk radio stations for you? At least you can get through to this one.

˙We'll use the alt group in the hands-on exercises.
†Requires a premium fee, although it may already be a part of your basic package.
‡You won't believe what some people consider to be recreation—here's something for everyone.

Figure 9-6

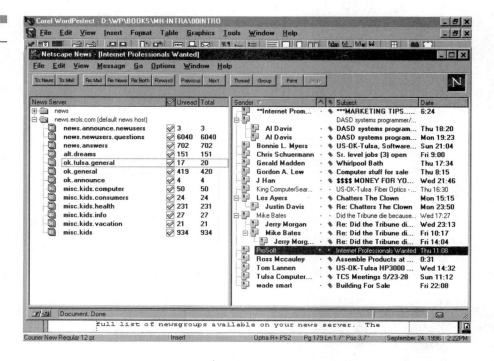

The first hands-on newsgroups exercise will download the full list of newsgroups available on your news server. Your Netscape news reader should be open from the earlier exercises. If not, open it now.

Objective: Learn to browse your newsgroups list.

❑ Click on the NEWS folder in the left window.

Two folders should show up in this window. One is NEWS and the other represents your news server (DEFAULT NEWS HOST).

❑ Click the right mouse button, then click SHOW ALL NEWSGROUPS.

The first download of newsgroups might take several minutes. Netscape will alert users to wait while it downloads the newsgroups it finds on the news server. The status bar displays the progress in the lower-right part of the screen.

❑ Click on ALT.*

Listings that end with an asterisk indicate that you are seeing a hierarchical header that leads to other topics beneath that level. Clicking on a topic will expand the listing to increasingly specific topic levels. Again, watch the progress bar because some headers, such as ALT.*, have a lot of subtopics and might require patience while you wait for everything to load.

❑ Scroll down to ALT.QUOTATIONS and click on it.

The folder's message headers will be displayed in the right window. The number after the checkbox shows how many unread messages are in that newsgroup.

❑ Click on a message header in the right window and the posted message will be displayed in the lower window.
❑ Touch the mouse arrow to the horizontal separator bar.

Drag the bar up or down to change the amount of the screen devoted to groups and headers or to the messages. The vertical bar can be dragged to change spacing between the windows. And the screen can be further tailored by adjusting the width of each of the header tags at the top of each frame.

After you click on a message and read it, the message's header disappears from the list. Don't worry, the message isn't lost; it's just that, by default, Netscape hides all messages that you've read. That can be a nice feature, but sometimes a user will want to go back. Here's how.

Objective: Learn to redisplay previously read messages.

❑ Click OPTIONS, SHOW ALL MESSAGES.

All messages remain visible, but the unread messages remain in bold.

❑ Click OPTIONS, SHOW ONLY UNREAD MESSAGES.

These options also are available on right mouse button menus.

Start Your Own Usenet Newsgroup

Can't find a newsgroup for a favorite topic? Are you kidding? Well then, this newsgroup is for you! Check out **news. announce.newgroups**.

The newsgroups contains posts of announcements of either the creation of new newsgroups or considerations of proposed newsgroups. Newsgroups are created after a successful *call for votes* (CFV) that begins with a posting to this newsgroup. Also, calls for discussions, vote results, and creation notices of all hierarchies should be posted here as well. Post submissions for a CFV to `announce newgroups@uunet.uu.net`. Follow-ups will be redirected to `news.groups`.

Post only *after* reading about the process by checking out these sources:

■ "How to Create a New Usenet Newsgroup," found in `news.admin.misc`, `news.announce.newgroups`, `news.announce.newusers`, `news.answers`, or in `news.groups`.

■ "Usenet Newsgroup Creation Companion," found in `news.announce.newusers`, `news.answers`, or `news.groups`.

■ "So You Want to Create an Alt Newsgroup?" found in `alt.config`, `alt.answers`, or `news.answers`.

If a newsgroup you create is rejected, a service is available that will deliver newsgroups deemed "unnecessary" or "of too little use to store on corporate news servers." How many? Well, for $5 per month you can get more than 13,000 of these rejects. For details on posting and receiving such "corporate rejects," e-mail to `ccaputo@alt.net`. Your organization will need to keep your main news service but it can add this one to the list. Netscape automatically handles multiple news servers if they're available.

Subscribing and Unsubscribing

Since the list of available newsgroups is ridiculously long, users will appreciate the SUBSCRIBE feature because it will limit the list to selected newsgroups only. Subscribing is a simple process, and users can learn it from the next hands-on exercise.

Objective: Learn to subscribe or unsubscribe to newsgroups.

❑ Highlight the newsgroups to which you want to subscribe.

❑ Click the checkbox after the name.

A checkmark will appear in the box next to subscribed newsgroups. Browse through the list and check more groups. Be sure to check at least one that you don't want to keep so that later I can show you how to unsubscribe.

❑ Scroll to the NEWS folder and open it if it's closed.

This folder shows all of your subscribed newsgroups and their number of unread messages. The next time you return to Netscape newsgroups, you easily will be able to find new messages posted to the groups that interest you without being swamped under thousands of headings in the main newsgroup window.

❑ Click on any group to see its message headers.

❑ Click on a message to read it.

Sometimes, after seeing a few day's worth of messages within a group, you'll decide to unsubscribe. Here's how to do that.

❑ Click on a subscribed newsgroup you wish to unsubscribe.

❑ Click the right mouse button.

❑ Click UNSUBSCRIBE.

Of course this newsgroup is still available to you at any time and you can go to it manually by scrolling through your list of downloaded groups. Or you can directly add it back to the list by clicking the right mouse button on your subscribed newsgroups folder.

Replying

Often, reading an article will prompt you to make some snappy reply. Don't worry; everyone else gets the same urge when they read newsgroups. No one knows for sure exactly why this happens but that urge to have the last word seems to be natural and certainly is the foundation for the Usenet. There are two ways to reply:

1. Post a follow-up article in the same newsgroup so that everyone in the world can see it if they want to. Hint: Be careful what you post!

2. Mail a reply directly to the author of the article you're reading and keep it between the two of you. This is a good choice either when you have a narrowly focused reply that would not interest general readers in the group or when you prefer to keep the reply private—well, as private as e-mail can be, anyway.

NOTE: *You can view detailed information about any message by highlighting the message and then clicking VIEW, DOCUMENT SOURCE. This will move the message into a viewer window. In the setup, Netscape can be configured to use the Windows Notepad as a viewer, in which case this function provides a quick way to edit, copy, and save newsgroup messages.*

The next exercise illustrates both of the ways in which replies can be sent to a newsgroup article. An on-screen article should be displayed from the last exercise. From there, we'll go to the reply function.

Objective: Learn how to reply to newsgroup articles.

❑ Click on MESSAGE, POST REPLY or click RE: NEWS (see Fig. 9-7).

The original message text will be included by default, but this is optional. It is, however, a good idea that will help other readers follow the thread, but the entire text of the article should never be used. Generally, most of the message can be cut, leaving only enough to cue the recipient. Be sure to remove the original poster's signature block. No one needs to see signature blocks repeated.

❑ Type a reply.

❑ Click SEND to actually post the article to this newsgroup, or click CANCEL, OK to return to the reader.

This posts a public message to the entire newsgroup. The next few steps illustrate how to post a reply directly to the original poster instead of replying publicly to the group.

❑ Click MESSAGE, MAIL REPLY or click RE: MAIL.

Figure 9-7

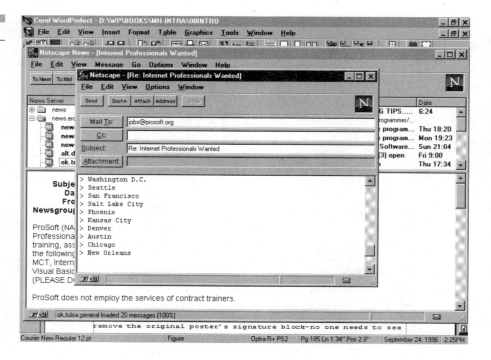

Often, a direct reply is the best method. Unfortunately, many people clog up the system with replies that would best have been sent directly.

❑ Type your reply.

❑ Click SEND to mail the article to the original poster, or click CANCEL, OK to return to the reader.

This posts a private message only to the original poster. Another option is to send a double reply, one to the group and one privately. We'll show that next.

❑ Click MESSAGE, POST AND MAIL REPLY, or click RE: BOTH.

❑ Type your reply.

❑ Click SEND to actually post the article, or click CANCEL, OK to return to the reader.

This posts a private message to the original poster as well as a public message to the entire newsgroup. This might seem redundant, but keep in mind that the original poster might not check back into the group for days and might miss your reply message. A companion e-mail message directly to him or her will increase the chance that the original poster will read your reply.

Posting Original Usenet Newsgroup Articles

Naturally, many users will want to post original messages to newsgroups. Or, perhaps, they might have questions that someone in the group might be able to answer. Either case requires posting an original article. It's basically the same as posting a follow-up, with one major exception that we'll mention twice. The subject line will be blank unless you fill it in manually! Make sure you don't post messages with blank subjects.

Objective: Learn how to post an original newsgroup article.

❑ Click FILE, NEW NEWS MESSAGE, or click TO: NEWS to create an original message (see Fig. 9-8).

❑ Type **(your own subject)**.

❑ Press TAB to move the insertion point into the message body.

❑ Type the body of your message.

This editing window is rudimentary, so users might prefer to use ALT+TAB to jump to a word processor, write the article there using its spell checker and thesaurus, use the Windows Copy command (CTRL+C), use

ALT+TAB to return to Netscape, and use the Windows Paste (CTRL+V) command.

❑ Click SEND to actually post the article to this newsgroup, or click CANCEL, OK to return to the reader.

❑ Click FILE, EXIT to close Netscape.

Nine Keys to Newsgroup Netiquette

Understanding newsgroups requires much more than knowing the technical steps we've shown so far. Newsgroups on the Usenet reach into a global realm that literally can touch anyone in the world. They are powerful communication tools that deserve much respect, courtesy, discretion, and common sense. The following nine keys will help you maintain and improve our global cyberspace community, thereby boosting the potential value of that community to you and your organization.

1. *Get the FAQs.* Almost every newsgroup has a FAQ (Frequently Asked Questions) file. Look for it or ask for it. Most questions you might

Figure 9-8

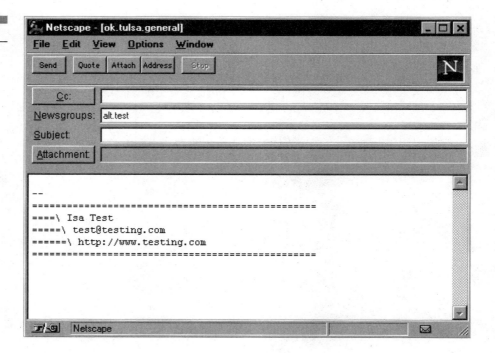

ask as a newbie to a group will have been asked already. The established users of the newsgroup are sick of browsing through the same old posts. Get the FAQ and read the FAQ before you ask the group a "dumb newbie" question.

2. *Lurk around first.* Newsgroups can get quite personal and develop a timbre of their own. Each is slightly different. Until you've sampled that timbre you don't know what might be considered offensive, rude, or stupid. The Internet term for sampling a newsgroup is *lurking.* You know the kind of people who don't lurk; they're the same people who interrupt your verbal conversations. If you post to a newsgroup in which you've never lurked, don't be surprised if you quickly attract flame mail.

3. *Remember the global community.* Lurking will help you abide by global community principle. Newsgroups might have members from anywhere in the world. Keep this in mind when you post. For example, if you live in the United States don't refer to your country as "America." That's considered by people in other Americas to be rude and arrogant. Also, ethnic and regional jokes will at best fall flat, could be misunderstood, and easily might offend thousands of your fellow Interneters.

4. *Forgive and forget.* If you read something annoying, offensive, misplaced, misguided, or just plain stupid, probably your best course of action is to forget it and move on. The Internet already has enough problems with flames and counterflames. Every group seems to have one or two real idiots who seem to have never heard of netiquette. You'll come to know them quickly, so don't worry about the occasional accidental offender. Save your flames for the really bad guys. Or, consider e-mailing a chronic repeater's ISP; you might get his account canceled, which flaming will never do.

5. *Follow the threads.* Most interesting newsgroup posts evoke replies. Most up-to-date software links these posts together into "threads" that follow the same theme. Read the entire thread before posting a reply yourself. Several others might already have said the same thing. No one will appreciate reading your belated opinion. Reading the whole thread is somewhat of a corollary to the last key; forgive and forget. If a post really has you steamed you can count on its annoying others as well, and they probably have done plenty of flaming for you already.

6. *Keep it short and sweet.* Remember an ancient comment on the art of writing that says, "I'm sorry this is so long . . . I didn't have time to

make it short." Keeping your posts short on purpose truly does take longer than simply spewing forth every word on a topic that comes to mind. But the time you spend on "editing down" will be appreciated many times over by happy newsgroup members, who actually might read your posts and actually might respond. At the same time, don't make them long on purpose, either. You'll get tired of wading through newsgroup replies in which the respondent copied the entire text from the original post and tacked on the brilliant reply, "I agree." People can follow threads; you need not copy any more of a post than a brief contextual reminder. Sure, it takes time to delete chunks of a post that don't need to be repeated, but the time you spend will be rewarded.

7. *Put it where it belongs.* Stick to the subject. Usually you can tell by the title, but make sure you're in the right place by lurking and reading the FAQs file. Post only when you're certain you're writing to the right audience. Posting to the wrong newsgroup wastes a lot of resources. Likewise, if you accidentally post to the wrong group, just forget about it. If you see an accidental post, ignore it. One of the most annoying events in newsgroups often begins when someone accidentally posts to the wrong group, then six people post to say how stupid this person is, then the person posts again to say to ignore the first post, which draws several more nasty comments, to which the original poster apologizes, then the apology draws a string of posts commenting on what a stupid waste of resources this whole event has been. Twenty messages or more can cascade out of a single errant post. Post correctly and remember to forgive and forget when others slip. And hope they do the same for you.

8. *Remember that you're invisible.* No one can see you smile on the Internet. No one can hear you chuckle, either. If you joke, don't assume that everyone understands you're joking. Remember the global community. Jokes or twisted humor on newsgroups rarely come across as funny. If you must make a crack about something, at least use one of the emoticons we've listed in Chapter 4, "Netiquette," so that everyone will know that you meant to make a joke. They still might not get the joke, but if you're lucky they won't get riled.

9. *Use e-mail when appropriate.* Newsgroups are excellent places to get answers to tricky or obscure questions. If you've read the FAQs file, lurked in the background for a while and followed all the threads, but still have a question—that's the time to post. But if the answer is not going to be of general use to the group, ask for replies by e-mail

and make sure your e-mail address is included in your signature file at the end of your post. (It's supposed to be in the header, but a backup is a good idea.) Conversely, if you want to send a personal reply to a posted question, use e-mail and spare everyone in the group the clutter of unnecessary messages.

Infomagnets

New newsgroups are appearing on the Usenet rapidly, and existing groups are gathering new members faster than ever. One drawback to the newsgroup phenomenon, however, is that the wealth of information they offer can seem to be more of a burden than a blessing. With so many public newsgroups, users hardly have time to read even the subject lines for all the new messages. And don't even think about taking a couple of days off.

Fortunately, a computerized news magnet can filter through the newsgroups and bring you the news you can use. Generically, these computerized new magnets are called *infomagnets* because they can extract valuable needles from all the haystacks that choke most of the Usenet. The two most common types include a tailored news service that will send targeted articles that fit tailored specifications, and a program that scans the Usenet and pulls in only those articles that fit within the program's guidelines and rules.

We'll cover both methods but let's begin by looking at one popular, tailored news service as an example.

ClariNet News Services

ClariNet e.News is an electronic newspaper that delivers professional news and information directly to your computer. It sends live news (including technology-related wire stories), timely computer industry news, syndicated columns and features, financial information, stock quotes, and more.

Your organization can receive, upon request, a free sample of selected articles that are posted to the Usenet newsgroup `biz.clarinet.sample`. For more information, contact ClariNet for a targeted sample of some news topics your organization might need to track (see Fig. 9-9). Even better, they will provide your organization with a free, two-week trial of the e.News.

Figure 9-9

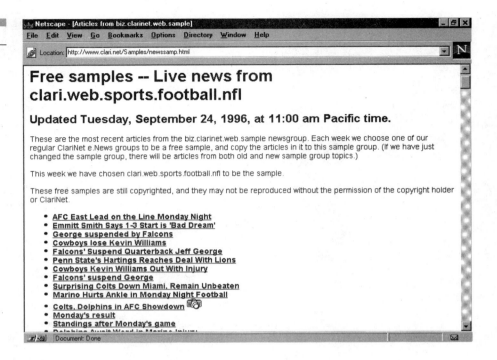

Via e.News the Internet can begin to work for your organization to receive the news that could have a direct impact on its business. e.News combines the in-depth coverage of print media with the speed of broadcast media to deliver the best of both worlds. Many U.S. media limit their international coverage for reasons of space and time, but e.News doesn't suffer from either of those limitations.

How e.News Works Many online services store the news on a computer at their site, but the e.News sends selected articles directly. When anyone wants to read the news, it's available instantly because they don't have to wait while the messages are transferred. Everyone in your organization can read targeted e.News, anytime, for a fixed monthly fee. And you'll love this feature if you offer it over your Intranet: There are no per-user charges.

The e.News is delivered as a Usenet-style newsfeed. So, any standard Usenet reading capabilities will work. And, if your organization doesn't receive Usenet-style news, ClariNet will help you get connected free, including free software. Hard disk space might become an issue, however, because a full e.News feed collects approximately four megabytes of data every day. Of course a carefully targeted feed will consume disk space at a slower rate. Many organizations set up an archiving system for older news stories, keeping perhaps only the last month or two available on the network.

Now let's look at the targeted e.News topics from which you can select.

Techwire This service includes specific categories for stories on science and technology and the industries around them, including computers, electronics, health issues, space, aerospace, telecommunications, defense, biotechnology, research, education, AIDS, and more. It also includes a daily price report of computer industry stocks.

Business News This service delivers business and financial stories on all topics: economic indicators, corporate news, regular stock market reports, legal issues affecting business, government information, commodity reports, and a great deal more. The e.News Business News option features the North American, European, and Asian Business Reports of Reuters, the world's most respected international business information source.

Newsbytes Here's a daily computer industry magazine that brings you timely information well before weekly print media reach your desk. Newsbytes stories are gathered from 11 bureaus around the world. Within the computer industry, Newsbytes covers trends, legal issues, reviews of new products, and corporate news. It also specifically addresses news on products that work with Apple, UNIX, and IBM computers, and telecommunications products.

Syndicated Features This service delivers top syndicated columns and features, such as etiquette from Miss Manners and movie reviews and cultural commentary from Joe Bob Briggs.

The Annals of Improbable Research As you might guess, the e.News isn't entirely serious or stuffy. You can receive this journal of scientific funnies that includes "Bizarro," an off-beat look at the world and "Views of the World," which presents a daily series of editorial cartoons from newspapers around the globe.

Matric News This service delivers a newsletter about cross-networking that covers the connections between all the computer networks worldwide that exchange electronic mail. Naturally that includes the Internet, but the service also covers UUCP-Net, BITNET, FidoNet, and conferencing systems such as the Well and CompuServe.

Global and National News   This is a major news source that includes global and national news, sports, and features from the wire services of Reuters and The Associated Press (AP). It covers U.S. and international news events, as well as regular coverage of sports (with detailed statistics).

As you'd expect from any newspaper, this service includes many standing features, such as editorials; columns on politics, entertainment and consumer products; reviews of books, movies, and videos; a daily almanac; and a daily news summary.

And here's something you can't get in a regular print newspaper: every two hours the e.News releases updated summaries of current events.

Access to "Old" News

Your organization's news feed can deliver only today's news. Yet countless gigabytes of information already have passed through newsgroups all over the world. Most messages are only actively displayed for a few days—perhaps a week at the outside. What happens to all of that "old" news? Believe it or not, there's a company on the Internet that archives it, indexes it, and makes it available to all through a powerful search engine.

Dejanews is a news service that can be found at `www.dejanews.com` (see Fig. 9-10). Dejanews is also available as an extension of the Yahoo! search engine. You might, however, want to make available this important service directly on your Intranet home page so users can access it quickly.

Deja News is extremely efficient and fast. Even searches that span huge quantities of data are finished on the server in a few seconds, despite the need to scour the largest collection of archived, indexed, Usenet newsgroup documents that can be found anywhere!

NewsClip(tm) News Filtering Language

Now we move on to the second type of infomagnet, an internal, tailored program. As mentioned earlier, this type filters newsgroups on your end and extracts articles it has been programmed to select. ClariNet has developed a programming language that includes a high level of filtering control over Usenet newsgroup information and automatically extracts the targeted information.

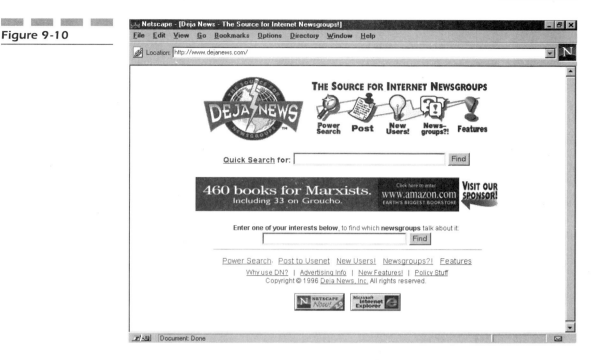

Early filtering programs gave users control over only the newsgroups they received and typically offered a "kill" feature that would eliminate unwanted articles. For example, systems less sophisticated than NewsClip would let users kill articles that were posted by a user who consistently posted annoying trash. NewsClip, by contrast, includes all the tools of a powerful programming language. NewsClip goes well beyond creating a kill file by making positive inclusion choices as well as negative exclusion choices.

The only news-filtering limitations your organization will have will be determined by how much time is invested in writing the program. Large organizations will enjoy a productivity payoff if someone invests the programming time to write a targeted filtering system to get the news that is most needed across the the organization's Intranet.

NewsClip programs are compiled, so they not only filter newsgroups precisely but they also work quickly. A compiled NewsClip program rates articles based on programming expressions that describe exactly what to receive and what to reject.

How You Can Use NewsClip   Compiled NewsClip programs can work interactively as articles are read in real time, usually with no noticeable delay. As a user browses through his or her chosen newsgroups, he or she will see only the articles that were specified by the program.

Or, the program can be run in the background after business hours to filter selected newsgroups. To do this, your Intranet will need a newsreader with a *newsrc* (news subscription) file that contains a list of all subscribed newsgroups. In unattended mode, the filter program reads the newsrc file, scans all unread articles, and marks as already read any articles that fit the programmed exclusion criteria. That's why users won't see those articles.

Here's a list of usage examples for a filtering program:

■ Screen out messages posted by a particular user, a group of users, or even all users from a designated site. It even can exclude follow-up messages posted to articles by the users you've specified.

■ Receive messages that contain specified keywords or that exclude specified keywords. For example, to track hot world news on domino tournaments you might select all articles that include the word "domino" but that exclude the word "pizza."

■ Eliminate follow-up articles that copy the entire original message, perhaps duplicating thousands of words you have already read, and then close with "I agree!" Users never will waste time on that example of poor netiquette if the system excludes articles in which the amount of copied text greatly exceeds the amount of added text.

■ Filter out all articles except for originals, so that the default is to exclude all follow-up articles, and then have the program include follow-ups to specific articles only.

■ Specify priority handling of articles posted by anyone within your organization, as well as follow-ups to those articles.

■ Include all the articles posted to any newsgroup by a known competitor. Include articles posted by anyone within an entire organization, or articles posted by specific individuals within an organization.

■ Ban the spam by filtering out cross-posted articles. For example, if an article is cross-posted 10 times it's probably spam and the program will ignore it. Fortunately, the ClariNet filtering program uses the familiar C programming language, so it's likely that someone on staff will be able to write a tailored filtering system for your organization.

The bottom line is that newsgroups are among the most popular features of the Internet, and you'll want to include them on your Intranet as well. But a raw feed of all newsgroups will not be a valuable productivity tool for your organization. With an information filtering tool in place, however, Usenet newsgroups can be powerful additions to your Intranet.

10

Intranet
Publishing
Lessons

Employees can greatly boost their organization's productivity if they can create their own Intranet HTML documents. Fortunately, it's getting easier all the time. This chapter will help spread the work of creating your Intranet.

When the Web debuted, creating HTML-language pages required high levels of computer expertise, diligence, and patience. But today, creating in HTML can actually be enjoyable and as simple as using a word processor. Producing World Wide Web documents has become so common that they can be created with WordPerfect for Windows and Word for Windows. Both applications offer free add-ons that greatly simplify the once arduous challenge of creating simple hypertext documents. So, now people can use an old friend as they become part of your Intranet. We'll highlight the strengths and weaknesses of both word processing programs so you'll know if you need something more advanced, and then we'll discuss the advanced Web editors.

But there's more to writing HTML documents than the technical side of producing hypertext documents. Knowing how to use tools doesn't make you a skilled craftsman. And, because your Intranet will reflect your organization's image, you'll want to get it right the first time. When you've finished this chapter you'll be fully prepared to help everyone in the organization join in developing your Intranet's content.

Tools, Tools, and More Tools

More tools are available for publishing HTML documents than we can count. New ones are being released almost daily. Before the recent dramatic expansion of Web tools, only programmers and computer specialists had the skills to create Web pages. But the Web's popularity explosion has prompted major software developers to create tools that enable mainstream users to create Web pages too.

It's become so easy, in fact, that many people in your organization might already have laid the foundation for HTML pages without knowing it. That's because there are several good applications that convert existing documents, including graphics and tables, into perfectly formatted HTML documents.

Creating world-class HTML pages still requires a technical expert because the leading edge of technology always stays out in front of the mainstream user. Someone always will be pushing existing technical limits. If you want to run at the front of the pack, you'll need skills that go beyond what you can learn from using a word processor add-on. But today, even the standalone HTML editors are simple enough for many users to use them to create attractive HTML pages.

We'll cover basic HTML development tools in several categories:

- Word processor add-ons
- Conversion programs
- Standalone HTML editors
- Graphics software
- CGI tools
- Java

Each category will be covered in subsequent sections of this chapter. Some topics, however, will be covered only briefly here because they have chapters dedicated to them later in the book.

Word Processor Add-Ons

WordPerfect for Windows and Microsoft Word for Windows both offer add-on packages that enable users to create a document and then use the SAVE AS command to create an HTML-formatted document that's ready for the Web (see Fig. 10-1). Many desktop publishing programs also offer add-on HTML support; those that do not soon will. These add-on packages are ideal for casual publishers and for documents with lots of text.

For users who are working on content that doesn't need graphics or sound files, WordPerfect and Word are excellent choices. And, these two word processors together cover more than 90 percent of the market. In fact, the STYLES feature in both of them means it's possible that a lot of archived documents can be converted into HTML.

You Say It's Easy, but How Do I Get Started?

Programmers long have learned their craft by analyzing the source code of existing programs. It's much easier to learn to program by example that it is to start from scratch. Often, programmers modify an existing program to fit their own needs. Using the same technique

Figure 10-1

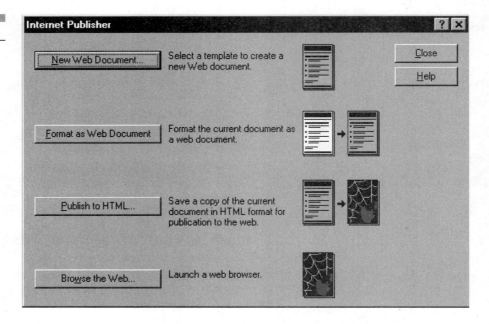

will help you learn to write HTML-encoded Web pages—you can study and modify existing Web pages.

When you encounter a Web page that has a feature you would like to implement, click VIEW, SOURCE to see its HTML source code. Netscape's default is to display the code in its internal source viewer. But if you want to edit the page or display documents that are too long for the internal viewer, you can designate any editor as your Netscape source viewer. The Windows Notepad application is a good choice (see Fig. 10-2). To change Netscape's default HTML viewer, follow the steps in the next exercise.

Objective: Learn to set Netscape's HTML source code viewer.

❑ Start Netscape with an Internet connection.

❑ Click OPTIONS, GENERAL PREFERENCES...

❑ Click the APPS tab.

❑ Click in the VIEW SOURCE text entry box.

❑ Type `c:\windows\notepad.exe` and click OK.

You can enter any Windows editing application instead. If you don't know the application's full path and filename, click on BROWSE, select an editor from your system, then click OK.

❑ Click OPTIONS, SAVE OPTIONS to save the change.

Of course, if you want to save the entire source code you can click FILE, SAVE AS... and use the dialog box with SAVE FILE AS TYPE set to SOURCE (*.HTM). Often this is overkill because you only want to save a small piece of a document's HTML code. With the Notepad as your viewer, you will be able to cut out the chunks that you do not need before you save the file.

When this was written, neither WordPerfect nor Word included their HTML functions on their original distribution disks. Before you can create Web pages with either of them, you'll need to download the application's Internet add-on and then install it.

Downloading an HTML Add-On

Here's the information you'll need to download the two add-ons outlined above.

Figure 10-2

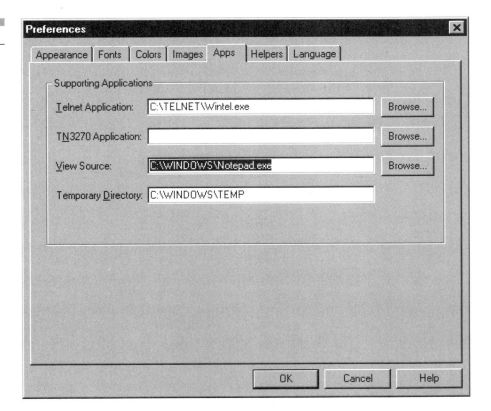

Figure 10-3

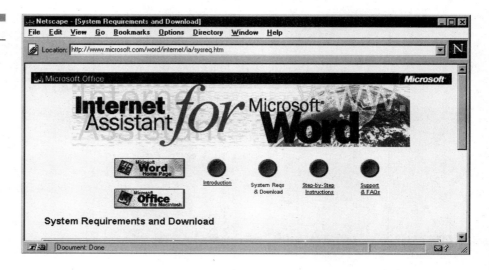

WordPerfect Internet Publisher

Start at WordPerfect's Website at `www.wordperfect.com`. Click on the generic INTERNET PUBLISHING link and then click on the INTERNET PUBLISHER link, then click on the download link. This will transfer the file `wpipzip.exe` to your hard disk. You'll need to put this file in its own directory, then execute it. It will install itself into your copy of WordPerfect for Windows. After that, you'll enjoy the freedom to create Web documents right inside your faithful, familiar friend.

Word Internet Assistant

Start at the Microsoft Website at `www.microsoft.com`. You might have to scroll down to see it, but look for a drop-down list that says SELECT A PRODUCT. Click on this and select INTERNET PRODUCTS. You'll find a link for the INTERNET ASSISTANT on this page, under the heading AUTHORING TOOLS. This page has links for Word 6, Word 95, and Word for the Macintosh. Download the file `wordia.exe` into a newly created directory on your hard disk. Do not place `wordia.exe` in your Word system directory. Execute the file from its new directory and it will complete the installation and enable you to create HTML documents within Word. The download page for this file was created with the Internet Assistant (see Fig. 10-3).

HTML Conversion Applications

HTML conversion applications will convert existing documents, databases, and files of other types to HTML format. They often do a better job than the word processor add-ons. Conversion applications can be especially valuable for productivity if you need to publish on the Web a large number of existing documents. We'll introduce you to two popular applications from Skisoft, *Web Publisher* and *Web Presentation Service*.

Skisoft Web Publisher *Skisoft Web Publisher* can be a major efficiency tool for organizations converting reams of documents. One of its biggest selling points is its batch conversion mode that can convert hundreds of documents in a single pass. It's not perfect, but it's a big leap up from using the Internet Assistant add-on for Microsoft Word and manually working through each document.

Skisoft Web Publisher automatically converts files from Word, Word Perfect, AmiPro, and Excel, but it doesn't convert the native format of all applications. Instead, it accepts documents in the Rich Text Format (`.RTF` as a file extension) that all these packages include as export options. So, Web Publisher won't directly convert your archives of ancient WordPerfect 5.1 text without first converting all of them into RTF. But even that process can be automated.

Tables are converted directly into Netscape-compatible HTML tables. And, Skisoft converts normal word processor images into GIF files. Plus, it builds a cross-linked table of contents and an index of key terms, with each item in the index linked to the appropriate text in your documents.

If you've spruced up your documents with numbered lists, bullets, and style headings, you'll be thrilled to know that it will convert all of these into HTML. It even converts bullets nested within numbered lists. Thus your styles can be converted into standard HTML heading codes.

If you are responsible for putting your organization's documents on the Web, the Skisoft Web Publisher might permit you to let writers in your organization continue to write in WordPerfect or Word. You can teach them to save final drafts in RTF or you can convert the documents later.

Downloading the Skisoft Conversion Tools

Go to **www.skisoft.com** (see Fig. 10-4) and you'll find links to both of the products reviewed here, Web Publisher and Web Presentation Service. Read the FAQs file before you download either one. Then, if you proceed, realize that you are licensed for free use of the downloaded applications for only 30 days. Then you'll need to register them to comply with copyright requirements. This site includes samples of documents and images that have been converted using Skisoft products.

Web Presentation Service   Skisoft also offers the *Web Presentation Service* that publishes your PowerPoint presentations on the World Wide Web. Web Presentation Service converts a presentation of up to 20 slides into a linked collection of HTML text files and GIF graphics files that are ready to post on your Web Server. Each presentation slide becomes a full-color Web page. It automatically creates buttons beneath each slide that let site visitors jump forward or backward as they view your presentation. It also creates an Outline page that has a hyper-linked heading to its related slide.

So, Skisoft gives you several user-friendly methods to create great-looking Web pages without needing to become a techno-wizard. Actually, you soon will find that even the standalone HTML editors don't require a technical genius. Let's graduate now to the next step up on the HTML development ladder.

Figure 10-4

How Did HTML Originate?

Have you ever wondered how HTML originated? Who cares, right? Well, HTML is based on SGML (Standard Generalized Markup Language). The development of SGML began in the 1980s. SGML became a formal standard in 1988. HTML used part of SGML, added URLs (Uniform Resource Locators) plus the HTTP (Hypertext Transfer Protocol), and created the Web. This is making a long story very, very short, but you can read all about it at `www.brainlink.com/~ben/sgml`.

Standalone HTML Editors

Standalone HTML editors are dedicated Windows applications designed specifically for creating HTML files. They offer more hypertext features, better control, and more flexibility than word processor add-ons or conversion applications. As a trade-off, however, they require a longer learning curve and they lack some of the advanced word processing features you've come to expect in Windows applications.

Here's a method you might use to ease your transition into Web publishing. Create your first Web pages in WordPerfect or Word, or convert some existing documents. After these HTML files are saved on your hard disk, open them in a standalone HTML editor. Seeing your own pages in HTML format is a good learning experience. And, most likely you'll fine-tune some things that didn't convert as you expected. You might be surprised at how quickly you pick up HTML using this method and learn to create Web pages directly in an HTML editor.

We've chosen three editors to profile here, because each one has different features, strengths, and weaknesses. They are HotDog Pro, Netscape Navigator Gold, and HTML Assistant Pro.

HotDog Pro

HotDog Pro has been a loyal puppy for us, so we imagine that you, too, might choose it as your own HTML editor. We find that all over the Web, HotDog consistently is rated as the best.

There are some disadvantages, however, in using HotDog instead of an HTML add-on. It doesn't yet deliver WYSIWYG graphics, so using it is much like working full-time inside a WordPerfect REVEAL CODES window.

The codes clearly delineate commands, but the effects will not appear on the editing screen while you're working. So, you'll work for a while and then use the PREVIEW mode to check the appearance of your work. Blessedly, HotDog easily lets you install any Web browser as its previewer and then places that browser's icon on a button bar. So it's a trade-off, but HotDog offers huge advantages in control and flexibility and it does things that you simply can't do with an add-on. Actually, it does everything!

You have complete control over all codes. This isn't true in the add-ons. For example, WordPerfect Internet Publisher prompts you to enter a title for your home page. It uses the text you enter as the actual document title and as the main heading at the top of the document. In HTML, however, you are not required to display the title at all. This feature is important because, if you create your title properly, you probably won't want it displayed.

Downloading HotDog Pro

You can download a free, trial version of HotDog so you can test it before you buy it. HotDog is a product of Sausage Software, located at **www.sausage.com** (see Fig. 10-5). The Sausage home page offers four HTML versions; HotDog and HotDog Pro are both available as either 16-bit or 32-bit applications.

The Pro version has many additional features that the standard version lacks, including an HTML spell checker. But most important, it has no file-size limit, while files in the standard version are limited to 32 Kbytes in size. All four versions give you a free trial period after which you should register and pay the registration fee.

HotDog lets you create a true HTML title that doesn't display on your Web page. This frees you to optimize the document title so that people can find your site easily with Web search engines. For example, with an add-on, you could end up with both the main heading and the document title saying "Welcome to Our Home Page!" And nobody is going to find your site by searching for WELCOME or HOME PAGE. You want to craft the document title to help people who are searching for the products or services you offer.

Figure 10-5

A more productive choice would be to use WELCOME TO OUR HOME PAGE! only as an on-screen heading, but make your actual document title, which won't be displayed on your Web page, say something such as "Power Tools, Socket Wrenches, Oil Field Supplies." Then, any search on those key words will place your Web page high on the list of search results. That's much more effective than hoping a Web surfer out there already knows your URL, or will have the patience to browse a long list of search results.

Overall, there are many similar control improvements that you'll enjoy with a standalone HTML editor. We've seen many users start out with an add-on and then switch to a standalone after they get frustrated with the limitations of the add-on application.

HotDog Snaglets

The folks at Sausage are trying hard to make life easy for HTML authors. They offer a set of tools that embellish HotDog and help you create special effects and implement advanced HTML features. They call these tools "snaglets," which is derived from the Australian name for a hotdog, a "snag."

They have one tool, called *FrameGang* (see Fig. 10-6), that helps users automatically create HTML page frames. Using frames allows you to display multiple HTML documents on one screen while hyperlinks in one frame interact with another frame. Frames are a power information-distribution embellishment. As cool as they look, however, with just basic knowledge of HTML frames and your trusty mouse you can point and click your way through frame generation.

Another great tool is *CrossEye,* an image-map editing utility that enables you to create clickable hotspots on graphic images without having to use the CGI script normally required to perform this task (see Fig. 10-7). These hotspots might be linked to URL addresses, providing your Web visitors with a graphical jump to any Web link you choose.

This is a wonderful tool because you don't want to have CGI scripts running all over the place. Besides, very few users on your Intranet will have the programming skills needed to develop anything in CGI. Fortunately, CrossEye allows nearly any HTML author to create *client-side* clickable image maps that don't require CGI scripts or special skills.

These are only two of the snaglets Sausage offers. Be sure to check their Website often for updates on these, as well as for information on any new snaglets.

Figure 10-6

Figure 10-7

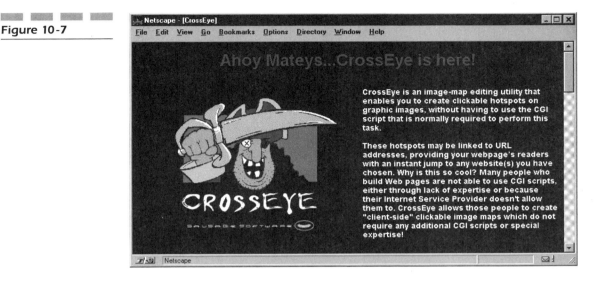

Netscape - [CrossEye]

File   Edit   View   Go   Bookmarks   Options   Directory   Window   Help

Ahoy Mateys...CrossEye is here!

CrossEye is an image-map editing utility that enables you to create clickable hotspots on graphic images, without having to use the CGI script that is normally required to perform this task.

These hotspots may be linked to URL addresses, providing your webpage's readers with an instant jump to any website(s) you have chosen. Why is this so cool? Many people who build Web pages are not able to use CGI scripts, either through lack of expertise or because their Internet Service Provider doesn't allow them to. CrossEye allows those people to create "client-side" clickable image maps which do not require any additional CGI scripts or special expertise!

CROSSEYE

Netscape

Netscape Navigator Gold

Netscape Navigator Gold offers a glimpse of how all HTML editors might one day appear. It gives you perfect WYSIWYG because you work directly in Netscape! There's no question about how your pages will look in Netscape once they're on an Intranet. That's the good news.

The bad news is that this application is not ready for prime-time players. It's quirky and it doesn't permit the level of control available in HotDog. In fact, in tests of the beta version, we found it to be the Humpty Dumpty of HTML editors. HTML documents fell apart as all kinds of unexpected changes occurred, and all the king's horses couldn't put them back together again. We exited without saving!

This can't be a permanent situation. Before long, Netscape will banish the bugs and fix the quirks and then you'll have the ability to draw HTML pages directly into Netscape. This seems to me to be the ultimate in Web page design. But you'll have to try Netscape Navigator Gold yourself as upgrades come out and decide when you're happy with its performance.

Downloading Netscape Navigator Gold

When used as a Web browser, Netscape Navigator Gold performs exactly as "just plain Netscape" performs. The Gold version has a few added items on its FILE menu that let you create and save original HTML documents.

To download it, simply go to the Netscape site at **home.netscape.com**. Then, follow the links to download the Gold version installation file into an empty directory. You will then install it exactly as you did with your regular Netscape. We suggest that you put the Gold version in a separate directory from your regular version, so you can have both. You're likely to need to download and install the Gold version often, as Netscape publishes upgrades. Meanwhile, your regular version won't be affected so you can count on reliable surfing.

HTML Assistant Pro 2

HTML Assistant Pro 2, a product of Brooklyn North Software Works in Bedford, Nova Scotia, is much like HotDog Pro. It's a point-and-click editor for making Web pages which runs under Windows 3.1 and Windows 95. HTML Assistant Pro simplifies Web page authoring by using push button tools so you don't have to remember complicated codes. Adding hypertext links involves simply copying and pasting the URL for the page to which you want to point. It uses child windows with their own menus that will improve your editing speed.

It has a special feature called the Automatic Page Creator that lets you create a Web page by filling in blanks. This features reduces the creation of forms and tables to simply clicking a button. As HotDog does, it also lets you designate any Web browser for previews so you'll be sure you're creating the look you want your visitors to see.

HTML Assistant Pro handles files of any size, so your only size limitation will be in what you believe your visitors will be willing to wait for. As a bonus, Brooklyn North Software offers instant help via e-mail, a step-by-step tutorial that guides you through the creation of your Web page, a complete HTML Tag Reference, and a beginners' guide to understanding the HTML.

Getting Your Copy of HTML Assistant Pro 2

You'll have to order HTML Assistant Pro 2 with a credit card via e-mail, fax, or telephone. Current price is US $99.95, Canadian $139.95, plus $10 shipping within the United States, Canada, or Mexico, and $15 to other destinations. Canadian residents also must include $10.50 GST, and Nova Scotia residents must add $17.65 PST. Federal Express shipping to the US is available for $25.

- Mail orders: Brooklyn North Software Works, Inc.
  25 Doyle Street
  Bedford, Nova Scotia
  Canada B4A 1K4
- e-mail orders: `sales@brooknorth.bedford.ns.ca`.
- Phone orders: 800-349-1422
- fax orders: 902-835-2600

HTML Assistant Pro has excellent aids for building tables and forms into Web pages. The syntax on both of those structures can be tricky, but this application lays out a sample for you after you select a basic format, and includes a user-friendly dialog box. All you need to do is substitute your own text into the sample.

Choosing between HotDog Pro and HTML Assistant will come down to personal choice. Each one is an excellent product, though we favor HotDog Pro, currently. We say "currently" because this is a hot market and the lead changes every few months. Bookmark the Web pages of both sites and follow the changes yourself. A good HTML editor can save you hours of work, so tracking updates will be time well spent.

Graphics Software

Once you begin writing HTML pages, you won't get far without wanting to add some graphics. The popularity of color printers, and the color graphics that now adorn millions of Web pages, have encouraged development of a slew of advanced graphics programs. *Corel Draw* and *Adobe Acrobat* are popular commercial products, while *PaintShop Pro* and *LViewPro* are popular shareware products for graphic image manipulation.

Graphics tools help create attractive and interesting HTML pages. And, with clickable maps, you will no longer be limited to using text-only links. But HTML graphics are big business, so they will be the featured topic of the next chapter. For now, let's get a quick overview of Common Gateway Interface (CGI).

Common Gateway Interface Tools

Common Gateway Interface (CGI) is a programming specification for Web servers. It makes it possible to have HTML pages tell the Web server to run programs that make your Web pages interactive.

CGI is called *server side* because it uses the server's processor to run the program. Input for the program is transmitted from the client to the server-based program. After the program runs, its results are transmitted back to the client.

User-friendly CGI tools include a wealth of valuable "pre-canned" programming scripts that can be referenced (i.e., called by the Web server) in existing hypertext documents. In other words, you won't have to start from scratch for every specialized function you want your Website to perform. Advanced tools such as *Cold Fusion* enable Web authors to create sophisticated database applications without doing any actual programming.

Two of the most common uses on the Web for CGI programs have been clickable image maps and e-mail forms. The use of CGI for clickable image maps is certain to drop now that Netscape enables client-side image maps that do not rely on the server's processor. But, for now at least, CGI formmail routines can interface with HTML forms on your Web page to create a user-friendly feedback form.

Getting Electronic Mail Feedback

You can see an example of a CGI e-mail form on this book's home page. Visit the Website **www.marketing-coach.com/intranet** and click on the FEEDBACK link (see Fig. 10-8).

You can save this page if you'd like to have an example of a mail feedback form, but you cannot simply copy the code into your own Web page. This form relies upon a CGI program on my site's Web server that actually handles the mail transaction. Your Web service provider probably has a standard CGI mail program that you can use. Once the formmail function has been made available to you, you can add it to your

Figure 10-8

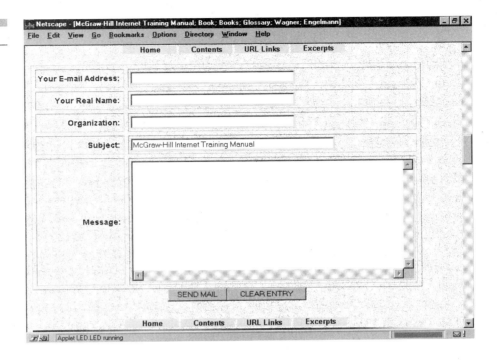

site by modifying the form on this book's home page and pasting it into one of your own Web pages.

Java and JavaScript

Java and competitive variants enable a Web browser to download programming code from a server. The downloaded code extends the functionality of a browser so that it can perform elaborate tricks that are not built-in. Leading Websites might use Java to nearly eliminate all Web browser limitations. The programming language required to implement Java applications is not yet for mainstream users, but you can hire a Java programmer to write some code if you have an application in mind.

As opposed to CGI, Java is a client-side program. Because Java code runs on the client computer after being downloaded by a Web browser, it transfers the computing demands from the Web server to client computers. This permits your servers to handle more traffic, because Java relies on the client's processor.

Quite likely, your Intranet will be used by many users whose computers will not be up to the task of running Java applications. So, until your typical user has a Pentium, consider the computing limitations your users might face before you implement an elaborate Java application.

In a later chapter we'll revisit Java and work with some sample Java code. But while we're on the subject of considering the computing limitations of your users, we'll present some pointers for testing your Website.

Testing Your Website

To create a truly user-friendly Intranet, you'll need to test your system on a variety of different platforms. We suggest you consider in your testing these four basic factors:

1. Network or modem speed
2. Web browser
3. Windows screen resolution
4. PC processing power

Even if you're not involved with the testing, be sure to encourage the testers to consider these factors.

Test with a Slow Modem

Most of your users will access your Intranet through your network. While you can expect those users to be quite satisfied with its performance, you might be shocked to see an Intranet perform at a remote office or for telecommuting users who are connected via 14.4-kbit modems.

If you need to support telecommuters with slow modems you can offer a text-only option at the top of your home page, so that those users can bypass graphics your Intranet might use. However, you might balance this extra work against the cost of providing a faster connection for those workers who need it. You could find that, over the long-term, it might be more cost-effective to design but one system and have the organization chip in for necessary upgrades.

Test with Different Browsers

At first, every browser seemed to have its own unique interpretation of HTML, and you could hardly recognize the same page on two different browsers. But now, the field has narrowed to two dominant browsers that are reasonably similar in their displays. Still, we recommend testing sites with both browsers because both are widely used.

Don't be concerned about users with browsers other than the top two. Anyone who uses something other than Netscape or the Internet Explorer simply wants to be different than the majority. They've grown accustomed to weird displays, they relish the differences, and they've learned to ignore the messages that say DESIGNED FOR NETSCAPE, CLICK HERE TO DOWNLOAD IT NOW.

Test with Different Windows Screen Resolutions

Here's a tricky consideration. What are the implications of different screen resolutions? You can create an HTML page that looks perfect at 800×600, but doesn't work at all at 640×480. For example, a heading that fits neatly across a page in the higher resolution might wrap into two lines at the lower resolution.

Changing screen resolutions in Windows is not a quick procedure, because you must restart Windows after every resolution change. Here's a hands-on exercise that will show you how to adjust Windows screen resolution. If you have at least a 15-in. monitor, I highly recommend using a screen resolution of 800×600 lines.

Objective: Learn to adjust Windows screen resolution

❑ Right-click an empty spot on your desktop.

If your desktop isn't visible, click the right mouse button on the Taskbar, click on MINIMIZE ALL WINDOWS, then right-click the desktop.

❑ Click PROPERTIES.

❑ Click the SETTINGS tab.

❑ Move the DESKTOP AREA marker to 800×600.

The Windows 95 default is 640×480. If your system already has been changed to 800×600, then click CANCEL now and skip the rest of this exercise.

❏ Click OK.

You'll probably have to restart your system for the resolution change to take effect. If so, follow the prompts to shut down and restart your system now. When it reboots, you might have to readjust your monitor's display controls to resize or reposition the screen image.

Changing Resolution Without Rebooting

Some premium video cards include a special driver that permits "on-the-fly" resolution changes without rebooting Windows after each adjustment. We can't give you a hands-on lesson to change resolution with a special driver, because each one works differently. Investing in such a card might be wise if you plan to regularly test your Website in different resolutions. Of course, if you're testing over a network you might be able to find PCs that are running other resolutions and you could use them to compare your site's appearance.

Another option is to download the Microsoft Windows 95 PowerToys set, which includes a screen resolution application called *QuickRes* that installs on the Taskbar (see Fig. 10-9). PowerToys is not an official part of Windows 95 and thus is not backed by technical support, but we've used the tools with no problems. Being able to switch resolutions in seconds from the Taskbar has been a boon to HTML development. If you're willing to take your own chances, you can visit the Microsoft PowerToys page at **www.microsoft.com/windows/software/powertoy.htm**.

HTML Width-Percentage Commands

HTML lets you specify the width of graphic images it will display. The width is specified in pixels. For example, on the home page of our first book we wanted the cover image to be one-quarter of the screen width. At a screen resolution of 800×600, you'd get that with the command WIDTH=200. Unfortunately, the same cover graphics would span nearly one-third of a 640×480 resolution screen, but less than one-fifth of the width of a 1024×768 resolution screen.

Fortunately, HTML includes a percent option for width specifications so that HTML pages can accommodate users with

Figure 10-9

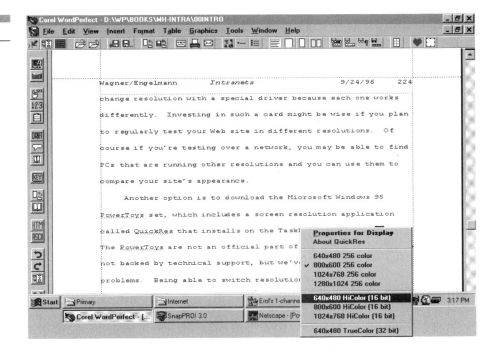

varying screen resolutions. By using the command WIDTH=25% we made certain that the cover would have a consistent size for all Windows screen resolutions.

User PC Processing Power

Eventually we'll see Web standards that are as universally implemented as those governing television. But until then, consider the potential computer limitations that your users might face.

First, remember that many users have 486 PCs that will strain to run a complex Java application. This is changing rapidly because it's very difficult to buy a new 486. Perhaps before long you will be able to design and create your site around a Pentium or better and just not worry about 486.

Also, think about your visitors' video displays. If you suspect that a lot of your visitors will be running in low resolution mode (e.g., 640×480), consider designing and testing your site with your resolution set to the lower standard. While a page that's designed for 800×600 mode might fall apart at 640×480, the reverse is not true.

Decisions, Decisions . . . Too Many Decisions

Are you feeling stressed over all of this information? Truly, it's a lot to digest. To simplify your decision-making, let us conclude with some tips that might help you quickly eliminate a lot of things you don't need to learn. This will be a guide to deciding what tools your organization might need to build its Intranet. First, consider your organization's existing technical and personnel resources.

- How many users do you expect each day?
- Do you have UNIX gurus in-house?
- Do you have artistic and advertising talent in-house?
- Will your Intranet content require frequent updates, or will most information be fairly static?
- Do you need database searches, or can you convey your organization's information with simple, cross-linked documents?

Depending on your organization's resources, you might decide to keep an Intranet project in-house, hire consultants, or outsource the entire project. Let's consider some factors important to organizations of varying sizes. You might benefit from reading about them all, because there is some crossover.

Large Global Organizations

Organizations of 10,000 people or more generally have lots of customers, with resources to match. They generally have editorial people who can ensure that grammar and writing are crisp (as long as they don't impede progress); computer professionals who can build elaborate scripts and database functions (or stall the project by trying to be too technical); and cautious management (who prudently, and unfortunately, might slow down the whole project).

We've found that, when large organizations eventually get themselves online, they often fail to achieve many of the benefits they expected from an Intranet. This occurs because large organizations have large organizational infrastructures that require extensive analysis before any action can be taken.

Because Intranet control is decentralized and customers won't see the content, each department often is free to immediately set up a Web server to handle their information storage and reporting needs. Even where field offices don't have Internet access, CD-ROMs containing data dumps of corporate Web servers can be shipped to them so that they have a (somewhat out of date) copy of the corporate databank on their local Intranets.

Tools that might be used by a large organization, which handles the total Web project internally, include C compilers, multiple high-end PCs, multiprocessor PCs and mini/mainframe Web-server hardware, UNIX or Windows NT Web-server software with on-staff technical support, advanced graphics editing tools such as Corel Draw and Adobe Photoshop, document conversion tools, SGML (the parent of HTML), multiple browsers for testing, database access tools such as Cold Fusion, and Java programming.

Large Domestic Organizations

Organizations in this size range (1000 to 10,000 people) generally have many of the internal resources found in giant organizations, and most of them can expect to handle an Intranet project internally. Shipping CD-ROMs to branch offices in organizations of this size probably wouldn't be cost-effective, but an Intranet still is a powerful productivity tool and should be considered in conjunction with the organization's Website.

Tools you might find used in this size range include C compilers, multiple high-end PCs, multiprocessor PCs and minicomputer Web server hardware, UNIX or Windows NT Web server software with technical support contracts, advanced graphics editing tools such as Corel Draw and Adobe Photoshop, document conversion tools, database access tools, and Java programming. A single fast server probably can handle all Website needs.

Medium-Sized Domestic Organizations

Organizations in this size range (100 to 1000 people) usually will have one or more full-time computer specialists who can meet the technology challenges of the Internet. These people probably will even be able to handle installing an Intranet Web server. Expect your computer professional to be able to create HTML pages with graphic images, simple Java scripts, and possibly even database applications.

Depending on types of customers, it might make sense to maintain a dedicated, external Web server, but at this size an organization is in the crossover range and should consider renting space on an ISP's Web server. A tailored domain name still would be a must, however. Organizations in this size range probably will train additional staff to regularly produce simple HTML documents and to rely on the computer professional to write or supervise production of database applications.

Typical tools used in this organization will be word processor add-ons, desktop publishing programs with HTML output support, a Windows NT server, a specialized HTML editor such as HotDog, a commercial Web server such as WebSite, Netscape Communication Server (or Purveyor), and simple Java scripts.

What about UNIX Operating Systems?

UNIX operating system experts usually do not abound in organizations in this size range (or in smaller ones, obviously). That's okay, because these companies should be looking at user-friendly, Windows-based, Web server software. But if you have more than one UNIX guru in-house, you might want to take advantage of the wealth of UNIX support available for Web servers and other applications.

However, you should *never* leave your company dependent on a lone UNIX professional. Replacing such a lost guru is nearly impossible to do quickly. Information on your site might go stale before you can hire a replacement capable of working through hundreds or even thousands of clever improvements that your former guru made. Sticking with Windows-based products will give you an ever-increasing number of professionals on which to draw if you need a replacement.

Small Organizations

A small company (20 to 100 people) often will have a LAN that easily can be adapted to an internal TCP/IP network, and the company can then use an inexpensive Web server. Such an organization often will have a knowledgeable, full-time computer specialist in-house, or a consultant who makes regular visits. This computer professional should be able to put up simple HTML pages on an internal web, even if your organization uses information intensely, and on an ISP's Web server for customer access.

Tools used in organizations of this size include word processor add-ons, desktop publishing software with HTML output, and tools recommended by an ISP for image-mapped hyperlinks and database applications. The ISP almost certainly will have an in-house staff with sufficient Web development skills to create a professional Website.

Very Small Organizations

Small companies (1 to 20 people), partnerships, and sole proprietorships nearly always lack a computer professional. Thus they will need to look for a Web service provider who can develop and maintain a World Wide Web presence. A turnkey Website provider, such as *GoSite*, could be an excellent choice. Keep in mind that no one who uses your Website knows its location, so it can be maintained anywhere in the country, a good thing to keep in mind if you find a real deal on Web server space a thousand miles away.

An Intranet remains a possibility for companies in this size range because the server demands will be low enough that nearly any PC could suffice. Probably, one server could handle an Intranet as well as all normal LAN traffic. Simple yet full- featured Web server software can be purchased for only a few hundred dollars, and shareware Web servers are even available.

Tools   Tools used in organizations of this size include word processor add-ons. Nearly anyone skilled in Windows word processor usage can put basic information on a Web page. You'll want the Internet Publisher for WordPerfect for Windows, or the Internet Assistant for Microsoft Word for Windows. Also, one of the Skisoft conversion programs could be a real time saver.

After creating the basics, contract with a local Web page designer to make up for your weak points. College campuses can be a good place to find HTML authors. You could easily find a suitable one via a notice on a student union bulletin board, or through an ad in a school paper.

You also might need an ad copywriter to help with the writing, an advertising consultant, and an artist to help with graphics and design. Many such marketing professionals before have now expanded their services to include Web technology. In fact, I've discovered that students in many college marketing courses are developing Web pages in class exercises. So, perhaps a college student would be satisfactory in one of these aspects of your Website development, too.

If information on your Website needs frequent changes, you can update it quickly if you use an ISP that permits you to FTP updates directly into the Web directory. You don't want the accuracy of the information seen by your clients and customers to depend on an ISP's schedule for updating it. These services often are staffed by young people who might not understand the importance of responding to your schedule, so be careful. Direct FTP capability will ensure that you have control over your Website's content.

Connection Considerations   Even if such a small company is split between one or more offices, an Intranet can still work. Full-time ISDN connections are available now for only a few hundred dollars a month, and ISDN accounts that provide 500 hours per month are available for $120 per month. For only $90 per month you can buy 300 hours of ISDN connect time, which is certainly enough to run an Intranet during normal business hours. And, as low as these prices are, expect them to be lower by the time you read this.

Finally, a really small organization might be able to run an Intranet using regular phone lines and 28.8 kbits/s modems. It would be a little slow, but not bad for limited traffic. The slow transfer times could seem worth the wait if the alternative has been to rely on regular courier service to exchange data.

Summary

Intranet technology changes too fast to include more detail in a book such as this. You can refer to Appendix B, "Continuing Education," for valuable, on-going sources of up-to-date changes. The next task is to help you learn about the graphics that will transform your Intranet into a vibrant, colorful landscape.

11

Intranet
Graphics

Remember that for nearly 30 years the Internet existed in text-only format, distributing technical and academic information between large institutions. And, in its text-only format, the Internet remained the enterprise of scientists and academics. But the creation of the Web permitted the Internet to go graphic, and graphics are what launched the Internet as a "hot revolution."

Well-done graphics can make even static, boring, technical information look appealing. Graphics also can create simple explanations for difficult concepts, and they can convey messages quickly and efficiently. And, graphics can bypass language barriers by creating universal, pictorial labels and instructions, perfect for the World Wide Web. Unfortunately, Web graphics have been like a double-edged sword.

Graphics on the Internet still cause serious bandwidth problems, but Intranets can easily solve the bandwidth problems that will continue to plague the Internet for years. Because of an Intranet's dramatically increased capacity, Intranet graphics can be a pleasure for everyone. Your Intranet might almost literally let everyone run wild with all their graphic dreams and ideas.

Of course, if your Intranet connects remote offices, graphics might cause some bandwidth problems there, too. But if you use a dedicated line your bandwidth problems are not likely to be as severe as they are on the Internet.

So graphics are here to stay, and we've included this chapter to give you some graphics resources that will help everyone in the organization sort the hype from the facts and learn where to turn for more information.

HTML Graphics Primer

You'll see two file formats in common use in HTML documents, GIF (Graphics Interchange Format) and JPEG (Joint Photographics Expert Group). GIF is the more common of the two, but JPEG is catching on fast. There are pros and cons with both so you'll have to decide for yourself.

We'll give you an overview of both major formats, tips on choosing the right one for a given application, overviews of graphics drawing, editing, and conversion software, plus tips on graphics saving and editing. You'll find many excellent graphics resources from around the Web, including links to other Internet books that deal specifically with graphics and scanning.

GIF Graphic Files

The GIF format is good for all types of images and is compatible with a wide variety of graphics applications. GIF was developed in 1987 by CompuServe, to be a device-independent method of storing pictures. GIF allows high-quality, high-resolution graphics to be displayed on a variety of graphics hardware and is intended as a common exchange and display mechanism for graphic images. A GIF picture file has an extension `.GIF`.

The 1987 GIF format was upgraded and released again in 1989, but the upgrade used the same GIF extension. Some graphic applications distinguish the two GIF formats as GIF87 and GIF89. Even though the GIF 8-bits-pixel format supports only 256 colors and has relatively large file sizes, GIF remains one of the most popular choices for storing images. GIF format is best when used with images containing flat areas of color that have little or no shading. GIF is well-matched to inexpensive computer displays, because it can store only 8 bits per pixel (256 or fewer colors) and most PCs can't display more than 256 distinct colors at once.

Sizing Web Graphics

The graphic images used on the Internet are sized by *pixels*. Pixels are dots on your screen. A typical Windows screen is made up of 640 pixels horizontally and 480 pixels vertically. For short, this is called a 640×480 screen resolution. But Windows has other resolutions. Another common Windows resolution is 800×600. Thus an image that is 240 pixels high would run 50 percent of the height of a 640×480 screen, but would occupy only 30 percent of the height of a 800×600 screen.

If your graphic displays in different sizes on different screens, you'll have difficulty planning the text so that it will fit around the graphic. Fortunately, HTML gives you two important but little-used tools to help control the relationship between text and graphics on your Web pages.

Clear Break Command

HTML has a code, `<BR>`, that causes a line break. You could use a series of consecutive `<BR>` commands to push your text down below the bottom of a graphic image. But if you put in just enough of them to push the text down past the graphic on a 640×480 screen, then the page will look different on a 800×600 screen. The solution is not to use multiple `<BR>` commands but to use an option with the code that forces the next line break to occur *after* it clears the current graphic image. Use the code `<BR CLEAR = LEFT>` or `<BR CLEAR = RIGHT>`, depending on which side of the screen the image lies.

Percentage Width Command

HTML lets you control the width of graphic images with a `WIDTH` command that normally is expressed in pixels. But, instead of using pixels you can use a percent so the size will be uniform across all screen resolutions. For example, if you used `<IMG SRC = "image.gif" WIDTH = 25%>`, the image would be 160 pixels wide at a 640×480 resolution, and 200 pixels wide at an 800×600 resolution.

Novice users might find GIF images the easiest to deal with. Creating a good JPEG image can require more user finesse than is practical to expect from mainstream users. GIFs, in contrast, are simpler—sort of a brute force alternative. But on an Intranet, they might be a good solution because you're not likely to be concerned about the bandwidth savings that come with JPEG images. So, unless your Intranet includes pages that also will be public on your Website, GIF probably will be fine for your Intranet graphics.

 NOTE: *GIF Internet images are transferred in 16×16-pixel blocks. Knowing this can help you increase your site's download efficiency. For example, if you size a graphic to be exactly 160×80 pixels it will download in 10×5 blocks, or 50 blocks in total. But if you sized the same image at 162×82 it would require 11×6 blocks, or 66 blocks. This would increase the download time, yet the on-screen size difference would barely be noticeable.*

JPEG and JPG Graphic Files

JPEG (pronounced *jay-peg*) is a standardized image compression mechanism. The name JPEG derives from the original name of the committee that wrote the standard, the Joint Photographic Experts Group (see Fig. 11-1).

JPEG is designed for compressing either full-color or gray-scale images of natural, real-world scenes. It works well on photographs, naturalistic artwork, and similar material, but not well on lettering, simple cartoons, black-and-white, or line drawings. A JPEG picture file has the extension .JPG.

JPEG stores full color information: 24 bits per pixel (up to 16.7 million colors). Therefore, with full-color hardware, JPEG images look much better than GIF files. And, JPEG files can be much smaller than GIFs so they usually are superior to GIFs in terms of disk space and transmission time.

We say "usually" because applications that save images in JPEG files or convert images to JPEG files permit adjustments to the image file that alter the image quality and file size. The compression method and or percentage of compression is fully controllable and directly corresponds to the quality of the compressed image.

It is possible to save a JPEG image in a file that is larger than its GIF counterpart. Of course, it also can be smaller. The trick is to learn to adjust the quality optimally because there is a point of diminishing

Figure 11-1

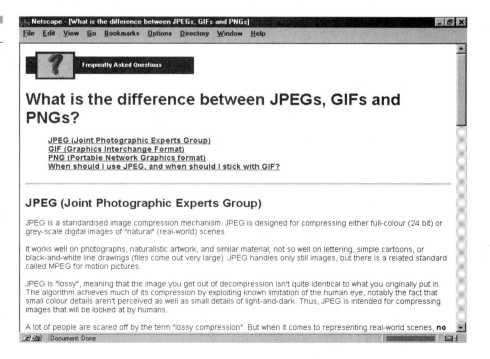

returns with every image. In other words, eventually you'll reach the point that increasing the quality adjustment doesn't improve quality but does continue to increase the file size. That's why GIF can be a nice trade-off, because it creates a reasonable middle-of-the-road file in terms of balancing quality versus file size, and users don't need to be skilled graphics designers.

JPEG files often use a file extension of `.JPG` because of file naming limitations in MS-DOS and Windows 3.x. For example, if you use a Windows 3.x application to save a JPEG graphic file your system will convert the extension to `.JPG`. There will be no difference between the two files and you can rename it with a `.JPEG` extension if you transfer it back to a UNIX, a Windows 95, or a Windows NT system.

Tips on Selecting an Image Format

The choice of the best graphics format to use depends on the application and the desired effect. So, to make some sense out of all the possible choices, I'll share these tips from Kody Kline of *Extreme D.T.P.* in Tulsa, Oklahoma (see Fig. 11-2). Kody is a master of computer graphics art, which you can see for yourself at `www.ionet.net/~kkline`.

All graphic images are rectangular in shape, even if they store pictures of irregularly shaped objects. If you want an irregularly shaped object not to have a rectangular outside shape, you'll need to use GIF format. Also, only GIF lets you make the background color of your image transparent. A transparent background creates the illusion of an irregularly shaped picture, because the transparent background allows the colors behind the picture to show through the transparent area, even though the actual image outline remains rectangular.

If you want to reduce the download time of your large graphic images, you'll find that a moderately compressed JPEG image can cut the file size and download time by approximately 70 percent, with only minor loss of quality. Much greater detail can be obtained, in full-color, photographic quality, in a low-compression JPEG versus GIF, because of the GIF's color limitations.

Although the flashy 16.7-million color JPEG images might look excellent on your computer, remember that many people who access your Website will not have adequate video hardware or the higher-

Figure 11-2

speed modems to handle these images efficiently. GIF format supports an *interlaced* option that quickly displays a blurred full-size image of the GIF, then, during repeated passes, fills in and sharpens the image. This doesn't reduce overall download time but at least it gives visitors a quick taste of the image, which might entice them to wait.

Whichever graphic format you select, a compromise between a high-quality photographic image with millions of colors and concerns for long transmission times can result in a usable graphic that can deliver pizazz without requiring visitors to take naps during downloads.

Capturing Images from Other Pages

You'll see a vast array of graphics as you surf the Internet, and Netscape makes is easy to save them to your hard drive. Of course, you'll have to keep in mind that many Internet graphics are protected by copyrights, but you easily can e-mail the source site for reuse permission. If you want to include a graphic on your Intranet because you plan to link your Intranet to their site, they'll be happy to grant permission to increase their site's exposure. And many times they'll tell you that the graphic is public domain and that you're free to use it anyway.

So, once the copyright considerations are handled, you can have a field day collecting graphics all over cyberspace. Here's a quick, hands-on exercise that shows you how to capture a graphic to your hard drive.

Objective: Learn to save an Internet graphic image.

❑ Start Netscape.

❑ Press CTRL+L.

❑ Type **www.marketing-coach.com/intranet**, then press ENTER.

❑ Place the mouse over the image of the book's cover.

❑ Click the right button.

❑ Click SAVE THIS IMAGE AS...

Select an appropriate directory in which to save this image before you complete the next step.

❑ Click SAVE.

You can open a saved graphic image in Netscape at any time, or you can reference it in one of your own HTML pages.

That was easy, right? But what about capturing the background image? So far, Netscape has not included that capability. If you have Windows 95 or Windows NT, however, you can download a background file with the Microsoft Internet Explorer. You can surf with Netscape for maximum compatibility, then quickly start Explorer if you encounter a background you'd like to save. Here's how.

Objective: Learn to save an Internet background graphic.

❑ Double-click in the Netscape LOCATION text entry box (You'll see the URL at the top of the screen).

❑ Press CTRL+C to copy the URL to the clipboard.

❑ Click the right mouse on a blank area on the Taskbar.

❑ Click MINIMIZE ALL WINDOWS.

❑ Double-click THE INTERNET on your desktop.

❑ Press CTRL+O or double-click in the ADDRESS text entry box.

❑ Press CTRL+V to paste the URL, then press ENTER to load it.

❑ Click the right mouse button on a blank area of the background.

❑ Click SAVE BACKGROUND AS.

❑ Click SAVE to save the image on your hard drive.

Select a directory and change the name as desired.

❑ Press ALT+F4 to close Internet Explorer.
❑ Use ALT+TAB to cycle back to Netscape.

Windows 95 lets you save an Internet background image to your clipboard so you can paste it into your favorite graphics application. The Internet Explorer also lets you designate an Internet background image as your desktop wallpaper.

Original Graphics Art

Creating a world-class site requires world-class graphics. Very few part-time graphics users can match the level of quality of the best graphics seen today on the Web. And even if they can do so they probably would lack the expertise to optimize the balance between image quality and file size.

But perhaps your creative juices are stirring and you want to try your own hand at Internet graphics. Or, perhaps budget constraints won't allow you to hire a graphics artist or consultant right now. Either way, for all do-it-yourselfers here's a quick introduction to creating Internet graphics.

Graphic Drawing Packages

A review of all the good graphics programs would be a book in itself, so we'll trim the list and show you some of the most popular (i.e., inexpensive) applications. In fact, some of them are *extremely* inexpensive; for example, free! The free applications won't create the very best graphics but you'll certainly save money. Everything involves trade-offs. Besides, if you're a novice you most likely would not be able to justify the time it would take to learn to use those highly specialized tools.

Client-Side Clickable Maps

Until Netscape Navigator 2.0 was released, HTML authors couldn't create a clickable image map. They needed to use CGI programs, running on the Web server, to enable users to navigate via clickable image maps. The need for CGI programming skills put clickable maps out of the reach of most HTML authors. But the new Netscape standard, called *client-side clickable maps,* is so simple that many HTML authors will be able to create clickable image maps.

With client-side clickable maps, the coding is built into the HTML document and all the action occurs on the client computer. Once the document is downloaded, the server won't need to be involved with handling the site's clickable maps. This helps alleviate bandwidth problems and makes the creation task easier.

In the last chapter, we outlined the HotDog Pro HTML editor. HotDog has an add-on application, called *CrossEye,* that automates the tedious job of mapping coordinates on an image map. You can get CrossEye from the Sausage Software Website at **www.sausage.com**. With CrossEye you won't have to write, test, compile, and upload a CGI script to handle the jumps. Instead, it generates simple HTML code and puts it in the Windows clipboard. All you have to do is paste the code into an HTML page that you're editing in HotDog. Then, once your Web page is loaded into a visitor's browser, the image map code in your document handles all jumps without any bandwdith or server demands.

CorelDraw

Since its acquisition of the complete line of WordPerfect products, Corel has the most complete line of business software in the industry (see Fig. 11-3). For years, the CorelDraw graphics application has been an industry leader. The merging of the two product lines will help the WordPerfect word processor remain a leader in Web page development.

Another reason we included CorelDraw here is that it is available in so many versions. Unlike most software vendors, when CorelDraw creates an upgrade it keeps its older versions on the shelf as well. This gives users a range of prices with a corresponding range of features. You can pay top dollar for the latest version, or buy a deeply discounted, slightly older version that might serve your Intranet graphics needs.

Corel also bundles its older versions with high-quality hardware products, such as video display cards and scanners. If you realize that your old video card is sapping your computer's performance and it's time for an upgrade, shop around for a card that includes a recent version of CorelDraw. Graphics cards with bundled graphics applications usually are no more costly than comparable video cards, and they give you an excellent $150 to $350 drawing package essentially free.

Figure 11-3

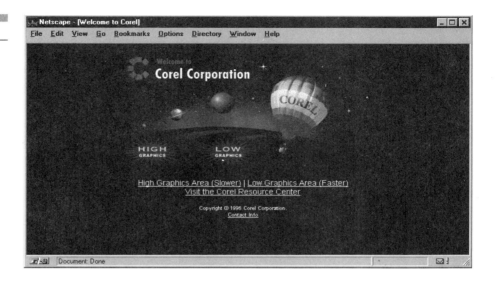

Features for HTML Publishing

When you're selecting which version of CorelDraw you'll use, make sure that yours is recent enough to handle JPEG files. The older versions (Version 3.0, for example) do not. For Intranet graphics that might be a serious limitation. But even Version 3.0 handles GIF files, which are perfectly adequate for use with basic HTML graphics on an Intranet.

Even older versions of CorelDraw can create a wide array of special effects, including objects that appear as 3-D. You'll be able to control blending in shaded objects so you can adjust the appearance of their resolution. And, Corel imports and exports most of the major graphics formats. In other words, these older versions of CorelDraw might satisfy the needs of most users on an Intranet without requiring you to incur any additional costs.

3-D Graphics

Although CorelDraw and others have some 3-D capability, some standalone, top-end 3-D graphics packages are available. 3-D graphics is a very hot topic as this book is being written. You'll need to check the latest versions on store shelves, read magazine reviews, or check out the Websites of the various graphics application vendors. The bottom line is that, with moderate graphics experience, you can expect to create some stunning 3-D graphics with the tools that are now available.

Paint Shop Pro

Paint Shop Pro is a shareware graphics application. This means that you can download a limited-license version and test it before you pay (see Fig. 11-4). Paint Shop Pro is a powerful, user-friendly, image viewing, editing, and converting program. With support for more than 30 image formats, and several drawing and painting tools, this might be the only graphics program you will ever need. It comes in both 16-bit and 32-bit versions. The 32-bit version runs under the Windows 95 and Windows NT operating systems and takes full advantage of their 32-bit capability. The 16-bit version is an excellent choice for anyone using Windows 3.x.

This is an excellent graphics tool for Web-authoring beginners, and it will handle all of the graphics formats you'll need to get started. Check out its home page at **www.jasc.com/psp.html** where you can read about it, check its lengthy feature list, and download a free, trial copy. You won't beat this deal on a graphics program. If you like it you can register and pay the fee to get technical support and upgrades. And

Figure 11-4

you've not invested any money if you find that you need a more powerful, professional-level graphics application.

If you decide to buy, don't let the price discourage you. It has a lot of profession-level features and can create some terrific graphics. For the money, this is the best value for Intranet graphics. However, if you're not on a tight budget and you're ready to tackle the intricacies of some truly world-class graphics features, check out the next sidebar.

World-Class Graphics

Adobe Photoshop graphics software enables designers and photographers to create original artwork, correct color, retouch and composite scanned images, and prepare professional-quality separations and output with complete flexibility. With a wealth of powerful painting and selection tools, plus multiple layers, special effects filters, and lighting effects, Adobe Photoshop is a professional's dream application. You can learn more at the Adobe Website at `www.adobe.com/Apps/Photoshop` (see Fig. 11-5).

Photoshop offers more than 40 standard filters, including multiple choices for image sharpening, softening, stylizing, distortion, video, and removal of noise, dust, and scratches. Its powerful lighting effects let users apply multiple light sources to an image and choose from a range of colors, intensities, and angles.

You can use Photoshop to create an original image or you can start with a scanned image. It lets you create effects in separate layers, which work like transparent sheets of acetate upon which you can combine graphic elements, paint, and editing without changing the original background image. Photoshop's user-friendly interface permits you to drag-and-drop selections from different files or from different layers. And you can save the finished image in a wide variety of different file formats, including GIF and JPEG. Its GIF support extends to the GIF89 format that lets you create transparency and interlacing.

LView Pro

Somewhere between the full-featured graphic applications and the beginner's applications, you might find that you lose some graphics conversion

Figure 11-5

abilities. Via the Web you can download an excellent, shareware graphics conversion application, called *LView Pro,* that was authored by Leonardo Haddad Loureiro of MMedia Research. You'll be free to distribute LView Pro to others for trial and leisure utilization. If you decide to use it in business, however, you'll need to register your copy with MMedia to comply with copyright regulations.

Considering that you can download this application free from the Internet, it sports an amazing array of features. It lets you flip, rotate, resize, and crop images, and it gives you a full-range of powerful image-enhancement tools. LView Pro can handle importing of BMP, GIF87, GIF89, JPEG, PCX, TIF, TGA, PPM, PGM, PBM, and DIB formats. Its GIF features include a transparency that uses a simple "dropper" that lets you touch a background color that you want made transparent. A simple menu selection lets you tell LView Pro to automatically save all your GIF files in interlaced format, an excellent choice if you need to consider telecommuters who might be using slow dial-up modems to work over your Intranet.

To get your copy of LView Pro, check out the MMedia Research Web page at `world.std.com/~mmedia/lviewp.html` (see Fig. 11-6). You'll have a choice of either a Windows 3.x or a Windows 95 version. The last time we checked, the registration fee for commercial use was only $30, a true software bargain. While you're there to download the application, you might as well check out the link entitled, "Transparent color" and save it or print it so you can create transparent backgrounds for your GIF images.

Oh, No, There's More!

Just when you thought you had nailed down the facts on Internet graphics, things changed. There's a new graphics format emerging, based on GIF. Right now it's all about lawsuits and patents and people fighting to collect money they're not likely to be paid anyway, but the result to you is a new graphic format. After CompuServe had used the GIF format for seven years and after it had become a standard on the Web, some lawsuits were filed over alleged patent infringements.

The real result? GIF had been showing its age in a number of ways even before the lawsuit, so the announcement only hurried the development of a new and much-improved replacement. Now we all have a new graphics format with an extension of `.PNG` (pronounced "ping"). The PNG format (Portable Network Graphics) was developed as free software, and CompuServe intends it to be free of patent infringements.

For more information on PNG, check out its home page, which is maintained by Greg Roelofs at `quest.jpl.nasa.gov/PNG`.

Figure 11-6

HiJaak Graphics Software

Once you've mastered your free, bundled copy of CorelDraw or your PaintShop Pro, you might want to move up without going all the way to Adobe PhotoShop. If so, you should consider the *HiJaak 95* graphics application.

HiJaak 95 changes the way you work with graphics by integrating its graphics technology directly into Windows 95. Without ever having to run a separate application you'll be able to view, organize, convert, and print graphics naturally and easily. HiJaak 95 also includes superb capture, convert, and image management tools, all with a choice of how to work, which you can do from the HiJaak application window or directly from Windows 95.

HiJaak 95 has extended Windows 95 with more than 75 graphics formats, and to the Windows 95 shortcut menu has been added searching, viewing, printing, thumbnail updating, and converting. This unprecedented level of integration means that HiJaak 95 can help you perform your graphics tasks more efficiently than ever before. Its conversion handles almost every graphic format you can expect to encounter.

HiJaak performs all the usual graphics enhancing tasks that you'll need, and includes a flexible and powerful screen-capture application that enables you to capture and save any image you can see on your screen.

HiJaak Graphics Suite is an integrated set of graphics utilities that lets you easily add great graphics to your Web pages. And you don't have to be a professional to get excellent results. It includes HiJaak Browser, HiJaak Smuggler, HiJaak Paint, HiJaak Draw, and HiJaak Pro. With the suite you can browse, search, find, manage, create, draw, edit, paint, view, convert, trace, capture, scan, and print. As a bonus, it includes a clipart library on CD-ROM that has thousands of images indexed by the HiJaak Browser, so you get visual access to specific images without entering keywords.

Image Scanning

Scanning is a computer function that transforms existing photos, graphic images, drawings, sketches, maps, illustrations, and even text into a digitized format. Once stored digitally, the captured image can be manipulated with computer graphics software. Scanned images can be retouched in the computer to optimize their on-screen appearance, or they can be printed or included in a word processing document.

Your primary use of a scanner probably will be to capture images and save them, in either GIF or JPEG formats, which you can then reference with HTML codes in your Web documents.

Since some quality always is lost during the scanning process, make sure that your original image is the best quality you can get. For best results the images should have high contrast and be perfectly sharp. Very much as with photocopiers, you might need to adjust the brightness and contrast to capture an acceptable image.

But there's more to it than merely twiddling with one or two buttons. You quickly will discover that scanning images optimally is an art, so much so that you'll find entire books on the topic. For some excellent scanning resources to get you started, refer to Appendix B, "Continuing Education."

Scanner Basics

For professional results you must use only flatbed, desktop scanners. An inexpensive, hand-held scanner isn't going to help you put up professional-quality Intranet content. A flatbed scanner is a scanning device that accepts flat art (e.g., photographs, drawings, clippings, and illustrations). Most flatbed scanners are designed to handle 8.5 × 11-inch originals in reflective media, meaning images that reflect light. Some flatbed scanners will handle transparent media (such as Ektachrome transparencies and 35mm slides), but you might have to add a special transparency adapter to activate this function.

For increased flexibility in paper handling, you can find scanners that accept legal-size documents. If you need to scan a large number of existing documents, be sure you select a scanner that includes a document feeder option, because flatbed scanners normally accept only one document at a time.

Scanners will include scanning software, but the quality and features vary wildly. You're not likely to find a full-featured application bundled with any scanner, though all are adequate. If possible, stick to applications that give you the ability to scan and save in all the common file formats that you will want to use, especially GIF and JPEG. Good scanning software also should allow you to crop and rotate before or during saving.

It's an absolute must that your scanner have a TWAIN (Technology Without An Interesting Name) module. TWAIN is a crucial feature because it's supported by all major applications and allows you to scan directly into non-image processing applications such as WordPerfect,

Figure 11-7

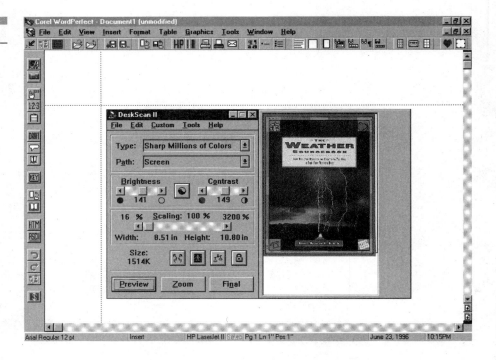

PageMaker, and CorelDraw. It's amazing to watch WordPerfect ingest a color photo directly into a document—what a way to spruce up a report or newsletter! (see Fig. 11-7). And remember, in the last chapter we outlined some conversion applications that will convert WordPerfect and Microsoft Word documents into HTML, *including* converting your imbedded graphics into GIF format.

If you're interested in going beyond the basics of scanning, the next sidebar will take you about as far as you could want to go. A note of caution, though; this could become an exciting, full-time job. But it will be fun—sort of like being a kid and getting the big box of crayons!

Advanced Scanning and Graphics

You can access online graphics lessons that will teach you advanced scanning and other graphics techniques. From these you can learn practically everything, from how to produce transparent backgrounds (a must for irregularly shaped images) to optimizing your graphics for size and download speed.

Advanced Scanning

For some productivity-enhancing scanning tips, check out Michael J. Sullivan's Website at **www.hsdesign.com/scanning** (see Fig. 11-8). This is a fabulous scanning resource, but it represents only the tip of the iceberg. For in-depth lessons and tips you can buy Michael's book, *Make Your Scanner a Great Design and Production Tool* (North Light Books, 1995).

Michael is partner and artistic director of Haywood & Sullivan in Quincy, Massachusetts, an award-winning full-range design firm that excels at communication design using various media. He also is founding partner of Pilgrim New Media in Cambridge, Massachusetts, a multimedia titles publisher.

Advanced Graphics

Jump to **www.warwick.ac.uk/~cudbh/I3course/ graphics.html** where you'll find a full set of graphics lessons from Bronwen Reid at the University of Hull, in the United Kingdom. Lessons here include backgrounds, transparencies, and interlacing. Also, you can use this site as a jumping-off point for other sites with graphics tips.

Figure 11-8

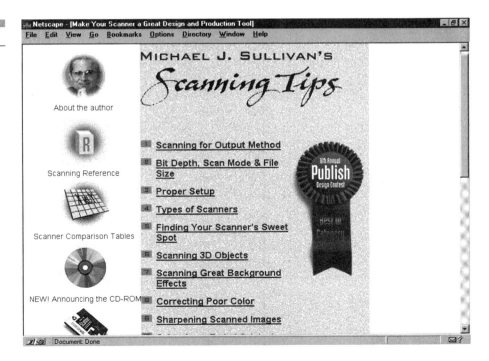

12

Bringing Your
Intranet
to Life

The hills might be alive with the sound of audio music, but the Web is alive with the sound of online music. And, because actions speak louder than words, you can forget about writer's block and begin expressing yourself through video clips, live-camera video, or animated action. Your Intranet will completely change the way you work with these media.

This is an exciting chapter that will show you how to configure Netscape to play audio, video, and animation. Also, it will discuss using these features to provide some of your Intranet content. All of these features are still pretty primitive, but the core technology is in place and it's advancing at the speed of light. Prepare to be thrilled at the sights and sounds you'll soon be able to pull in from all over the world and adopt for your Intranet.

Don't Overdo It

Cyberspace is getting overcrowded with "gee whiz" doodads that show off how talented their authors have become. Gee whiz technology certainly can draw people into a site—after all, the results are fun to watch. But after the initial impression wears off, most people want to accomplish something with the technology.

A survey was done recently, at Georgia Tech, which will give you an idea of what Web visitors are seeking when they strap on their browsers and launch themselves into cyberspace. To see it, go to **www.cc.gatech.edu/gvu/user_surveys**. You'll learn what people like to do most on the Web (browsing), and what they like least (shopping). Speed problems generate the most and biggest complaints, so go easy on the graphics and other fancy stuff for your Web viewers but don't worry about speed for your on-site Intranet viewers. Again, the important point is that, whether your content is for the Internet or your Intranet, you should make sure that any special effects truly make sense and improve the value or accessibility of the information you're distributing.

For example, let's say your organization has just produced an informative video and has made it available over an Intranet. On-site employees can view it in real time. If a user in a remote office wanted this information, there would be some download time for the file. Most likely, however, he or she wouldn't mind the download time because it would be much less trouble than formally requesting a copy of the video and waiting for delivery.

This chapter is an overview of the major Web special features that you'll see as you cruise through cyberspace with the latest technology. Here's the menu for the delightful treats that await you.

- Java, the Web's own programming language
- Audio
- Video
- Virtual reality

Java

Java is an object-oriented programming language developed in the 1990s at Sun Microsystems, Inc. It was developed there by a team headed by James Gosling and was intended for the microprocessors in small appliances. Given this focus, Java also had to work on a wide variety of processors and it needed excellent safeguards against system lockup. To put that in perspective, you've become accustomed to having your PC lock up occasionally, but how would you reboot your dishwasher?

While the Sun team was developing Java, the World Wide Web grew up around them. Along the way, someone realized that the same characteristics that made Java perfect for appliance processors also made it perfect for the Web. The two technologies were married and introduced to the world in May 1995. Java will be a major factor in how the Internet and Intranets change the way we all work, play, and live.

What's in a Name?

Contrary to rumors, Java does NOT stand for "Just Another Vague Acronym." Java originally was named *Oak* in honor of a large tree outside James Gosling's window. Trademark considerations forced the team to come up with a new product name. That's a tough task in today's crowded markets, but Java hit the spot.

What's the difference between Java and HotJava? Java is the programming language; HotJava is Sun's Java-compatible Web browser. At first, HotJava was the only Java browser available, but HotJava never really caught on because, soon after Java became available, Netscape agreed to make its browser Java-compatible. Later,

Microsoft added Java compatibility to its Internet Explorer, and that pretty much established it as *the* Internet programming language.

There are two other important factors in Java's incredible rise in fortune. First, Java is very much like the highly popular C and C++ programming languages used by the most serious programming professionals. This means that most programmers can learn it easily and adopt a lot of existing code. Your organization might already have programmers on staff who can develop Java applications for your Intranet.

Second, Java is much more forgiving than C or C++ so it's more fun to use, and debugging is simplified. That means that novices can pick it up more quickly and experienced C programmers will appreciate its relative ease-of-use. These factors combined will bring millions of Java applets into cyberspace.

NOTE: *Java programs are called applets because they depend in part on code that's embedded into your Web browser. Without that code a Java program would be useless, so they're just called applets instead of applications.*

Sample Java Script

Many popular Java applets are written to receive input from a script file. This means that a lot of people will be able to add Java applets to their site without knowing anything about programming. They'll be able to write a script from scratch, or perhaps to modify a sample script that the programmer included with the applet.

The Website of an earlier Internet book we wrote includes a good example that shows why the script feature is so significant. If you visit the book's home page at **www.marketing-coach.com/mh-guide**, and if you have a Java-compatible browser, you will see an LED display that carries a running message similar to the sign on the side of the Goodyear blimp (see the arrow in Figure 12-1).

This applet's programmer spent five days writing its code, and he was a highly skilled and experienced programmer. On the other hand, one non-programmer was able to get the LED display working on this site in just an hour or so. All that he needed to do was to study the syntax of the script and modify the sample that came with the applet. He added the required HTML applet codes to the Web page by copying and pasting

Figure 12-1

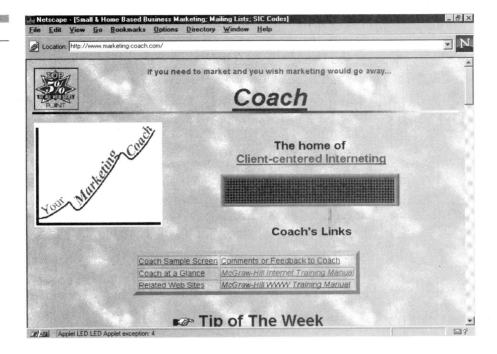

from the sample file. Finally, the new HTML page was uploaded along with the LED applet code and the script file. That's all there was to it.

This small block of HTML codes tells a Java-compatible browser to run the Java code stored on the book's Website. Note the second line of the code that specifies which script file to use. When a visitor loads the book's home Web page, their browser will run the LED applet and display the text as specified in this script (see Fig. 12-2).

Figure 12-2

```
<CENTER>
<applet code="LED/LED.class" width=320 height=60>
<param name=script value="Scripts/coach1.led">
<param name=font value="Fonts/default.font">
<param name=spacewidth value="3">
<param name=bordercolor value="100,130,130">
<param name=border value="3">
</applet>
</CENTER>
```

Of course this script would be worthless without the Java code stored on the site's Web server. But once the code was loaded, it simply needs to be fed the parameters in the script and it creates magic on the screen.

So What?

Think about your audience when you add Java to your site, and be realistic. Someday, Java will run easily on all systems, but today it can strain slower systems and annoy your users. People with PCs based on 486 (or slower) processors might not see the cool show you planned; it might generate more aggravation than "gee whiz" enthusiasm. You might also keep several other considerations in mind.

- Java is not enabled in the 16-bit version of Netscape. This means that most of your visitors with Windows 3.x will not see your little marvel anyway.
- Many visitors will have other non-Java browsers.
- The Java code takes extra time to download for users who access your Intranet across an Internet connection. Will these remote users agree that your Java application was worth the time they had to wait to get it?

Don't misunderstand, we believe that Java will be a major factor in how Intranets revolutionize our lives; just not in the next year or two. Make sure that your use of Java has a higher purpose than making you feel good about your site.

How Your Organization Can Use Java

There are practically no limits to what can be done with Java. Soon you will see an explosion of Java applets on the market that will enable your organization to do almost anything anyone can imagine. The resources listed in Appendix B, "Continuing Education," contain links to a lot of Java-powered sites. Start with these links and keep browsing for ideas on how your organization can use Java to deliver increased value to internal users as well as to visiting members, clients, and customers.

Before Java, the only programming you were likely to encounter on the Web was CGI (Common Gateway Interface) programs that ran on Web servers. You probably have seen CGI in action if you have ever filled in an information form and sent it to the parent company.

But CGI works only as a two-way street. In other words, CGI programs must go back and forth to verify user input. This means that user actions must interact with the Web server, which increases Internet bandwidth demands. A heavily used remote site could cause user delays. Java, on the other hand, can perform data verification tests within the client's browser and will use the server only when the task is ready to send back. This capability will enable your site to provide better service to your visitors, and will also allow your site to handle more traffic.

Banish Programming Forever

If you're sick of reading about all this programming and you don't care which is easier because you have zero interest in learning either one, there are alternatives. You can create interactive brochures and databases on your Intranet without having to learn CGI or Java, thanks to user-friendly applications that let you work in an intuitive environment. Then, when you're done, the applications handle the technical stuff.

Interactive Brochure and Catalog

Made by AMT Learning Solutions, Interactive Brochure lets you easily create interactive multimedia presentations that can work on your Intranet or over the Web. This application is perfect for presenting sales information for your products and services. And a companion product, Interactive Catalog, lets you quickly set up an online sales catalog from which users can order directly. Combine this with a commerce server and you have an online sales outlet!

Now imagine being able to handle all your corporate training over an Intranet! Interactive Brochure has an expanded version that creates interactive training sessions. It includes a testing, scoring, and reporting system that can handle all functions online, sending crucial scoring information to corporate headquarters from any office in the world. It's a perfect way to handle on-going training requirements at all your offices; it lets workers complete their requirements on their own time and in their own time zones!

For more information, contact AMT Learning Solutions at `www.amtcorp.com`. Or e-mail an inquiry to `amtsales@amtcorp.com`.

AskSam

The famous *askSam* is the free-form database that helped U.S. federal prosecutors break open the Iran-Contra case. No human mind or ordinary database had been able to piece together the facts that prosecutors suspected could lead to indictments. But once the information was entered into askSam, the big picture came into focus. A free-form database can deal with information that doesn't fit into traditional database fields.

Now you can use askSam to create an online database that users can interact with from anywhere in the world. You can organize data that users input from the Web, or you can let users search through your database to retrieve information. Sam doesn't care how much you dump in; he'll be able to index it and give you exactly what you want when you want it. It's a perfect solution for archives of e-mail, Usenet newsgroup articles, or just about any kind of information your organization needs to store, index, and distribute via your Intranet. Visit the askSam Web page at `www.asksam.com` for more information (see Fig. 12-3).

CGI isn't dead and will probably be around for years. But Java will quickly replace many of its functions, especially for all the new people

Figure 12-3

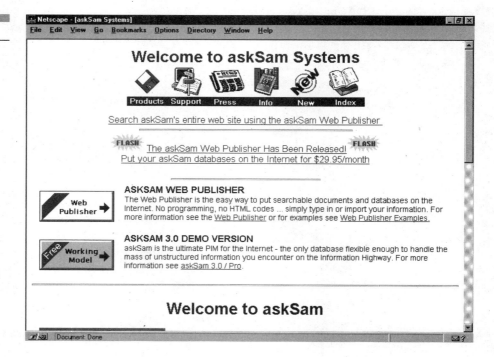

coming into cyberspace who don't know—and don't want to know—anything about CGI.

Here is a list of some Java functions that already are in use.

- Clickable image maps
- User-friendly link buttons
- Active and interactive site navigation help
- Scrolling messages to present hot topics
- Sound and video players that activate automatically
- Automated visitor reply-and-response forms
- Calculators tailored for a specific use
- Spreadsheets that present tailored financial data

JavaScript

JavaScript is a simplified version of Java that you might want to investigate if all this talk of programming is giving you the jitters. You can find a lot of valuable JavaScript examples that you can use without programming knowledge. This isn't the same thing as the use of a script that I demonstrated in an earlier Java example. That was a script that fed parameters to a Java applet, while JavaScript is another programming language.

JavaScript complements Java by bringing the useful properties of Java applets to less-experienced authors. JavaScript is a descendant of smaller, dynamically typed languages such as dBASE. These scripting languages bring programming capability to a broader set of users because of their simpler syntax, specialized built-in functionality, and minimal requirements for object creation.

If you'd like individual offices or divisions within your organization to be able to create interactive Intranet features, research some JavaScript Websites or books. You might be able to accomplish a lot without creating a large training need.

The next feature we'll discuss is something that works well with Java, online audio. Before Java, Web authors needed to create links on Web pages so that visitors could click and download an audio file. After the file was downloaded, it then could be played in an audio player. But Java enables Web authors to automatically play an audio file when the page loads into a Java-compatible browser. For example, you could place a welcome message or a musical fanfare on your Website that visitors would hear automatically when they hit your site. In an Intranet world, automated audio can be used to alert users to crucial news that might otherwise be missed during normal or casual browsing. For example, your organization's Intranet home page could have a short news update each morning that would point out hot spots for the day, thus increasing the number of users who would activate the featured link.

Online Audio

Online audio works by converting sound into digital information and storing that information in audio computer files. These files then can be transferred electronically and can be played on a wide variety of operating systems and computer platforms. You soon will see that sound files come in a lot of different formats, and that each of these formats uses a proprietary compression scheme to reduce the size of the saved sound files they produce. File compression is crucial to the spread of Internet audio, because sound files currently require very large file sizes in relation to the length of the sound clip. Don't be surprised to watch sound files grab 11K of disk space for every second of sound.

The use of online audio is increasing rapidly, especially on Intranets, because the bandwidth demands are much less of a problem than with Internet audio. Unfortunately, no uniform standard for digital audio formats exists yet, though the field is narrowing. The more common types you'll encounter in a Windows environment include:

- wav files (common SoundBlaster-type audio files)
- au files (common Internet audio files)
- ra files (Real Audio files, best for voice only)

Wave Audio

Wave is the native sound format for Microsoft Windows systems. The short musical segments you hear sprucing up your Windows activities are wave files. The wave format is the least efficient of the three listed here, requiring approximately 50 percent larger files than au sound files. It's main advantage lies in the huge number of wave files that are available, including lots of public domain clips. You can buy these in bulk on disk to be included in your Internet or Intranet sites. And, the Internet has audio archives that can be rich sources of sound clips. If you find a wave clip that you want to use, but you'd like to save some disk space and transfer time, you can convert any wave file to the more efficient Sun format, au.

Sun Audio

One of the most popular sound file formats in cyberspace is the au format, also called the *uLaw, NeXT,* or *Sun Audio* format. This format can be used on most of the machines on the Internet that are equipped to play sound. It also produces reasonably small files that consume less bandwidth and disk space than the popular Windows wave format. The au format is a nice balance between audio quality, required transfer time and server space. It definitely has sufficient audio quality for the typical sound clips you might offer, pretty much matching the sound quality of wav files.

Real Audio

Real Audio is the commercial name of a company that developed the ra standard. It is rapidly gaining popularity on the Internet because of its extremely small bandwidth demands. In fact, if you have a good connection and a 28.8-kbits/s modem, ra sound clips can play in real time. We performed a download test while researching this book and, using a 28.8-kbits/s modem, and got a 5.71-s clip in less than 5 s.

Check out the Real Audio Website at **www.realaudio.com** and download the latest version of their ra player (see Fig. 12-4). While you're there, check out their links to other Websites that use Real Audio so you can get some ideas on how to use it yourself.

When you've completed the download you'll need to run the installation. After that you'll be ready for an exercise later in the chapter, in which we'll have you install the default Windows audio player. In that exercise, you can substitute the Real Audio player instead because the steps are almost exactly the same.

Real Audio might not be the best choice for many Intranet sites. Its sound quality is noticeably lower than either wave or au. In fact, many listeners will consider it poor sound quality. If your Intranet supports a lot of remote or telecommuting users who have only modem connections,

Figure 12-4

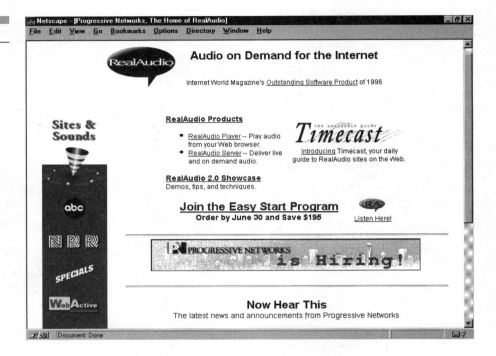

then the Real Audio format could make sense for broadcasting important organizational news.

Netscape Helper Applications

Netscape cannot play sound files by itself. Instead, Netscape hands off the files to configurable "helper" applications, such as the Real Audio player. Netscape needs a helper application for many audio formats. Many players are available, and you can download them via Netscape. Some players are dedicated to playing only a single type of file. Increasingly, however, you will find audio players that can handle a variety of sound files. Whichever you choose, you'll have to install it as a Netscape helper application. And, even if you select a different player for each type of file, their use will be invisible to you once they all are installed in Netscape.

If you don't have an audio player configured, when Netscape encounters an audio file it will ask you what you want it to do with the file. You can use the directory browser to locate an audio player for that file. Once the sound player is installed in Netscape for that type of file, Netscape will handle such files automatically.

Differences in File Formats

If you plan to offer audio on your site, before choosing a file format you should carefully consider your visitors and what you're delivering with the audio files. There are dramatic differences in file sizes and resulting download times. We ran a download comparison test to illustrate the real-life differences. I selected a clip from *Hollywood Online* (profiled later) that offers each of its sound clips in multiple formats.

Bandwidth Comparisons

The clip we used was from a scene in the film *American President*, starring Michael Douglas and Charlie Sheen. The clip is 5.71 s long and begins when Michael Douglas asks, "She didn't say anything about me?" Charlie Sheen responds, "Well, no sir, but I can pass her a note before study hall." Here's a comparison chart of the test.

Format	Size	Download time	Comments
ra	5K	5 s	Choppy, music barely audible, words not clear
au	44K	23 s	Music clear, voices excellent
wav	62K	32 s	Music clear, voices excellent

Mostly likely, your own results would differ. These were clocked on a 133-MHz Pentium with 32 Mbytes RAM, Windows 95, and a 28.8-kbits/s U.S. Robotics Courier modem. The actual connection speed reported by Windows 95 was 21,600 kbits/s, but the actual transfer times are not the point. Look instead at the relative performance of the different formats. Again, if your audio files will be accessed only over a LAN-based Intranet, the download time will not be significant. Your only consideration will be in the server space required.

Other Formats

If you're having trouble finding a player for an Internet audio format, check out the site at **www.geocities.com/Hollywood/1158/ sndutils.html**. If you offer sound, you might link your Web page to this site to help visitors get a sound player. This site also is a good source for non-IBM-compatible players that you might reference for your visitors who don't use Windows.

When you download any file, Netscape compares the file's extension against its list of installed helper applications to see how to handle the file. During that last exercise, you might have noticed that many file extensions are preprogrammed (see Fig. 12-5). For example, files with **htm** or **HTML** extensions are handled by the browser. Files with **ZIP**, **EXE**, or **COM** extensions are handled by the Windows save function. You also will noticed a large number of extensions for which the action is ASK USER. This means that Netscape doesn't know how to handle those files and will ask you what to do if it's asked to download one.

Configuring Netscape to Play Sound

In this next exercise you'll learn how to install a helper application. We've selected the wave format for your exercise because you most likely

Figure 12-5

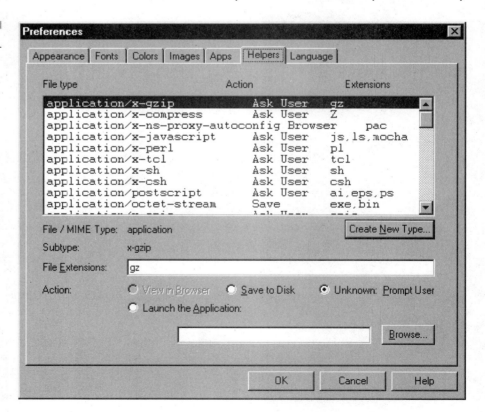

already have the required sound player application on your hard drive, so we'll proceed on that assumption.

Objective: Learn to configure Netscape to play sound files.

❏ Start Netscape.

❏ Click OPTIONS, GENERAL PREFERENCES.

❏ SCROLL DOWN TO audio/x-wav.

❏ Look on this line under ACTION.

If this entry says ASK USER, then finish the exercise. If it already lists a player application, then click CANCEL now.

❏ Click the LAUNCH THE APPLICATION radio button near the bottom.

❏ Click in the text entry window immediately below this button.

❏ Type `c:\windows\mplayer.exe`.

Your installation might be nonstandard and require you to click on BROWSE to search for the `mplayer.exe` application. Also, if you know you have another player on your system that you would rather use, select it instead.

❏ Click OK.

❏ Click OPTIONS, SAVE OPTIONS.

You have just completed a basic helper application installation. We'll do another later, but you can use this dialog box to configure helpers for many other file formats. For example, if you exchange a lot of WordPerfect documents that use the standard WordPerfect file extension of `WPD`, then you can use the same steps above to make Netscape automatically launch WordPerfect if you download a `WPD` file. The same could apply for Word `doc` files, `RTF` files or for Excel spreadsheet files.

Recorded Audio

The use of recorded audio is increasing rapidly in cyberspace. You can expect this growth to accelerate now that Java applets enable Web authors to embed automated sound into Web pages. Whether you automate their playing or not, sound files can be a nice addition to many types of Websites.

You probably are only a few dollars away from having all the equipment you need to record a message and put it on your Website. For example, Windows 95 includes an application with recording capability;

just add a microphone to plug into your sound card and you have a recording studio.

Your PC's sound card has a microphone input jack on it, near the jack into which your speakers are plugged. Inexpensive microphones are now available at all large computer stores and electronics outlets, such as Radio Shack. Make sure your microphone has a $^1/_8$-in. plug and not a standard $^1/_4$-in. plug. Then, assuming you've got a sound card, speakers and a microphone, here's how to record an audio file.

> ***Objective:*** Learn to record using Windows 95.
>
> ❑ Click the START button.
>
> ❑ Click PROGRAMS, ACCESSORIES, MULTIMEDIA, SOUND RECORDER. Get ready with your microphone before the next step.
>
> ❑ Click the red RECORD button.
>
> ❑ Say, "One small step for multimedia, one giant leap for me."
>
> ❑ Click the square STOP button.
>
> ❑ Click the right-arrow PLAY button.
>
> ❑ Click FILE, SAVE to save the file to disk.
>
> ❑ Type `smalstep.wav` and click on SAVE.
>
> ❑ Press ALT+F4 to close the sound recorder.

You now have recorded and saved a wave sound file that you can use on your Intranet or on the Web. If you'd like a more sophisticated recorder, be sure to visit the GoldWave site at `web.cs.mun.ca/~chris3/goldwave` and get its latest version (see Fig. 12-6). Gold-Wave is a full-featured, professional-quality digital sound recorder. It supports many file formats (`.wav`, `.au`, `.iff`, `.voc`, `.snd`, `.mat`, `.aiff`, and raw data) and can convert to or from these formats. It also has all kinds of editing and mixing controls, such as distortion, Doppler, echo, filter, mechanize, offset, pan, volume shaping, invert, resample, and transpose. You can use these effects to modify any sound file, whether you recorded it or not. Be sure you save a backup copy, though, because it's very easy to make a complete mess of a perfectly good sound file.

Downloading Audio

Once you've recorded an audio clip, you might wonder how you get onto your Intranet so that other users can download it and play it. The

Figure 12-6

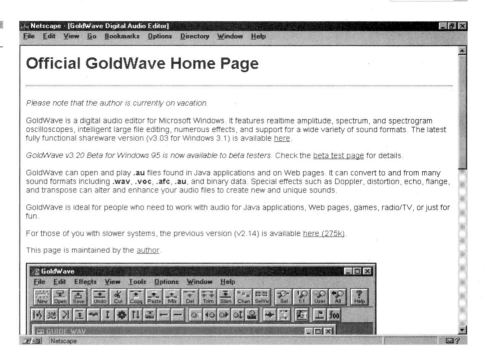

user side is a cinch if their browser is configured to play audio files. Your side also is easy because you reference the audio file with normal HTML codes, as if it were a Web page or a graphic image. Here's a sample of HTML coding that would let visitors play the file you recorded in the last hands-on exercise: `<A HREF="sound/smalstep.wav">My First Clip</A>`.

In addition to adding a link to your Web page, you would need to make a new directory on your server for sound files and transfer the `smalstep.wav` file to that directory. Future visitors to your page would see *My First Clip* as a normal, underlined hyperjump. If they click on it and their Netscape is configured to handle a wave file, the file would download and play automatically. If their Netscape was not configured for wave audio, Netscape would ask what to do with the file. At that point, the visitor could either save your sound file to disk to be played later or point Netscape to an audio player.

To see more examples of online audio clips, visit *Hollywood Online Sound Bites* (see Fig. 12-7) and have a ball. Careful, though! Don't try this at work—it's way too much fun! And, as if this site isn't enough fun by itself, it has links to many other sound sources on the Internet.

Figure 12-7

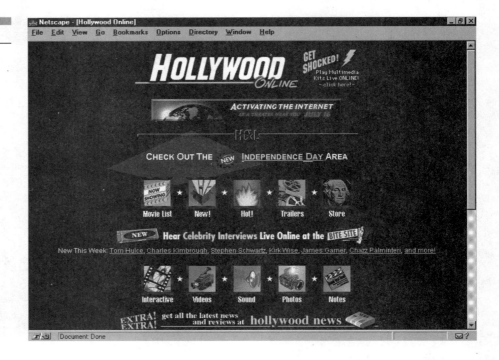

Real-Time Audio

How could we say so much about audio on the Internet without mentioning that you can use your Intranet as a voice telephone? It doesn't exactly fit in here, but voice capability is a related topic and an amazing function.

Just in case you haven't heard already, you can use the Internet as a telephone to talk to anyone in the world without incurring any additional long-distance charges (see Fig. 12-8). Most people simply don't comprehend what's being said (or believe it) the first time they hear about Internet phone service, but it's true. After all, the Internet runs on phone lines that are mostly maintained by MCI and Sprint, who started out in the long-distance business.

Internet phone service has a lot of room for improvement, but if your organization does any international business you might be willing to accept the limitations. It's probably not appropriate for a formal business call but you certainly can use it to exchange quick messages, such as flight arrival times or other travel plans. Then again, this type of information can easily be exchanged via e-mail as well, so you'll have to decide for yourself.

One problem with Internet phone service is that you can't just call someone, or "ring them up." Both parties need the right software, the right hardware, Internet service, and both will have to be online at the same time. If you're "lurking" around, connected to the Internet in the pool of available phone users, then your Internet phone can be called very much like a regular phone.

Another problem with Internet phone service is poor audio quality. You might have to shout and you might be cut off unexpectedly. Overall, though, it's not bad and quality will improve rapidly. You'll have a serious limitation if both parties do not have a *full-duplex* sound card. Full-duplex means that you can talk and listen at the same time. Unfortunately, many popular sound cards have only half-duplex sound. This means that, while you're speaking, the other party can only listen and cannot interrupt. (Actually, that might be a big advantage with some people you know, right?) So, you'll have to signal the end of your turn by saying "Over," just as an airline pilot does when he or she talks to the tower.

To learn how to use the Internet as a phone, check out the *WebPhone* site at **www.netspeak.com**. This site includes Internet phone software and details on using the system (see Fig. 12-9). You can download a free version of WebPhone for test purposes, but it's limited to three-minute

Figure 12-8

calls and permits you to store only a short directory listing. The paid, commercial version removes the limitations and lets you make unlimited calls anywhere in the world. We also recommend *FreeTel* at **www. freetel.com**.

And, you can always do a Yahoo! search for the phrase **Internet phone**. You'll be inundated with listings. The last time we tried it we got 125 hits—see how many you get today!

Online Video

Digital video standards have quickly been adopted by the Internet, and in particular by the World Wide Web. Because video fits so well with the expectations we all have developed for graphic displays in our presentations, you'll see a rapid increase in the use of video in cyberspace. The speed of Intranet transfer rates will make video even more popular on Intranets. Because bandwidth limitations can be eliminated, you might be able to present much of your Intranet content in video format.

Figure 12-9

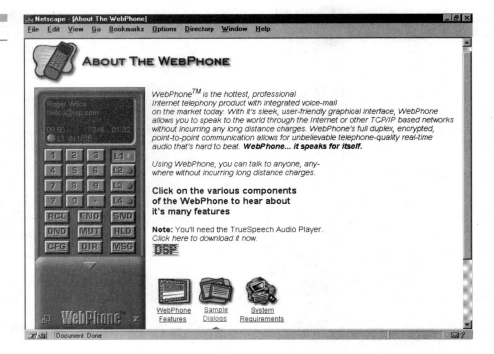

Currently, four common formats for video are available on the Web and on Intranets: MPEG, **mov** files, **avi** files, and **hqx** files. The **hqx** files are for Macintosh computers, so we'll give you an overview and some resources for the other three formats.

MPEG

The MPEG (Moving Pictures Experts Group) is a group of people who meet under the auspices of the ISO (International Standards Organization) to generate standards for the compression of digital video (time-sequenced digital images) and audio. The MPEG conducts approximately four, one-week meetings each year. In between, members work on topics discussed at the meetings.

Specifically, the MPEG defines a compression standard that reduces the storage space required for digital video. The compression standard ensures that we all can use each other's digital video files, much as the videocassette standards that enable us to play videotapes on different players. The compression algorithms, however, are not defined. That's left to individual vendors, which is where proprietary advantage is obtained even though MPEG is a publicly available, international standard.

The MPEG video files that are used on the Internet have a file extension of either **.MPEG** or **.MPG**. The MPEG core technology used in these files includes many different patents from different companies and individuals worldwide. Since the MPEG committee sets only the technical standards without dealing with patents and intellectual property issues, there are differences in the performance of video files from one vendor to the next, even though they might use the same file extension.

QuickTime

QuickTime video files sometimes have a file extension of **qt**, but most often you'll see the **mov** extension. Some video sources will give you a choice of formats. A good example, again, is Hollywood Online that we used for the sound sources (see Fig. 12-10). You'll find a wide assortment of video clips there as well. The Windows file formats listed there are **avi** and **mov**, so you'll need a QuickTime video player for the **mov** files.

The QuickTime helper application installs exactly the same way as the MPEG player that we use in the next exercise. So, all you need to play **mov** files is a QuickTime (QTVR) player. To get one, visit the *Sunvalley*

Figure 12-10

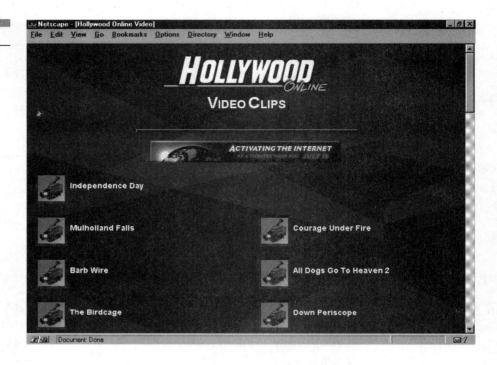

Software site at **www.kwanza.com/~embleton/service.html** (see Fig. 12-11) and click on the link for downloads to get the Apple Quick-Time player, then download it and install it. And don't worry about the "Apple" in there; it also comes in a Windows variety.

After the QuickTime files are on your system, complete the hands-on exercise listed under the MPEG heading below, but change it for Quick-Time. The QuickTime helper application will be installed into Netscape under the **video/quicktime** listing.

If you're interested in more information about digital multimedia files, check out the following. From it you can learn more details, find more sources, and keep up with the latest industry changes, such as player upgrades. If you've seen enough technical details for now, skip ahead to learn how to configure Netscape to play video.

Multimedia File Formats on the Web

For even more coverage on these topics, check out the Website at **ac.dal.ca/~dong/contents.html**, maintained by Allison

Figure 12-11

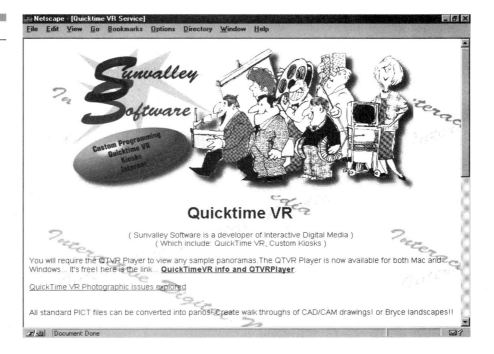

Zhang (see Fig. 12-12). First we want to thank Allison for helping with some of the information in this chapter. Her home page is entitled *Multimedia File Formats on the Internet: A Beginner's Guide for PC Users.* Check out the table of contents to see all the topics offered. She also maintains a helpful FAQs file that can be a ready reference source as you learn Web multimedia.

Configuring Netscape to Play Video

If your installation of Netscape does not include support for playing videos, you can use this hands-on exercise to show you how to configure Netscape to use an MPEG player. If you don't already have one on your system, check out "Point Your Visitors to a Video Source" below for sites from which you can download a file that will install the latest version of an MPEG player application on your system. Once the application is installed, you can complete this exercise.

Objective: Learn to configure Netscape to use an MPEG player.

❑ Start Netscape.

Figure 12-12

- ❏ Click OPTIONS, GENERAL PREFERENCES.
- ❏ Click the HELPER tab.
- ❏ Scroll down to VIDEO/MPEG.
- ❏ Click LAUNCH THE APPLICATION.
- ❏ Click BROWSE and locate your MPEG player.
- ❏ Click OK.
- ❏ Click OPTIONS, SAVE OPTIONS.

Point Your Visitors to a Video Source

If you include a video clip on your Website, be sure to give obvious instructions to your visitors on how to obtain and install a video player. Even on your Intranet, you can't be certain that every user will have access to a video player. You probably can, however, get your organization to obtain permission from one of the video player vendors to distribute its players over your Intranet. If you can do that you won't need to reference the appropriate URLs on your Web pages. Instead, you'll be able to point Intranet visitors to an on-site server that contains the files they'll need.

But you might need to link to an external source on your Internet Web pages. And, you'll need to visit these sites anyway to obtain local distribution rights. The two sources for the MPEG player are

```
ftp.cic.net/pub/Software/pc/www/viewer/mpegw32h.zip
ftp.ncsa.uiuc.edu/Web/Mosaic/Windows/viewers/mpegw32h.zip
```

If you want to view MPEG video you'll need an MPEG player on your system, so you can use Netscape now to get it from one of these sources. The file is about 640 kbytes in size, so plan for the download time.

Video Conferencing

The Internet is exploding with other uses for real-time video technology. Already, you can conduct video conferencing and check weather and traffic. In the 1980s, the fax machine brought about a great business revolution, but the 1990s will be the decade of video conferencing. By the end of this decade it will be a common business tool.

In fact, video conferencing will be a common household appliance before long. Just imagine Thanksgiving dinner in front of a large, wall-mounted, flat-screen monitor. You'll be able to enjoy a family meal with relatives and friends from all over the country—all over the world, actually. You'll be able to do everything but pass the cranberry sauce. And don't be surprised if the next decade brings us a technical solution for that limitation. How long until we get 3-D e-mail?

For a taste of video conferencing, check out the Cornell University *Cu-See-Me* project (see Fig. 12-13). They've done a lot of development work on Internet video and they're sharing their work on the Website at **cu-seeme.cornell.edu**. What you'll see there will appear a little primitive by the standards of cable television, but the key to using video conferencing lies in seeing the possibilities demonstrated at this site.

Real-Time Video

Many major cities around the world now have multiple, live-action weather cameras linked to the Internet. There's something powerful—

Figure 12-13

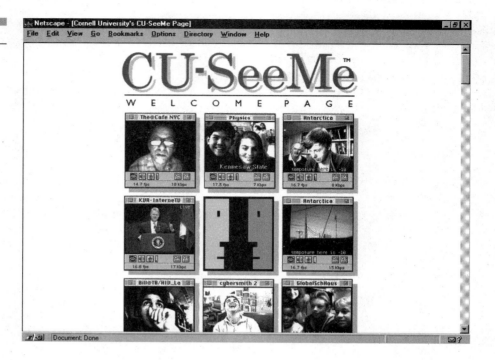

almost charismatic—about being able to see a live-action shot of a city anywhere in the world. We believe you'll find it to be mind-broadening, graphic evidence that we all are one people all over this planet.

Online camera images sap a lot of Internet bandwidth, and even then they deliver only some small, fuzzy pictures. And, they update only once every minute or two. But remember the little black-and-white television sets of the 1950s and consider the pace at which electronic advancements are racing into our future. Before long you'll be able to adorn your office wall with a real-time, wall-sized, stereo-sound shot of Niagara Falls (see Fig. 12-14). For more scenic views from around the United States, check out the Weather Cam site at `cirrus.sprl.umich.edu/wxnet/wxcam.html` and pick your favorite spot.

Erol's Internet and Computers, the largest Internet service provider in the Washington metro area, pioneered the online traffic cam there. Before venturing into traffic, Washington-area drivers can pull up shots from real-time cameras located all over the region (see Fig. 12-15). Won't that be nice for when we all have Internet service in our cars? Of course, such detailed, up-to-the-minute information might *cause* more *new* traffic jams than it alleviates, but at least you could send e-mail to flame that turkey in front of you!

Figure 12-14

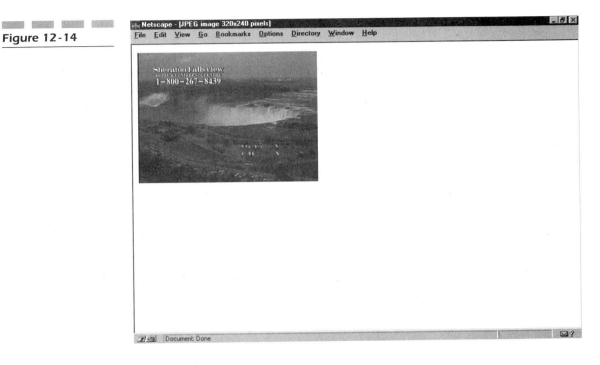

Figure 12-15

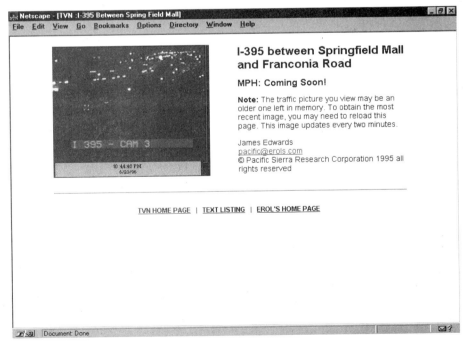

What's next after the traffic cam? Virtual reality, which could enable you to stay at home and make yourself *think* you were out driving in rush hour! Or, you could be "virtually" doing just about anything else you can imagine, such as working at home or visiting branch offices or remote divisions within your organization. Plant managers will be able to track production from anywhere in the world via your Intranet.

Virtual Reality

The next generation of Intel microprocessors, the Pentium Pro, includes built-in support for Websites that use the Virtual Reality Markup Language (VRML). To learn more about it, visit the Website at `www.intel` `.com/procs/ppro/intro/index.htm` (see Fig. 12-16). This site features some VRML tours of Pentium Pro applications. You won't be able to view these tours in 3-D virtual reality without a Live3D player, which you can download at `www.netscape.com/comprod/products/` `navigator/live3d/index.html`. Take good notes when you get to this page, because it also lists the "coolest VRML worlds on the Web."

Figure 12-16

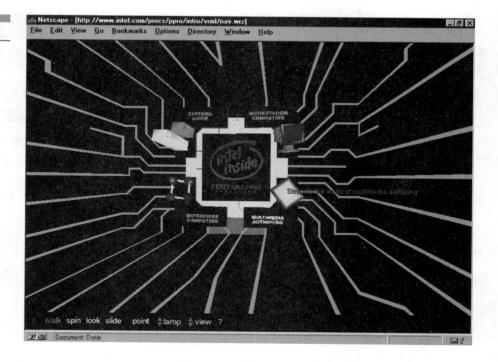

But virtual reality definitely is only *future* cyberspace reality for Internet because of heavy bandwidth demands and the small number of users who have the required PC power. Over local portions of your Intranet, however, you can expect virtual reality sites to work well. Nonetheless, VRML programming is not likely to be for the average office HTML author, even with all the bandwidth in the world, so expect to see VRML only where its use truly makes sense. If you think VRML might be for you, though, you can visit the Website of a good book on VRML at `www.mcp.com/general/news7/vrml2.HTML`.

Of course, VRML will make enormous sense for some uses. For example, we asked Orhan Onaran, of Erol's Internet and Computers, about future uses for VRML. His organization has been discussing how it can help bring virtual reality shopping into the homes of its subscribers. Don't be surprised to soon be able to stroll through a grocery store on-screen, click on the items you want, and have them delivered to your door before you could have fought the traffic and waited in line to get them yourself. You could provide a similar service for your customers. Or you could allow employees, who might use your Intranet all over the world, to examine closely a new product and even experience using it.

But at first you're going to see a lot of "gee whiz" virtual reality gimmicks designed to show off the technology. That's normal, though. After all, there was a time when the Wright Brothers flew down city streets in Washington, D.C. just to show off their new technology. After the "Wright Brother Effect" wears off, virtual reality will still be the best thing that happened to our overcrowded, time-pressed society since the airplane. And Intranet should lead its advance.

APPENDIX A

Electronic Copyrights

Here's an overview of the rapidly changing world of cyberspace copyright law. It will help you understand that your company's copyrighted material, once it's in cyberspace, can be instantly available worldwide and can be copied and pasted by anyone via a couple of mouse clicks. An electronic format doesn't change your legal rights, but how will you enforce them if you find a violation?

It also will help you consider the rights you might be violating when you click your own mouse. Just because information has been translated to an electronic format doesn't mean it's public domain. Do you know who put it there and how they got it? We'll give you some expert guidance on how to protect yourself, and how to honor those people whose work merits reward.

Top 10 Copyright Myths

Here is a response to common myths about copyrights as applied to the Internet. It was created by Brad Templeton, the publisher for ClariNet Communications Corporation's news service, and it covers issues related to e-mail, news, research, and Usenet posting. ClariNet, founded in 1989, is the Internet's first and largest electronic newspaper.

Please note that, while most of the principles covered here are universal in Berne copyright signatory nations, some are derived from Canadian and U.S. law. Brad created this document to clear up some common misconceptions about intellectual property law with respect to properties often seen on the Internet. It is not intended to be a complete treatise on all the nuances of the subject.

Here begins the text of *Brad's 10 Big Copyright Myths*, followed by a summary of the main points. Be sure to check out Appendix B, "Continuing Education," in which we point you to some other Internet sources on copyright issues.

NOTE: *Do not e-mail Brad Templeton for legal advice! Use other resources or consult a lawyer. You can, however, check out Brad's personal Web page at ClariNet, at www.clari.net/brad (see Fig. A-1).*

1. If it doesn't have a copyright notice it's not copyrighted.

This was true in the past, but today almost all major nations follow the Berne copyright convention. For example, in the United States, almost everything created privately and originally after April 1, 1989 is copyrighted and protected whether it has a notice or not. The default you should assume for other people's works is that they are copyrighted and might not be copied unless you *know* otherwise. There are some old works that lost protection without notice, but frankly you should not risk it unless you know for sure.

It is true that a notice strengthens the protection, by warning people, and by allowing one to get more and different damages, but it is not necessary. If it looks copyrighted, you should assume it is.

Figure A-1

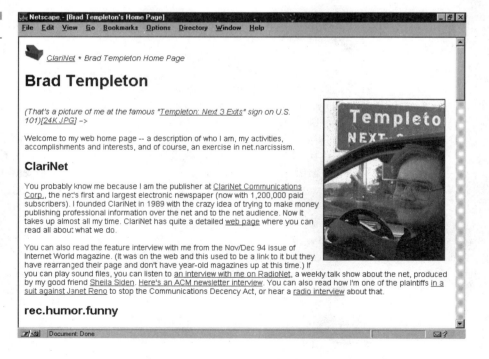

This applies to pictures, too. You may not scan pictures from magazines and post them to the Internet, and if you come upon something unknown, you shouldn't post that either.

The correct form for a copyright notice is:

"Copyright (dates) by (copyright holder)."

You can use the copyright symbol instead of the word "Copyright," but (C) has never been given legal force. The phrase "All Rights Reserved" used to be required in some nations but is now not needed.

2. If I don't charge for it it's not a violation.

Absolutely false. Whether you charge can affect the damages awarded in court, but that's essentially the only difference. It's still a violation if you give it away—and there can still be heavy damages if you hurt the commercial value of a protected property.

3. If it's posted to Usenet it's in the public domain.

False. Nothing is in the public domain anymore unless the owner explicitly puts it in the public domain. Explicitly, as in you have a note from the copyright holder stating, "I grant this to the public domain." If not those exact words, then words very much like them.

Some argue that posting to the Usenet implicitly grants permission to everybody to copy the posting within fairly wide bounds, and others feel that Usenet is an automatic store-and-forward network wherein all the thousands of copies made are done at the command (rather than at the consent) of the poster. This is a matter of some debate, but even if the former is true (and in this writer's opinion we should all pray it isn't true) it simply would suggest posters are implicitly granting permissions "for the sort of copying one might expect when one posts to Usenet" and in no case is this a placement of material into the public domain. Furthermore, it is very difficult for an implicit licence to supersede an explicitly stated licence of which the copier was aware.

Note that all this assumes that the poster had the right to post the item in the first place. If the poster didn't, then all the copies are pirate and no implied licence or theoretical reduction of the copyright can take place.

Copyrights can expire after a long time, putting something into the public domain, and there are some fine points on this issue regarding older copyright law versions. However, none of this applies to an original article posted to Usenet.

Note that granting something to the public domain (PD) is a complete abandonment of all rights. You can't make something "PD for non-commercial use." If your work is PD, other people can even modify one byte and put their name on it.

4. My posting was just fair use.

The "fair use" exemption to copyright law was created to allow things such as commentary, parody, news reporting, research, and education about copyrighted works without the permission of the author. Intent and damage to the commercial value of the work are important considerations. Are you reproducing an article from the *New York Times* because you needed to in order to criticize the quality of the *New York Times*, or because you couldn't find time to write your own story, or didn't want your readers to have to pay to log onto the online services with the story or buy a copy of the paper? The first probably is fair use; the others are not.

Fair use is almost always a short excerpt and almost always attributed. (One should not use more of the work than is necessary to make the commentary.) It should not harm the commercial value of the work—in the sense of people no longer needing to buy it (which is another reason why reproduction of the entire work generally is forbidden.)

Note that most inclusion of text in Usenet follow-ups is for commentary and reply, and it doesn't damage the commercial value of the original posting (if it has any) and as such it is fair use. Fair use isn't an exact doctrine, either. The court decides if the right to comment overrides the copyright on an individual basis in each case.

There have been cases that go beyond the bounds of what's been covered here, but in general they don't apply to the typical Internet misclaim of fair use. It's a risky defense to attempt.

5. If you don't defend your copyright you lose it.

False. Copyright is effectively never lost these days, unless explicitly given away. You might be thinking of trade marks, which can be weakened or lost if not defended.

6. Somebody has that name copyrighted.

You can't copyright a name or anything short like a name. Titles usually don't qualify, but you could not write a song entitled: "Everybody's got something to hide except for me and my monkey." (J. Lennon/ P. McCartney)

You can't copyright words but you can trademark them, generally by using them to refer to your brand of a generic type of product or service. Like an "Apple" computer. Apple Computer "owns" that word applied to computers, even though it is also an ordinary word. Apple Records owns it when applied to music. Neither owns the word on its own, only in context, and owning a mark doesn't mean complete control — see a more detailed treatise on this law for details.

You can't use somebody else's trademark in a way that would unfairly hurt the value of the mark, or in a way that might make people confuse you with the real owner of the mark, or which might allow you to profit from the mark's good name. For example, if I were giving advice on music videos, I would be very wary of trying to label my works with a name like "MTV."

7. They can't get me; defendants in court have powerful rights.

Copyright law is mostly civil law. If you violate a copyright you usually would get sued, not charged with a crime. "Innocent until proven guilty" is a principle of criminal law, as is "proof beyond a reasonable doubt." In copyright suits, these don't apply the same way or at all. It's mostly which side and set of evidence the judge or jury accepts or believes more, though the rules vary based on the type of infringement. In civil cases you can even be made to testify against your own interests.

8. Copyright violation isn't a crime.

Actually, recently in the United States, commercial copyright violation involving more than 10 copies and value of more $2500 was made a felony. So use caution. (At least you get the protections of criminal law.) On the other hand, don't think you're going to get people thrown in jail for posting your e-mail. The courts have much better things to do than that. This is a fairly new, untested statute.

9. It doesn't hurt anybody; in fact, it's free advertising.

It's up to the owner to decide if they want the free ads or not. If they want them, they will be sure to contact you. Don't rationalize whether it hurts the owner or not, ask them. Usually that's not too hard to do. Time past, ClariNet published the very funny Dave Barry column to a large and appreciative Usenet audience for a fee, but some person didn't ask and forwarded it to a mailing list, got caught, and the newspaper chain that employs Dave Barry pulled the column from the Internet. Even if you can't think of how the author or owner gets hurt, think about the fact that piracy on the Internet hurts everybody who wants a chance to use this wonderful new technology to do more than read other people's flamewars.

10. They e-mailed me a copy, so I can use it.

To have a copy is not to have the copyright. All the e-mail you write is copyrighted. However, e-mail is not, unless previously agreed, secret. So you can certainly report on what e-mail you are sent, and reveal what it says. You can even quote parts of it to demonstrate. Frankly, somebody who sues over an ordinary message might well get no damages, because the message has no commercial value, but if you want to stay strictly within the law you should seek permission.

On the other hand, don't go nuts if somebody posts your e-mail. If it was an ordinary, non-secret personal letter of minimal commercial value with no copyright notice (like 99.9% of all e-mail), you probably won't get any damages if you sue.

In Summary

Almost everything written today is copyrighted the moment it's written, and no copyright notice is required.

Copyright is still violated whether you charged money or not, though damages usually increase if you charge money.

Postings to the Internet are not granted to the public domain; postings don't grant you any permission to do further copying except perhaps the sort of copying the poster might have expected in the ordinary flow of the Internet.

Fair use is a complex doctrine meant to allow certain valuable social purposes. Ask yourself why you are republishing what you are posting, and why you didn't rewrite it in your own words.

Copyright is not lost because you don't defend it; that's a concept from trademark law. The ownership of names is also from trademark law, so don't say somebody has a name copyrighted.

Copyright law is mostly civil law, wherein the special rights of criminal defendants you hear so much about don't apply. Watch out, however, as new laws are moving copyright violation into the criminal realm.

Don't rationalize that you are helping the copyright holder; the Internet has made it easier that ever to secure permission.

Posting e-mail is technically a violation, but revealing facts from e-mail isn't, and for almost all typical e-mail, nobody could wring any damages from you for posting it.

APPENDIX B

Continuing Education

O'Reilly Associates

> http://website.ora.com

O'Reilly Associates has emerged as a powerhouse of technology on the Internet. They have published a library of more than 80 excellent technical reference guides that delve into details far more deeply that we have in this book. Mainstream users might even find the topics covered in this site to be too technical, but if you are performing or managing the hands-on work involved in publishing your organization's Website you absolutely *must* place O'Reilly's URL on your Bookmark List.

Random Tips and Hints on Constructing HTML Pages

> http://www.nd.edu/PageCreation/TipsAndHints.html

Here's a Notre Dame University site that gives tips and hints on constructing HTML documents (see Fig. B-1). Be sure to check out the *Clickable Graphics* tutorial that gives you a clickable graphic map demonstration/tutorial. This site is not an encyclopedic presentation on creating HTML documents, and it admits being "Mac-centric" on some points, but it does address a number of issues that you could encounter frequently. Bookmark this URL, because this Website is also a good place to track HTML changes as well as other changes in Web technology.

Jeff Mallett's HTML Authoring Page

> http://www.cruzio.com/~tao/html.html

Here's an online guide to publishing in HTML by Internet guru Jeff Mallet. Click on any one of these headings to jump to fact-filled text

291

Figure B-1

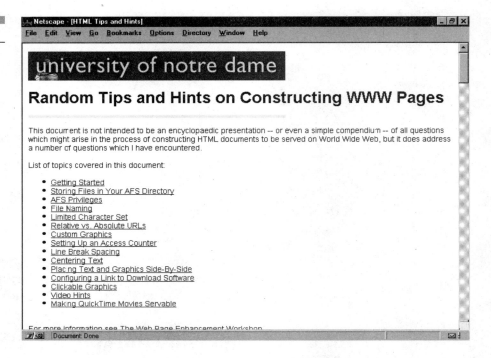

that can help you get started with your HTML pages: Authoring HTML, Web Authoring, Authoring CGI Scripts, Java, and Authorization.

Self-Taught HTML Publishing

```
http://www.lne.com/Web/Books/HTML
```

This is the home page for the books *Teach Yourself Web Publishing with HTML in a Week* and *Teach Yourself More Web Publishing with HTML in a Week*, both by Laura Lemay. These books describe how to write, design, and publish information on the World Wide Web. In addition to describing the HTML language itself, they provide extensive information on using images, sounds, video, interactivity, gateway programs (CGI), forms, and image maps. Through the use of dozens of real-life examples and actual HTML source code, the books help you learn the technical details of writing Web pages. They also teach you how to communicate information effectively through the Web.

The World Wide Web Handbook

```
http://www.ucc.ie/~pflynn/books/wwwbook.html
```

This is a Website for the book, *The World Wide Web Handbook: An HTML Guide for Users, Authors and Publishers* by Peter Flynn, published by International Thomson Computer Press. It profiles the book, including its table of contents, and includes a downloadable version of the *HTML Reference Card* included with the printed edition of the book.

HTML Specification 3.0

```
http://www.w3.org/hypertext/WWW/MarkUp/MarkUp.html
```

Here's a link to the table of contents for the complete HTML 3.0 specification online manual. This is not a user-friendly guide to HTML, but it is a highly detailed reference source about all aspects of HTML, including its development and specifications. HTML 3.0 has been designed to be created in a variety of different ways. It is simple enough to type manually and can be authored using WYSIWYG editors for HTML, or it can be generated via export filters from common word processing formats or other SGML applications.

Fill-Out Forms Overview

```
http://www.ncsa.uiuc.edu/SDG/Software/Mosaic/Docs/fill-out-forms/
overview.html
```

This site focuses on creating fill-out forms for your Web pages. One of its most valuable features is a listing of 13 forms done in HTML (at last count) that you can use as examples. They range in complexity from ludicrously simple to extremely advanced.

Computer Graphics Virtual Library

```
http://www.dataspace.com/WWW/vlib/comp-graphics.html
```

This is a dazzling array of sources for graphics that you can use in publishing your HTML documents. You could spend all day at this site alone. Unfortunately, this site, which offers countless graphic images to download, can be annoying during off-peak hours and impossibly slow during peak hours. Keep this URL, though, for the day that soon will come when you have more bandwidth than you know what to do with.

Graphics Viewers, Editors, Utilities, and Information

```
http://www.w3.org/pub/WWW/Graphics
```

This is the World Wide Web Consortium's collection of links to graphics shareware, demos, and information files available over the Internet. You'll find in-depth FAQs files for several major graphics formats, as well as recently posted messages on graphics formats and an online archive of past messages. They also include links that can guide you to Usenet newsgroups that discuss different graphics formats and related topics. Links to applications are accompanied by a designation for each particular platform: Windows, MS-DOS, UNIX, and Macintosh.

Yahoo! GIF Files

```
http://www.yahoo.com/Computers_and_Internet/Software/Data_Formats
/GIF
```

Yahoo! has an entire category for GIF graphics. Above is the direct URL for the page. Or, once you're in Yahoo! you can step manually through the categories: Computers and Internet, Software, Data Formats, and GIF. This page probably includes more on GIF than you'll ever need to know. GIF licensing has been a mess for years, but if you're a GIF graphics developer you can check here to make sure you're up to speed on the latest word on licensing the GIF technology.

Adobe

```
http://www.adobe.com
```

Adobe probably offers the widest, most powerful selection of Internet graphic tools of any software vendor. In addition to the graphics applications they have publishing applications too, including a Web publishing application, called *SiteMill*, that gives you drag-and-drop HTML authoring. Be sure to hit the link entitled `Elsewhere` to discover a rich resource of other graphics links on the Web. This includes not only other Websites but newsgroups and mailing lists to which you will want to subscribe.

Usenet Graphic FAQs Files

```
http://www.cis.ohio-state.edu/hypertext/faq/bngusenet/comp/graphics/
top.html
```

Now that's a long URL, but the site itself is equally long on content. This could be a primary contact point for you for graphics information, answers, and updates. If you've been elected as your organization's computer graphics expert you should put this URL on your bookmark list, because eventually you will need something listed on this page.

Scanning Graphics

```
http://www.curtin.edu.au/curtin/dept/cc/docs/scan/graphics
```

This Web page is sponsored by the Curtin University of Technology, where they use Macintosh computers for the lessons (see Fig. B-2). The tips here, however, can be used for help on scanning files on any computer or in any format that you desire.

Web Graphics Sources

```
http://redtape.uchicago.edu/users/mdmendoz/art.html
```

This page says it best itself, "Have you ever needed a picture of an armadillo but didn't know just where to start looking for it? Well, hopefully this page will contain some help for you. From clipart to fonts to graphics, the links below will connect you to a wealth of art and graphics

Figure B-2

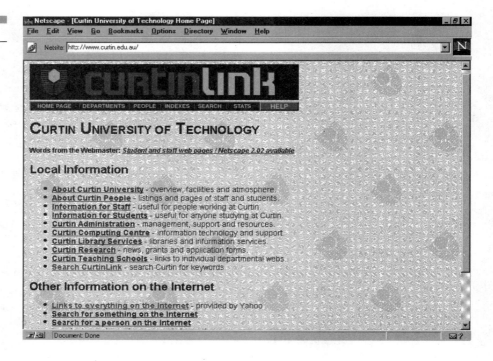

resources. Have fun!" This page is a perfect bookmark candidate for anyone who needs to locate HTML graphic images. At least start here, because many of the pages listed here will have other links and you can always return for that armadillo.

Michael Sullivan's Scanning Tips

```
http://www.hsdesign.com/scanning
```

We've repeated this URL in case you missed it in Chap. 11, so it will be included in the book's online version of these references. This outstanding site is a "must see" for anyone who will be scanning Web documents; bookmark it now.

Scanning FAQs

```
http://www.infomedia.net/scan
```

This page contains a wealth of scanning FAQs, presented by Jeff Bone, formerly Electronic Media Coordinator, University of Alabama at Birmingham, School of Medicine; and more recently founder and president of Infomedia, Inc., a top-flight, information systems integration and development company, serving the Southeast. To give you easy access, the topics on scanning artwork and photographs have been broken down into four primary categories: line art, halftones, greyscale, and color. In addition to these tips you also can read about tricky, yet very important, resolutions issues and copyright issues. If you don't yet own a scanner, be sure to check out the "Scanner Roundup" here before you buy.

Hooked on Java

    http://java.sun.com/hooked

This is the home page for the book *Hooked on Java* (see Fig. B-3). You'll find supplements to the book, including bug reports, fixes, and new applets that are not included on the book's CD-ROM disk. If you don't already have the book, this site is an excellent source for Java samples. And even if you do have it, you can find other Java resources here as well as stay in touch with the latest developments from the Java team at Sun.

Gamelan Java Applet Collection

    http://www.gamelan.com

Here's a vast array of Java examples, instructions, references, sources, code, and applets. It's a very well-done site that gives you easy access to its resources by using the Netscape frames feature. It's a user-friendly site and is the best I've seen for Java applets. The authors also maintain a parallel site for JavaScript at `www.gamelan.com/Gamelan.javascript.html`.

Belle Systems Java Resource

    http://www.belle.dk

Figure B-3

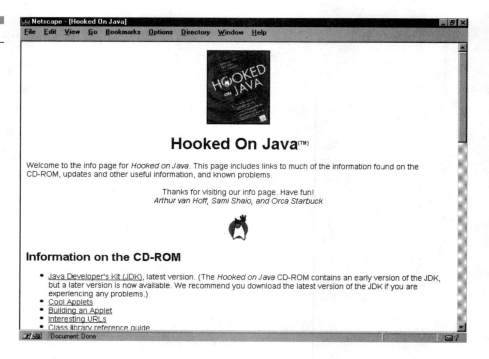

Here's Bjarne Jensen's Java home page in Denmark (see Fig. B-4). Bjarne maintains a well-tested list of Java links that should guide you to some sites that will give you a good start with Java. This site shows off a lot of the possibilities of the Net, such as extensive use of the HTML language, Java Prestel emulator, Java Telnet emulator, and links (including Java, magazines, graphics, HTML, and even OS/2 and ISDN). These features, plus his big joke collection, add up to several pages that you should see for yourself.

Netscape JavaScript

```
http://www.netscape.com/comprod/products/navigator/version_2.0/
script/index.html
```

Netscape itself has a nifty Website on JavaScript. It includes examples, JavaScript resources, sample programming code, an authoring guide, and some good technical overviews of both Java and JavaScript. Especially valuable is a section that directly compares the features of the two.

Java Newsgroup

```
omp.lang.java
```

Newsgroups are not a good source for reference material. You might, however, be able to use this one to get an answer to a specific question. And if you hear about any rumors of new Java developments, you could start checking this newsgroup regularly to follow the discussions.

Teach Yourself Java in 21 Days

```
http://www.lne.com:80/Web/Books/Java
```

If you're interested in learning more about working with Java, *Teach Yourself Java in 21 Days* is the first complete hands-on tutorial guide for working with the Java language and class libraries to create applets for Web pages and full-fledged applications. *Teach Yourself Java* covers the

Figure B-4

Beta and 1.0 Java API (as supported by Netscape 2.0), and it contains complete information about most aspects of Java development, including the language itself, the Abstract Window Toolkit class libraries, sounds and animation techniques, and technical details about packages, interfaces, and the Java virtual machine. It comes with a CD-ROM that includes the complete Java development release for UNIX and Windows NT/95 platforms, plus all the examples from the book.

Hollywood Online

```
http://www.hollywood.com/movies/video.html
```

This site is a lot of fun—we could hardly stay focused on researching this book. Its huge collection of photos, sound bites, and video clips come from the latest Hollywood hit movies and you'll hardly find a richer source for photos, sound, and videos. The photos are available in GIF and JPEG. Sound is available in four formats: au, wav, ra, and Macintosh. Videos are available in two formats: mov and avi. This site is a preview of what the Web one day will bring us: full-length, online videos, with instant access. It's a primitive preview, that's for sure, but the Web could move way past this in but a few years. Remember this URL because one day it might replace your Blockbuster card.

Earchives

```
http://www.geocities.com/Hollywood/1158/earchive.html
```

The audio clips on this site are taken from popular movies and television shows (see Fig. B-5). All files are in **.WAV** format. Most were recorded at 11 kHz mono, but all files have been run through digital reprocessing to enhance quality. Use these files to attach your favorite sounds or sayings to Windows events, objects, or dialog boxes, using sound utilities such as Icon Hear-It or the Windows Sound System. Of course you'll need to consider copyright issues before offering these on your Website. The collection increases constantly, so check back often and enjoy!

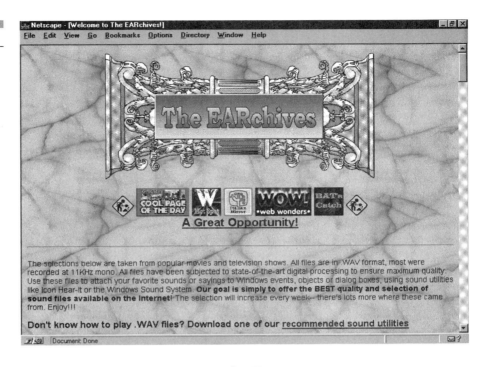

Brad Cox on Electronic Property

http://www.virtualschool.edu/mon/ElectronicProperty.html

Brad Cox is a professor at George Mason University in Fairfax, Virginia. He's the author of *Superdistribution: Objects as Property on the Electronic Frontier,* an in-depth study of the problems of product distribution in the electronic age (see Fig. B-6). On the Web home page listed here, Brad covers four different aspects of our cyberspace world: Electronic Commerce, Electronic Money, Electronic Goods, and Electronic Property.

United States Copyright Office Automatic Information Service

gopher://marvel.loc.gov/11/copyright

This is an actual connection to a directory listing within the U.S. copyright office in Washington, D.C. Begin by clicking on the first document

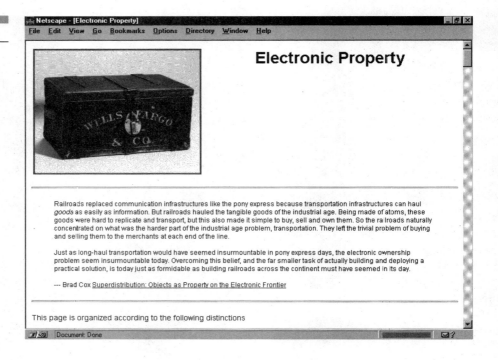

on the list, entitled, *Introduction to the Copyright Office*. After reading it, return to the first page and click on any of the directory folders that you need to access.

The United States Patent and Trademark Office (USPTO)

```
http://www.uspto.gov
```

The USPTO provides a Web page (see Fig. B-7) entitled *Basic Facts About Registering A Trademark*. Topics include securing trademark rights, submitting applications, who may apply, how to search for conflicting, previously registered trademarks, and rules for using (tm), (SM), and "circled R" symbols. Some of the information here can help your organization sort out the relationships (or lack thereof) between Internet domain names and registered trademarks.

Cornell University

ttp://www.law.cornell.edu/topics/copyright.html

This is a comprehensive Web page with hypertext links to just about every aspect of intellectual property law you could ask about. It includes a hypertext version of U.S. copyright law from the Legal Information Institute (LII), and a hypertext version of the Berne international copyright convention.

Copyright Clearance Center Online

http://www.openmarket.com/copyright

This is the online version of the Copyright Clearance Center, a nonprofit organization that provides collective copyright licensing services. They help ease permissions burdens and consolidate payments rights for organizations of all sizes and types.

Figure B-7

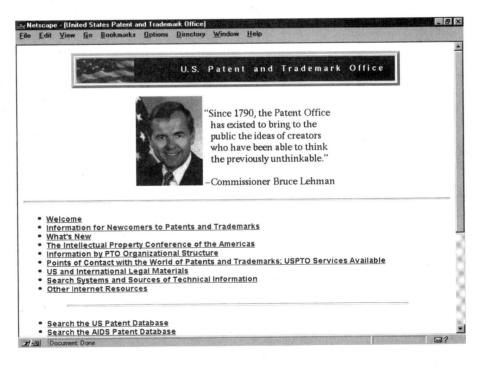

Ohio State

```
http://www.cis.ohio-state.edu/hypertext/faq/usenet/Copyright-FAQ/
top.html
```

A detailed listing of copyright Frequently Asked Questions (FAQ) covering many issues, including compilation copyright, the intricacies of fair use, and international copyright issues.

Electronic Freedom Frontier's Intellectual Property Law Primer

```
http://www.eff.org/pub/CAF/law/ip-primer
```

This primer was written by J. Diane Brinson and Mark F. Radcliffe to help you understand intellectual property law issues as they apply to the development and distribution of multimedia works. The information was derived from the *Multimedia Law Handbook* (Ladera Press, 340 pages, 1-800-523-3721).

GLOSSARY

anonymous FTP Using the FTP function of the Internet anonymously by not logging in with an actual secret login ID and password. Often permitted by large, host computers who are willing to share openly some of their files with outside users, who otherwise would not be able to log in.

Archie An ancient Internet search tool, not used much since way back in the good old days of 1994. It's an archive of filenames maintained at Internet FTP sites. Don't pine its passing; you didn't miss anything. The Web is much more fun.

bandwidth The transmission capacity of the lines that carry the Internet's electronic traffic. Historically, line capacity has imposed severe limitations on the ability of the Internet to deliver all that we are demanding of it, but fiber-optic cables will ensure that bandwidth soon will be essentially limitless and free.

browser Software that enables users to browse through the cyberspace of the World Wide Web. Netscape is the primary Internet browser today.

ClariNet A commercial news service that provides tailored news reports via the Internet. You can access ClariNet news within Usenet newsgroups. There is a whole series of them, dedicated to a wide range of broad topics. In general, you can find them on news servers at `clari.*`.

client/server Computer technology that separates computers and their users into two categories, clients and servers. When you want information from a computer on the Internet, you are a client. The computer that delivers the information is the server. A server stores information and makes it available to any authorized client who requests the information. Expect to hear either half of this expression frequently; for example, someone might say, "You can't contact us today because our Web server is down."

dial-in An Internet account that can connect any standalone computer directly to the Internet. The account is used by having a software application dial through the phone lines to an Internet service provider (ISP). The software connects with the ISP and establishes a TCP/IP link to the Internet that enables your software to access Internet information. The computer that accesses a dial-in connection needs either a modem to connect via a regular phone line or a terminal adapter (TA) to connect via an ISDN phone line.

305

e-mail (Electronic mail)   Messages transmitted over the Internet from user to user, collectively known as e-mail. Messages sent by e-mail can contain text but also can carry files of any type as attachments.

FAQs (Frequently Asked Questions)   Files that commonly are maintained at Internet sites to answer questions asked frequently, so that experienced users don't have to bear the annoying burden of hearing newbies repeatedly ask the same questions and receive the same answers over and over. It's good netiquette to check for FAQs and read them. It's extremely poor netiquette (and a good way to get flamed) to post questions that already are answered in the FAQ file.

Finger   An Internet function that enables one user to query (finger) the location of another Internet user. Finger can be applied to any computer on the Internet, if set up properly. For example, the most famous finger site of all was a Coke machine at Carnegie-Mellon that students wired to the Internet so they could finger it and track such important information as how many bottles of which beverage remained and how long the bottom bottle in each stack had been in the machine. Thus they never had to walk all the way to the machine and find it empty or filled with warm soda. You won't use finger but it was fun while it lasted. Most sites on which you could still use Finger are shutting it down because it helps hackers crack a system.

firewall   A combination of hardware and software that protects a local area network (LAN) from Internet hackers. It separates the network into two or more parts and restricts outsiders to the area "outside" the firewall. Private or sensitive information is kept "inside" the firewall.

flames   Insulting, enraging Internet messages; the equivalent of schoolyard brawls in cyberspace. Unfortunately, good schoolyard brawls would be preferable, because at least then the only people who suffer are the dummies who fight. On the Internet, everyone suffers as resources are squandered on ridiculous, infantile behavior. Of course, as a serious representative of a business organization you won't be using flames.

FQDN (Fully Qualified Domain Name)   The "official" name assigned to a computer. Organizations register names, such as `ibm.com` or `utulsa.edu`. They then assign unique names to their computers, such as `watson5.ibm.com` or `hurricane.cs.utulsa.edu`.

FTP (File Transfer Protocol)   The basic Internet function that enables files to be transferred between computers. You can use it to download files from a remote, host computer, and to upload files from your computer to a remote, host computer (see anonymous FTP).

gateway   A host computer that connects a network to other networks. For example, a gateway connects a company's LAN to the Internet.

GIF (Graphics Interchange Format)   A graphics file format that is commonly used on the Internet to provide graphics images in Web pages.

Gopher   A tool that organizes information by means of a hierarchy of menus. Gopher now is buried under mountains of WWW pages; don't bother learning how to use it directly. You sometimes will find a Web link that takes you to a Gopher site, but at that point, if you're using Netscape, its usage will be obvious and actually will look a great deal like the Web.

host   A system that includes TCP/IP and runs applications that provide files and services or that share the system's resources.

HTML (Hypertext Markup Language)   The basic language used to build hypertext documents on the World Wide Web. It is used in basic, plain, ASCII-text documents, but when those documents are interpreted (called rendering) by a Web browser, such as Netscape, the document can display formatted text, color, a variety of fonts, graphic images, special effects, hypertext jumps to other Internet locations, and information forms.

HTTP (Hypertext Transfer Protocol)   The protocol (rules) computers use to transfer hypertext documents.

hypertext   Text in a document that contains a hidden link to other text. You can click a mouse on a hypertext word and it will take you to the text designated in the link. Hypertext is used in Windows help programs and CD encyclopedias to jump to related references elsewhere within the same document. The wonderful thing about hypertext, however, is its ability to link to any Web document in the world, using http over the World Wide Web yet still requiring only a single mouse click to jump clear around the world.

IP (Internet Protocol)   The rules that support basic Internet data delivery functions (see TCP/IP).

IP Address   An Internet address that is a unique number consisting of 4 parts separated by dots, sometimes called a *dotted quad*. For example, 198.204.112.1. Every Internet computer has an IP address, and most computers also are assigned one or more Domain Names that are easier to remember than the dotted quad.

IRC (Internet Relay Chat)   Currently an Internet tool with a limited use that lets users join a "chat" channel and exchange typed, text messages. Few people have used IRC, but it is going to create a revolution in communications when the Internet can provide the bandwidth to carry full-color, live-action video and audio. Once that occurs, the IRC will provide full video-conferencing. Even today, while limited for all practical purposes to text only, the IRC can be a valuable business conferencing tool, already providing adequate voice communication.

ISDN (Integrated Services Digital Network)   A set of communications standards that enable a single phone line or optical cable to carry voice, digital network services, and video. ISDN is intended to eventually replace our standard telephone system.

JPEG (Joint Photographic Experts Group)   The name of the committee that designed the photographic image-compression standard. JPEG is optimized for compressing full-color or gray-scale photographic-type, digital images. It doesn't work well on drawn images such as line drawings, and it does not handle black-and-white images or video images.

kbps, or kbits/s (kilobits per second)   A speed rating for computer modems that measures (in units of 1,024 bits) the maximum number of bits the device can transfer in one second under ideal conditions.

kBps, or kbytes/s (kilobytes per second)   Remember, one byte is eight bits.

leased line   A leased phone line that provides a full-time, dedicated, direct connection to the Internet.

listserv   An Internet application that automatically "serves" mailing lists by sending electronic newsletters to a stored database of Internet user addresses. Most lists let users subscribe and unsubscribe automatically, requiring anyone at the server location to personally handle the transaction. But for a "reflector" mailing list, the request to join goes to the mailbox of a human being, who then must manually perform the subscribe or unsubscribe transaction.

mailing list   An e-mail-based discussion group. Sending one e-mail message to the mailing list's list server sends mail to all other members of the group. Users join a mailing list by subscribing. Subscribers to a mailing list receive messages from all other members. Users have to unsubscribe from a mailing list to stop receiving messages forwarded from the group's members.

MIME (Multipurpose Internet Mail Extensions)   A set of Internet functions that extends normal e-mail capabilities and enables computer files to be attached to e-mail. Files sent by MIME arrive at their destination as exact copies of the original, so you can send fully formatted word processing files, spreadsheets, graphics images, and software applications to other users via simple e-mail.

modem An electronic device that lets computers communicate electronically using regular phone lines. The name is derived from *modulator-demodulator* because of how the modem functions when processing data over analog phone lines.

netiquette Internet etiquette; good netiquette will keep you out of trouble in newsgroups.

newsgroup An electronic, community bulletin board that enables Internet users all over the world to post and read messages that are public to other users of the group. There were more than 28,000 public newsgroups in 1996, collecting hundreds of megabytes of data daily, but no one really knows how many might be in existence at any given time.

NNTP (Network News Transfer Protocol) An Internet protocol that handles Usenet newsgroups at most modern Internet service providers.

POP (Post Office Protocol) An Internet protocol that enables a single user to read e-mail from a mail server.

PoP (Point of Presence) A site that has an array of telecommunications equipment: modems, digital leased lines, and Internet routers. An Internet access provider might operate several regional PoPs to provide Internet connections within local phone service areas. An alternative is for access providers to employ *virtual* PoPs in conjunction with third party providers.

protocols Computer rules that provide uniform specifications so that computer hardware and operating systems can communicate. The process is similar to the way that mail, in countries around the world, is addressed in the same basic format so that postal workers know where to find the recipient's address, the sender's return address, and the postage stamp. Regardless of the underlying language, the basic protocols remain the same.

router A network device that enables the network to reroute messages it receives that are intended for other networks. The network with the router receives the message and sends it on its way exactly as it was received.

shell account A software application that lets you use someone else's Internet connection. It's not the same as having your own, direct

Internet connection, but pretty close. Instead, you connect to a host computer and use the Internet through the host computer's connection.

signature file   An ASCII text file, maintained within e-mail programs, that contains a few lines of text for your signature. The programs automatically attach the file to your messages so you don't have to repeatedly type a closing.

SLIP/PPP (Serial Line Internet Protocol/Point-to-Point Protocol)
Two different, basic rule sets that enable Internet traffic to travel from point to point. Both SLIP and PPP are used by all kinds of Internet hosts and routers.

SMTP (Simple Mail Transfer Protocol)   The simple, classic protocol used to handle the Internet's e-mail functions.

spam   Anything that nobody wants. The label applies primarily to commercial messages posted across a large number of Internet newsgroups, especially when the ad contains nothing of specific interest to the posted newsgroup.

T1   An Internet backbone line that carries up to 1.536 million bits per second (1.536 Mbits/s).

T3   An Internet line that carries up to 45 million bits per second (45 Mbits/s).

TA   See Terminal Adapter.

TCP/IP (Transmission Control Protocol/Internet Protocol)   The basic programming foundation that carries computer messages around the globe via the Internet. Co-created by Vinton G. Cerf, former president of the Internet Society, and Robert E. Kahn.

Telnet   An Internet protocol that lets you connect your PC as a remote workstation to a host computer anywhere in the world, and to use that computer as if you were logged on locally. You often have the ability to use all the software and capability on the host computer, even if it's a huge mainframe.

Terminal Adapter (TA)   An electronic device that interfaces a PC with an Internet host computer via an ISDN phone line. These are often called *ISDN modems*. However, because they are digital, TAs are not modems at all (see modem definition).

UNIX   The computer operating system that was used to write most of the programs and protocols that built the Internet. The need for UNIX is rapidly waning, and mainstream users will never need to use a UNIX command-line prompt. The name was created by the programmers who wrote the operating system, because they realized that while they were developing the operating system they essentially had become eunuchs.

URL (Uniform Resource Locator) A critical term. It's your main access ticket to Internet resources. It's the equivalent of having the phone number of a place you want to call. You constantly will use URLs with your Internet software applications to identify the protocol, host name, and file name of resources you want.

Usenet Another name for Internet newsgroups. This is a distributed bulletin board system running on news servers.

Veronica Archie's companion, but not really, because Veronica actually helps you find information on Gopher menus. It's an acronym for *Very Easy Rodent-Oriented Net-wide Index to Computerized Archives*. You probably never will use it, because Web searches are faster and more extensive.

WinVN A standalone Windows-based Internet Usenet newsgroup reader application. This is a powerful program with many useful functions. Now that Netscape includes built-in newsgroup functions, however, the use of WinVN is waning except for users with advanced Newsgroup needs. In many ways, Netscape is a better newsgroup reader for mainstream users.

World Wide Web (WWW) (W3) (the Web) An Internet client-server distributed information and retrieval system based upon the hypertext transfer protocol (http) that transfers hypertext documents across a varied array of computer systems. The Web was created by the CERN High-Energy Physics Laboratories in Geneva, Switzerland in 1991. CERN boosted the Web into international prominence on the Internet.

INDEX

About the Authors

Ronald L. Wagner is a computer trainer and author who has 14 published Internet books to his credit.

Eric Engelmann is the primary Internet trainer at the World Bank, where he played a key role in developing the organization's state-of-the-art Intranet.

Wagner and Engelmann are also coauthors of *The McGraw-Hill Internet Training Manual.*